Civilian or Military Power?

This text critically examines the belief that the EU not only has an impact on the international system but also a 'normative', 'civilian' and 'civilising' power. The contributors question whether this assertion fits with the empirical record, or is merely based on anecdotal evidence and whether there is a theoretical basis for the expectation of a 'normative' or 'civilising' power. Moving the research agenda forward, the book establishes criteria and assessment standards for examining the EU's international role and its putative normative dimension. Such an endeavour is particularly important against the backdrop of recent developments in European security and defence. The acquisition of military means, or the EU's ambition to acquire such means, might weaken at least the argument that the EU is a 'civilian' power and could provoke a shift towards a policy more akin to traditional 'great powers.'

This book was previously published as a special issue of the *Journal of European Public Policy*.

Helene Sjursen is Senior Researcher at Arena – Centre for European Studies, University of Oslo, Norway. She has written extensively on international relations, in particular on the foreign and security policy of the European Union, and on the question of EU enlargement.

Journal of European Public Policy Series

Series Editor: Jeremy Richardson is a Professor at Nuffield College, Oxford University

This series seeks to bring together some of the finest edited works on European Public Policy. Reprinting from Special Issues of the 'Journal of European Public Policy,' the focus is on using a wide range of social sciences approaches, both qualitative and quantitative, to gain a comprehensive and definitive understanding of Public Policy in Europe.

Towards a Federal Europe
Edited by Alexander H. Trechsel

The Disparity of European Integration
Edited by Tanja A. Börzel

Cross-National Policy Convergence:
Causes Concepts and Empirical Findings
Edited by Christoph Knill

Civilian or Military Power?
European Foreign Policy in Perspective
Edited by Helene Sjursen

Civilian or Military Power?

European Foreign Policy in Perspective

Edited by Helene Sjursen

Routledge
Taylor & Francis Group

London and New York

First published 2007 by Routledge
2 Park Square, Milton Park, Abingdon, Oxon, OX14 4RN

Simultaneously published in the USA and Canada
by Routledge
270 Madison Ave, New York, NY 10016

Routledge is an imprint of the Taylor & Francis Group, an informa business

Transferred to Digital Printing 2009

© 2007 Taylor & Francis Ltd
Typeset in FranklinGothic, Garamond by Techset Composition Limited

British Library Cataloguing in Publication Data
A catalogue record for this book is available from the British Library

Library of Congress Cataloging in Publication Data
A catalog record for this book has been requested

ISBN 10: 0-415-38048-0 (hbk)
ISBN 10: 0-415-56853-6 (pbk)

ISBN 13: 978-0-415-38048-5 (hbk)
ISBN 13: 978-0-415-56853-1 (pbk)

Contents

What kind of power?

Helene Sjursen[1]

INTRODUCTION

In the past decade the view of the European Union (EU) as a relevant and important international actor has gained increasing acceptance. The EU is the world's largest trading power as well as a major donor of humanitarian assistance and development aid. This, together with the fact that it is gradually building capabilities in security and defence, does indeed make it difficult to neglect the EU's international role. Consequently, whereas much attention was traditionally paid to the question of whether or not there *is* such a thing as a European foreign policy (Bull 1982; Hoffmann 2000), analysis now tends to ask what characterizes this European foreign policy. In this context, a number of authors have stressed the 'particularity' of the EU. In developing their argument, they often build on François Duchêne's (1972) conception of the EU as a 'civilian' power. According to Duchêne, the particularity of the EU's international role is linked to the 'nature' of the polity itself. In his view, the EU's strength and novelty as an international actor is based on its ability to extend its own model of ensuring stability and security through economic and political rather than military means. A number of authors have picked up on this idea and developed it further. What they have in common is an interest in a putative normative dimension to the EU's foreign and security policy (Rosencrance 1998; Whitman 1998; Stavridis 2001; Smith 2000; Manners 2002; Delcourt 2003; Aggestam 2004; Diez 2004; Lightfoot and Burchell 2005). The argument in this literature tends to be that the EU is distinguished from other actors because it is not only a *civilian* power (in the sense that it does not have military instruments at its disposal) but (also) a *normative, civilizing* or *ethical* power within the international system.

On the one hand, the conception of the EU as a *normative/civilizing* power has provided a fruitful avenue for research, which has moved the agenda a step forward. It has not only taken the debate beyond the often rather sterile discussion on whether or not the EU 'actually' has a foreign policy, but it has also gone further than the more policy-oriented studies, which assess the strengths and weaknesses of institutional arrangements and their consequences for policy effectiveness. It raises different and important questions about the foreign policy of the EU and the role this actor – which is less than a state and more than an international organization – can and does play in international relations. Many of the observations about the EU's putative 'normative' power also connect to broader debates in international relations and foreign policy. They have particular relevance for the discussion of the evolution of the international system towards a post-Westphalian order where state sovereignty is constrained through legal developments beyond the nation state.

On the other hand, such descriptions of the EU also raise a number of new questions. The conception of the EU as a 'normative', 'ethical' and particularly a 'civilizing', power is contested – not least because this conception is very similar to that used by EU officials when describing the EU's international role. This leaves researchers vulnerable to the charge of being unable to distinguish between their own sympathy for the European project and their academic role as critical analysts. In order to assess if such conceptualizations of the EU are simply co-optations of the agenda of those in power, it is important to investigate whether these claims fit with the empirical record or are merely based on anecdotal evidence. More fundamentally, however, analyses should contribute to a better grasp of the nature of the EU's external policies as well as the 'nature of the beast' itself (Risse-Kappen 1996). In order to contribute to such an endeavour, we have sought to address the following three questions:

1 What would be the criteria for identifying a 'normative/civilian/civilizing' power?
2 How can we theoretically account for the putative existence of the EU as such a power?
3 Does the argument that the EU is a 'normative/civilian/civilizing' power hold up to systematic empirical investigation?

It is even more pertinent to ask such questions against the backdrop of recent developments in European security and defence. These are not only relevant with regard to the development of EU military capabilities. It is also important to ask if the EU is, or has been, a 'normative' power in other fields. Examples include international trade, issues of global economic justice, the environment and the EU stance when defending the interests of its agricultural producers. However, the prospect of military power dramatizes the question. It also raises the issue of the extent to which the putative particularity of EU foreign policy is linked to the instruments at its disposal or is due to other factors as well. For example, the establishment of military capabilities is often seen as signalling the EU developing towards a state-like entity and, as a result, possibly losing some of the particularities that are assumed to make it a 'normative' power.

Consequently, this is a particularly important point to re-examine the argument. Developments in the direction of autonomous EU military capabilities have been considerable in recent years. On 31 March 2003, the EU launched its first military mission, Operation Concordia. In June 2003 this was followed by the United Nations' (UN) request for assistance from the EU in the Democratic Republic of the Congo (DRC). The ensuing Operation Artemis further confirmed the impression of the EU's capacity to deliver in the military field. At the Thessalonica European Council in June 2003, the EU declared the European Security and Defence Policy (ESDP) operational for the full spectrum of Petersberg tasks. The EU has developed its own security strategy and is expanding its concept of *battle forces* to further enhance its military capabilities.

Furthermore, the argument has gained particular actuality in the context of transatlantic disagreements. A key issue here concerns the supposed differences of approach by the United States (US) and the EU/European states to (normative) questions such as the legitimate conditions for the use of military force and, more generally, how to deal with current security challenges such as international terrorism. The EU is often described as a 'normative' or 'ethical' power in contrast to the US. Yet many would argue that US foreign policy is at least as normatively driven and infused by moral argumentation as the EU. How can this be?

Several of the contributors here use these developments in security and defence as a springboard for their analyses. The acquisition of military means, or the EU's ambition to acquire such means, might weaken at least the argument that the EU is a 'civilian' power. It could provoke a shift, making EU policy more akin to that of traditional 'great powers'. It raises questions about whether the EU can be considered a 'normative' or 'civilizing' power.

DEFINING AND ACCOUNTING FOR 'NORMATIVE/CIVILIAN' POWER EUROPE

Much remains to be done in terms of finding a satisfactory theoretical basis from which to examine the argument that the EU is a 'normative/civilian/civilizing' power.

The need for theory

The concept itself requires some disentangling. Often, it seems to rest simply on the rather vague notion that the EU is 'doing good' in the international system.

This notion is built on three core claims. Firstly, as already noted, it contains a claim about the EU being a different and even novel kind of power in the international system. Often, there is an implicit comparative element pointing to the role of states and in particular great powers in international affairs as distinct from that of the EU. Secondly, this difference or novelty is considered to consist in the EU's pursuit of the spread of norms and values and/or an emphasis on non-military instruments in foreign policy. This can be seen, it is argued, through the fact that the EU has traditionally disposed of only non-military instruments in international affairs, and is considered to have a preference for 'carrots' rather than 'sticks' in dealing with third countries. It tends to promote multilateral solutions, to aim for conflict prevention and negotiation rather than enforcement; it encourages regional co-operation and stresses the importance of principles of democracy and human rights. Thirdly, the two previous claims about EU foreign policy are seen as being linked to the type of organization or polity that the EU is, but it is not quite clear what aspect of the polity is regarded as most important in this respect. Sometimes the 'normative' dimension in the EU's external policy seems linked to the conception of the EU as a 'post-Westphalian' entity in which there is no single authority, where territorial sovereignty is no longer crucial, and where borders are 'fuzzy'. At other times, the emphasis is more specifically on the organizational character of the EU (i.e. the particular mix of supranational and international elements) and the decision-making process. Elsewhere, the particular values and principles that constitute the EU are highlighted. In order to investigate the empirical relevance of the conceptualization of the EU as a 'normative', 'civilizing', 'civilian' power, we need a clearer definition. We need to be sure both of what it is and what it is not.

However, the problem is not only that there is a certain vagueness concerning the specific characteristics of the EU's putative 'normative' or 'civilizing' power. At a more fundamental level, one might question the meaningfulness of the concept as such. If power is, as it is usually defined, the ability to make others do what they would not otherwise do, the concept of normative power appears a contradiction in terms. 'Power' alludes to 'coercion'; 'normative' alludes to 'legitimacy'. How do we know that the EU's use of – normative – power is legitimate, as is implied in this concept? And how can we account for a normative dimension to the EU's international role? The argument is under-theorized and another concept may be more appropriate. In short, what is needed in order to assess the nature of the EU's foreign and security policy is meticulous empirical research, based on well-developed criteria and indicators within a broadened theoretical frame of reference. In order to address these concerns, much may be gained from normative theory and from sociological insights into modern politics.

The need for critical standards

Foreign policy-makers face normative dilemmas every day. Thus, it is a paradox that most of the theorizing about foreign policy is focused on tools that from the very outset of the analysis exclude the possibility that normative considerations have influenced decisions and processes. It is not at all clear that the need for parsimony or simplicity is a satisfactory reason for doing so. When it comes to claims about the EU as a 'normative', 'civilian' or 'civilizing' power, it would seem that the very nature of the argument calls for theories that take the normative dimension in international affairs and foreign policy seriously. This is so even if one doubts from the outset the reality as well as the validity of norms. If we do not have a conceptual apparatus that allows us to at least theoretically account for their possible relevance, such doubts will simply turn into self-fulfilling prophecies.

This should not be interpreted as a call, or a desire, for normative theory of the type prescribing, or seeking to define, what 'ought to be done'. Rather, what is needed is a theory that can deal with the criticism that the 'normative' power argument is simply apologetic and uncritical. To some, the 'solution' is to return to the realist perspective and to (re-)introduce the concept of 'power' in order to produce a more 'realistic' analysis of political processes (Hyde-Price 2006). However, this would only work if power in any shape or form, even that exercised within the legal bounds of a liberal democratic Rechtstaat, is seen as based purely on will without further justification. A better solution would be to establish explicit normative standards. It is only if we are clear regarding the basis on which criticisms are made, that normative claims may be critically assessed and vindicated – or rejected. This also makes it possible to discuss whether or not the standards themselves are the correct ones, hence linking in with normative political theory.

A broadened theoretical frame of reference

However, we also need to be able to account for the influence of norms on (the EU's) political processes. In other words, we need to find a plausible theoretical explanation for the EU's putative 'normative', 'ethical' or 'civilian' characteristics – to capture the important undergrowth of norms in the international system and its potential relevance for and influence on political processes. Basic sociological insights have taught us that common norms, values and social conventions are at the basis of a stable social order. It is such common understandings, established through intersubjective processes of communication, that keep society together. Norms and preferences are not exogenous to the social order, but developed in a social and cultural context. And norms are not mere 'oughts'. They are rooted in practice – through socialization and internalization processes – and as such they have behavioural consequences even in the absence of external sanctions (cf. Durkheim 1973; Weber 1978). These insights have also filtered through to and been recognized in the international relations literature (Finnemore 1996; Katzenstein 1996; Adler 1997; Wendt 1999) and the literature on European integration (Christiansen *et al.* 1999; Risse 2004).

Applying this to the study of the EU's foreign and security policy, it could signify that understanding how the EU can be a 'normative' or 'civilian' power requires us to study how it inserts itself into an existing normative order. Alternatively, a 'normative' power EU could be one that pursues policies that are considered appropriate given its particular role or identity (for example, as representative of the member states or of a particular idea of 'Europe') (March and Olsen 1989, 1998). Analyses with such starting points are indeed likely to provide new and important insights into developments in the EU's foreign policy and international role. They would contribute to a better understanding both of how the EU might be constituted by norms, and why it pursues norms in its external policies.

However, it is one thing to interpret a tradition and act in accordance with it. It is quite a different matter to be able to criticize this same tradition and work towards changing or transforming it. The literature on the EU as a 'normative' or 'civilian' power is ambiguous regarding which of these roles the EU is considered to play. Sometimes it seems to suggest that the EU not only interprets and/or writes itself into a given normative context or order, but also that it challenges this order and the norms that constitute it. In fact, in so far as the EU's 'normative' dimension is linked to the idea of the EU as a 'particular', 'novel' or 'different' actor, this would suggest that it breaks with the established normative order. If we are to account for a 'normative' power that actually contributes to shape norms and rules at the international level, a theory that *both* takes the putative normative dimension to political processes seriously *and* considers norms to have a rational basis is useful (Eriksen and Weigård 2003). We would need to be able to identify the mechanism that could explain this 'norm-shaping'. This can be done by conceiving of the EU as an actor capable of 'criticiz[ing] the norms that [it is] socialized under, and [of] choos[ing] different modes of action from what [it is] expected to and used to' (Eriksen 1999: 226). This takes us further in terms of understanding not only the influence of norms, but also why the EU might respect certain norms – or consider certain norms as valid – as well as why it would put less emphasis on others. By providing an account of the validity of norms, clearer theoretical underpinnings for the 'normative' power argument are established.

This discourse theoretical path is pursued by several of the contributors here (Eriksen 2006; Mitzen 2006; Sjursen 2006). From this perspective, political orders are not only practical arrangements, held together through 'mutual agreement about their advantageousness or through the use of coercive power' (Eriksen and Weigård 1997: 224–5). Social orders are normatively integrated and norms are held to be autonomous sources of motivation owing their validity to their impartial justification – meaning that they can be defended in an open, free and rational debate (among all affected parties). It is through a communicative process in which norms are rationally assessed that their relevance and binding character is established (cf. Habermas 1984). The mechanism that would allow us to account for the EU's 'normative' or 'civilian' power in its external policies would be that of the *better argument*. The concept of 'normative' power could be replaced by that of 'communicative' power, which depicts its policies and principles as able to endure critical public scrutiny.

To communitarians, however, communicative processes are context-bound; they are only possible in collectivities that have a 'thick' sense of identity (Miller 1995). In such collectivities, the relevant form of justification of a policy would refer to the appropriate conduct, given the particular identity of the community in question. Norms would express common understandings of the 'good life'. It would be the thickness of the social environment – a common cultural identity – that would explain the emergence of, and commitment to, common norms. Whereas much of the relevant international relations literature highlights the potential role of identity-shaping norms, the conception of actors as communicatively rational is important. The latter allows us to capture those processes in which actors rely on arguments that have a certain universal validity, as well as the possibility that arguments can function as a mobilizing force for change. It points to a distinction between, on the one hand, culturally or socially specific values or conceptions of what is good (for example, those which are particular to a specific community or collective identity) and, on the other, a conception of what is right, fair or just, which can be kept separate from this:

> The question of fairness does not refer to an axiological value, but to a moral norm – a deontological principle. It is concerned with what we are obliged to do when our actions have consequences for others. Rights then refer to higher order principles and claim universal validity.
>
> (Eriksen and Weigård 2003: 134–5)

This distinction is important with regard to the 'normative', 'ethical', 'civilian' power argument. It highlights the risk that, if we present an indiscriminate view of norms, failing to distinguish between different types and their validity and legitimacy basis, we cannot really tell whether or not the EU's 'normative' power is simply an expression of Eurocentric cultural imperialism.

The EU and international developments

The arguments about the EU as an actor which is not only conditioned by normative structures but also contributes to shape them, echo discussions about recent developments in the international system. And the study of the EU's foreign policy can benefit greatly from the theoretical developments in international relations and foreign policy more generally (Gilbert 1999; Wendt 1999; Jackson 2000; Risse 2000; Müller 2004; Diez and Steans 2005; Linklater 2005). Many observers today point to the emergence of new forms of governance beyond the sovereign states. Problems and their solutions are often defined and solved in transnational and international, rather than exclusively national, contexts. Political authority increasingly cuts across national borders. A strengthening of international law and international institutions beyond the nation state is seen as challenging the principle of external sovereignty and the assumption of international 'anarchy' (Fassbender 1998; Zürn 2005; Eriksen 2006). Developments in the direction of a civil society at the international level, involving transnational movements and non-governmental organizations, are also increasingly highlighted (Bohman 1999; Falk *et al.* 2002; Held and Koenig-Archibugi 2005). A number of non-state actors justify their actions and initiatives with regard to norms and principles developed at the international level – and by doing so, contribute to reinforcing their importance and relevance.

Whereas such changes have mostly been discussed with regard to issues of economics or 'low politics', they are now also increasingly relevant in the 'high politics' sphere of security. The boundaries between the domestic and the international have become increasingly blurred here too. The international security context is increasingly discussed as 'global' and de-linked from states, borders and territories. Security challenges are considered to emerge not only from other states, but also from non-state actors. War is no longer only an inter-state affair, carried out by state armies (Beck 2005). In parallel with these developments, the normative basis of security policy has been shifting. Increasingly, human rights have become a core reference for security policy, supplementing the principle of territorial sovereignty. The Westphalian order is also under challenge in this domain.

The emergence of transnational governance structures in 'low politics' raises questions about the democratic legitimacy and protection of rights beyond the national state. Current developments in the security sphere make such questions even more acute, by bringing to the fore the fundamental dilemma between human rights as universal principles, on the one hand, and external sovereignty, on the other. Urgent and crucial questions about the legitimacy basis for the use of force are raised. As in the economic sphere, the normative challenge with regard to international security increasingly becomes how to secure democracy and fairness, some form of accountability of power, in a context where there is no 'community' – no demos – and where the rule of law is limited. Unchecked power, exercised in the name of 'humanity', as such may easily lead to totalitarianism (Eriksen 2006).

It is in the EU that the challenges to the Westphalian order have been taken the furthest. In relations amongst the Union's member states, the principles of external sovereignty and territoriality are no longer decisive. They have been replaced by a common legal structure above the member states, which is constituted on democratic principles and a charter of rights. Hence, the EU is often described as an experimentarium for a number of questions of broader theoretical and empirical relevance. EU foreign policy is less often considered in this way. Nevertheless, it is in a sense a test case for broader international developments. The question is not only if the EU in its external policy reflects similar trends of 'domestication' as those observed in its internal relations, but also if it can be seen as representative of, or reflecting, broader changes in the international system.

To be sure, the trend towards strengthening international law and international institutions does not go unchallenged in today's international system. And as noted earlier, the possibility should not be overlooked that the EU itself is moving in a different direction from that of a 'normative' or 'civilian' power, due either to internal developments such as the establishment of military capabilities, the strengthening of border controls, and the introduction of judiciary and policing capabilities, or to external pressures. Some of the contributions here also reflect such assessments (Manners 2006; Wagner 2006). Nevertheless, such tensions by no means reduce the need for and interest of a close examination of the 'normative/civilian/civilizing argument'. Rather, the contrary is the case. And important insights may be gained by allowing, for example, for comparisons between the EU and other international actors.

A second question concerns what is required in order to analyse these putative developments. Concepts and standards developed independently of the EU may be helpful here. As noted, turning to insights from sociology, normative or legal theory, we may find a better starting point for examining whether the transformations are comprehensible as well as justifiable. Without these insights, the analyst might miss an important dimension, which has to do with the potential validity of different kinds of norms, with why *particular* norms or principles might emerge as important and crucial, and why actors adhere to them. If we conceptualize norms as having a rational basis, this may provide us with a better understanding of why developments have gone in a particular direction.

To sum up, the very nature of the subject requires attention to two aspects: the more abstract theoretical discussion of the justification of norms and how to conceptually clarify and disentangle the various dimensions of the proposition that the EU is a 'normative' power. At the same time, the empirical grounding is pivotal, as the main aim for the discipline is to develop tools to grasp actual developments as they unfold, rather than develop abstract theory for its own sake. Hence, it is necessary to work at both ends of the spectrum – the empirical and the conceptual – and to ensure a dialogue between them.

THE ARGUMENTS MADE

It is against this broader backdrop that this project was launched. The concrete aim here is more modest, as we seek mainly to address the three core questions outlined in this introduction. By doing so, we hope most of all to promote and provoke further debates about the intersection of the EU's foreign policy, European studies and questions of relevance to developments in the international system more broadly. The various contributions differ in their assessment of the 'normative power argument', both with regard to its empirical relevance and its theoretical foundations. In fact, the aim has not been to impose a coherent theoretical framework on the contributors, nor to encourage them to reach agreement on how best to conceptualize the EU's international role, but to clear the ground for further discussion.

In the first contribution, Ian Manners restates his argument about the EU as a 'normative' power and discusses its continued relevance against the backdrop of developments in security and defence. He is sceptical about the EU's ability to remain a 'normative' power, due to the increasing militarization of its external policies. Similarly, Wolfgang Wagner considers that the Europeanization of defence policy weakens the prospects for 'civilian power' Europe. Identifying parliamentary control as an important element of a civilian power, he shows that little room is left for parliamentary deliberation as defence policy is increasingly made at the transnational and supranational level.

Adrian Hyde-Price considers that neither 'normative' nor 'civilian' power is a viable way to conceptualize the Union. Instead, he argues, the evolving international role of the EU can best be understood by utilizing a structuralist approach rooted in neorealist theory. From this perspective, he claims, it becomes clear that the EU acts as a collective hegemon, shaping its external milieu by utilizing both hard and soft power. The subsequent three contributions follow up the conceptual and theoretical discussion. However, rather than rejecting the idea of civilian or normative dimensions to the EU from the outset, they seek to reconceptualize, and to specify the theoretical tools that might be used to account for the putative existence of such dimensions. Helene Sjursen argues that the existing literature lacks the necessary criteria and assessment standards to qualify or substantiate the claims that the EU is a 'normative' or 'civilian' power. She suggests that the main issue is to find a criterion for what might be legitimate action in the international system (for both military and non-military action). In line with this, Erik Oddvar Eriksen argues for an analytical approach that does not rule out the development of a form of 'civilian' power as a logical possibility when analysing the EU's foreign policy. Further, he suggests a cosmopolitan order, defined as one where actors subject their actions to the constraints of a higher ranking law, as a normative standard for assessing such dimensions. Jennifer Mitzen turns her attention to the Union's internal dynamics and the way in which they may contribute to sustain its 'civilian' identity. She suggests that the publicity and deliberation inherent in the routines of interstate interaction within the Common Foreign and Security Policy have helped to stabilize healthy security relations both among EU member states and in Europe's external relations, thus strengthening the EU's role as a normative power.

Finally, the last two contributions assess the strengths and weaknesses of the 'normative power' argument with reference to the concrete cases of the Mediterranean and the EU's human rights policies. With regard to the former, Federica Bicchi stresses the need for nuancing the conception of the EU's normative power, and for asking what kinds of norms the EU exports and promotes in its external initiatives. Highlighting the phenomenon of institutional isomorphism, she argues that much of the EU's action can be characterized as an attempt to promote its own model. Hence, in the case of its Mediterranean policy, the EU may be a normative power. Yet this does not necessarily echo the promotion of norms that are universally embraced. Finally, the findings of Marika Lerch and Guido Schwellnus suggest that while the EU's policy on the death penalty seems to support the concept of the EU as 'normative' power on all levels, its position on minority protection offers a different picture. In their view, it follows that the EU is not necessarily 'normative by nature', but that its normative power depends heavily on the interaction between its policy goals, means and justifications, and therefore varies between different issue areas.

The contributions are part of the CIDEL (Citizenship and Democratic Legitimacy in the EU) project and were first presented at a workshop held in Oslo in October 2004. CIDEL is a joint research project between ten partners in six European countries headed by Erik Oddvar Eriksen at ARENA – Centre for European Studies at the University of Oslo. The project is financed by the Fifth Framework Programme under the auspices of the European Commission. For further information, consult the project website at <http://www.arena.uio.no/cidel>. I would like to thank Lisbeth Aggestam, Carlos Closa, Magnus Ekengren, John Erik Fossum, Knud Erik Jørgensen, Morten Kelstrup, Mareike Kleine, Agustín Menéndez, Ulrika Mörth, Marianne Riddervold, Børge Romsloe, Hazel Smith, Karen Smith, Anne-Elizabeth Stie, José I. Torreblanca and Richard Whitman who acted as discussants and critical interlocutors at the workshop and thus contributed much to the final result presented here. I am also very thankful to Jeremy Richardson for supporting the idea of this volume. Last but not least, Geir Kværk must be thanked for his, as always, efficient and reliable administrative support.

Biographical note: Helene Sjursen is Senior Researcher at ARENA – Centre for European Studies, University of Oslo, Norway.

Address for correspondence: Helene Sjursen, ARENA – Centre for European Studies, University of Oslo, PO Box 1143 Blindern, N-0317 Oslo, Norway. Tel: +47 22 85 49 58. Fax: +47 22 85 78 32. email: helene.sjursen@arena.uio.no

NOTE

1 Many thanks to Erik Oddvar Eriksen for comments and advice on this introduction.

REFERENCES

Adler, E. (1997) 'Seizing the middle ground: constructivism in world politics', *European Journal of International Relations* 3(3): 319–63.

Aggestam, L. (2004) 'A European foreign policy? Role conceptions and the politics of identity in Britain, France and Germany', Doctoral Dissertation, Department of Political Science, Stockholm University.

Beck, U. (2005) 'War is peace: on post-national war', *Security Dialogue* 36(1): 2–26.

Bohman, J. (1999) 'International regimes and democratic governance: political equality and influence in global institutions', *International Affairs* 75(3): 499–513.

Bull, H. (1982) 'Civilian power Europe: a contradiction in terms?', *Journal of Common Market Studies* 21(2): 149–64.

Christiansen, T., Jørgensen, K.E. and Wiener, A. (1999) 'The social construction of Europe', *Journal of European Public Policy* 6(4): 528–44.

Delcourt, B. (2003) *Droit et souverainetés. Analyse critique du discours européen sur la Yougoslavie*, Brussels: Peter Lang.

Diez, T. (2004) 'Constructing the self and changing others: problematising the concept of "normative power Europe"'. Paper presented at the Millennium Conference 'Facets of Power in International Relations', London School of Economics and Political Science, London, 30–31 October.

Diez, T. and Steans, J. (2005) 'A useful dialoque? Habermas and international relations', *Review of International Studies* 31(1): 127–40.

Duchêne, F. (1972) 'Europe's role in world peace', in R. Mayne (ed.), *Europe Tomorrow: Sixteen Europeans Look Ahead*, London: Fontana, pp. 32–47.

Durkheim, E. (1973) *On Morality and Society; Selected Writings* [ed. R. N. Bellah], Chicago: University of Chicago Press.

Eriksen, E.O. (1999) 'Towards a logic of justification. On the possibility of post-national solidarity', in M. Egeberg and P. Lægreid (eds), *Organizing Political Institutions*, Oslo: Scandinavian University Press, pp. 215–44.

Eriksen, E.O. (2006) 'The EU – a cosmopolitan polity?', *Journal of European Public Policy* 13(2): 252–69.

Eriksen, E.O. and Weigård, J. (1997) 'Conceptualizing politics: strategic or communicative rationality?', *Scandinavian Political Studies* 20(3): 219–41.

Eriksen, E.O. and Weigård, J. (2003) *Understanding Habermas: Communicative Action and Deliberative Democracy*, London: Continuum.

Falk, R., Edwin, L., Ruiz, J. and Walker, R.B.J. (eds) (2002) *Re-Framing the International: Law, Culture, Politics*, London and New York: Routledge.

Fassbender, B. (1998) 'The United Nations charter as constitution of the international community', *Columbia Journal of Transnational Law* 36: 529–619.

Finnemore, M. (1996) *National Interest in International Society*, Ithaca, NY: Cornell University Press.

Gilbert, A. (1999) *Must Global Politics Constrain Democracy? Great-Power Realism, Democratic Peace, and Democratic Internationalism*, Princeton, NJ: Princeton University Press.

Habermas, J. (1984) *Theory of Communicative Action. Volume I: Reason and the Rationalization of Society*, Boston: Beacon Press.

Held, D. and Koenig-Archibugi, M. (eds) (2005) *Global Governance and Public Accountability*, Oxford: Blackwell Publishing.

Hoffmann, S. (2000) 'Towards a common European foreign and security policy?', *Journal of Common Market Studies* 38(2): 189–98.

Hyde-Price, A. (2006) '"Normative" power Europe: a realist critique', *Journal of European Public Policy* 13(2): 217–34.

Jackson, R. (2000) *The Global Covenant: Human Conduct in a World of States*, Oxford: Oxford University Press.

Katzenstein, P. (ed.) (1996) *The Culture of National Security: Norms and Identity in World Politics*, New York: Columbia University Press.

Lightfoot, S. and Burchell, J. (2005) 'The EU and the World Summit on Sustainable Development', *Journal of Common Market Studies* 43(1): 75–95.

Linklater, A. (2005) 'Dialogic politics and the civilising process', *Review of International Studies* 31(1): 141–54.

Manners, I. (2002) 'Normative power Europe: a contradiction in terms?', *Journal of Common Market Studies* 40(2): 235–58.

Manners, I. (2006) 'Normative power Europe reconsidered: beyond the crossroads', *Journal of European Public Policy* 13(2): 182–99.

March, J.G. and Olsen, J.P. (1989) *Rediscovering Institutions. The Organizational Basis of Politics*, New York: Free Press.

March, J.G. and Olsen, J.P. (1998) 'The institutional dynamics of international political orders', *International Organization* 52(4): 943–69.

Miller, D. (1995) *On Nationality*, Oxford: Clarendon Press.

Mitzen, J. (2006) 'Anchoring Europe's civilizing identity: habits, capabilities and ontological security', *Journal of European Public Policy* 13(2): 270–85.

Müller, H. (2004) 'Arguing, bargaining and all that: communicative action, rationalist theory and the logic of appropriateness in international relations', *European Journal of International Relations* 10(3): 395–435.

Risse, T. (2000) '"Let's argue!": communicative action in world politics', *International Organization* 54(1): 1–39.

Risse, T. (2004) 'Social constructivism', in T. Diez and A. Wiener (eds), *European Integration Theory*, Oxford: Oxford University Press, pp. 159–75.

Risse-Kappen, T. (1996) 'Exploring the nature of the beast: international relations theory and comparative policy analysis meet the European Union', *Journal of Common Market Studies* 34(1): 53–79.

Rosencrance, R. (1998) 'The European Union: a new type of international actor', in J. Zielonka (ed.), *Paradoxes of European Foreign Policy*, The Hague: Kluwer Law International, pp. 15–23.

Sjursen, H. (2006) 'The EU as a "normative" power: how can this be?', *Journal of European Public Policy* 13(2): 235–51.

Smith, K.E. (2000) 'The end of civilian power EU: a welcome demise or cause for concern?', *International Spectator* 35(2): 11–28.

Stavridis, S. (2001) 'Militarizing the EU: the concept of civilian power Europe revisited', *International Spectator* 36(4): 43–50.

Wagner, W. (2006) 'The democratic control of military power Europe', *Journal of European Public Policy* 13(2): 200–16.

Weber, M. (1978) *Economy and Society: An Outline of Interpretive Sociology* [eds G. Roth and C. Wittich], Berkeley, CA: University of California Press.

Wendt, A. (1999) *Social Theory of International Politics*, Cambridge: Cambridge University Press.

Whitman, R. (1998) *From Civilian Power to Superpower? The International Identity of the European Union*, Basingstoke: Macmillan.

Zürn, M. (2005) 'Global governance and communicative action', in D. Held and M. Koenig-Archibugi (eds), *Global Governance and Public Accountability*, Oxford: Blackwell Publishing, pp. 136–63.

Normative power Europe reconsidered: beyond the crossroads[1]

Ian Manners

INTRODUCTION: THE EUROPEAN UNION AS A GREAT POWER

> One impression predominates in my mind over all others. It is this: unity in Europe does not create a new kind of great power; it is a method for introducing change in Europe and consequently in the world. People, more often outside the European Community than within, are tempted to see the European Community as a potential nineteenth-century state with all the overtones this implies. But we are not in the nineteenth century, and the Europeans have built up the European Community precisely in order to find a way out of the conflicts to which the nineteenth-century philosophy gave rise.
>
> (Monnet 1962: 26)

How easy it is to imagine that the European Union (EU) can be both a method for introducing change in international relations and a great power. It is seductive to think that the EU can be both a post-national normative power for the twenty-first century and acquire the accoutrements of nineteenth-century state power at no extra cost. It is tempting to think that the EU can have-its-cake-and-eat-it-too in militarizing its normative power. For the armies of academics now writing on EU military force the logic is both simple and seductive – in order to practise 'preventative engagement' and strengthen the European defence industrial and technological base, the EU needs to acquire a 'full spectrum' of crisis management capabilities. As whole special issues of journals such as *Survival, European Security, International Affairs,* and *International Peacekeeping* now attest, 'martial potency' is the means and the method for the EU's new power status.

As the quote from Jean Monnet reminds us, 'unity in Europe does not create a new kind of great power'; we have built the EU precisely to escape great power mentality. As part of my contribution to this volume on the EU at a crossroads, I intend to reconsider my original normative power Europe (NPE) argument in order to reflect on the consequences and risks that the militarization of the EU beyond 2003 now poses to the Union's normative power in world politics (see Manners 2000b, 2002). In doing so I will argue that that militarization of the EU need not necessarily lead to the diminution of the EU's normative power, if critical reflection characterized the process. However, I will further argue that militarizing processes beyond the crossroads provided by the European Security Strategy are already weakening the normative claims of the EU in a post-11 September world characterized by the drive towards 'martial potency' and the growth of a Brussels-based 'military-industrial simplex'.

In order to do so I shall address the theoretical and empirical questions set out in the introduction to this volume from the NPE perspective. I shall first consider theoretical accounts for the EU's normative power, emphasizing the risks of conflating civilian and civilizing, as well as revisiting my normative power Europe argument. Next I will turn to the EU's normative political ethos and its promotion of sustainable peace in world politics. This will involve a brief reconsideration of the historical development of EU conflict prevention policy as an empirical example of normative power shaping external actions. I will then empirically discuss some of the EU militarizing processes beyond the 2003 crossroads. Finally, I shall conclude by discussing the normative choices for the EU beyond crossroads between continued unreflexive militarization, potentially perpetuating the idea of nineteenth-century 'great power' or the return to sustainable peace as a central norm of EU normative power.

THEORETICAL ACCOUNTS OF THE EU'S NORMATIVE POWER

> The issue in Europe is an historic one. The nuclear stalemate is making it possible to move away from naked force toward politics and so to *civilize* conflict in one of the centres of gravity of the balance of power. If this can be done by freeing up an empire over them, it will mark a real moment of progress in international twentieth-century society.
>
> (Duchêne 1971: 82; emphasis added)

Europe would be the first major area of the Old World where the age-old process of war and indirect violence could be translated into something more in tune with the twentieth-century citizen's notion of *civilized* politics.

(Duchêne 1972: 43; emphasis added)

Europe as a whole could well become the first example in history of a major centre of the balance of power becoming in the era of its decline not a colonized victim but the exemplar of a new stage in political *civilization*.

(Duchêne 1973: 19; emphasis added)

As these extracts from François Duchêne's discussions of civilian power illustrate, it is extremely easy to characterize the EU as a 'civilian power' and then take a simple step to granting it the mission of 'civilizing' international relations. The use of civil, civilian, civilianize, civilianizing, civilize, civilization, and civilizing as if they were interchangeable makes their use highly problematic. Firstly, 'civilizing' is far too encumbered a term to be used in any self-reflexive discussion of European relations with the rest of the world (see Manners 2003: 70). Postcolonial theory makes absolutely clear that the term 'civilization' is part of 'Eurocentric strategies of narrativizing history, so that Europe can congratulate itself for progress' which in contemporary terms invokes the 'culture of capitalism' (Spivak 1999: 91, 93). Secondly, 'civilian power' as a conceptual category has come to be far too related to the ontology of states, rather than a 'style of action' or 'domestication'. As I discussed in my paper on NPE, the notion of civilian power has become located in assumptions about the fixed nature of the nation state, the importance of direct physical power, and the notion of national interest (Manners 2002: 238). The EU and its actions in world politics demand a wider and more appropriate approach in order to reflect what it is, does and should do.

  I have used the phrase 'normative power Europe' in order to attempt to capture the movement away from Cold War (and neo-colonial) approaches to the EU. Based upon my research into the symbolic and normative discourses and practices within the European Community (EC)/EU during the 1990s, I developed the NPE approach as a response to the relative absence of normative theorizing and to promote normative approaches to the EU. As discussed above, rather than theoretically accounting for the putative existence of the EU as a civilizing power, I will focus on the EU's normative power in world politics.

  EU norm diffusion is shaped by six factors − contagion, informational diffusion, procedural diffusion, transference, overt diffusion and the cultural filter (Manners 2002: 244−5). What has been significant in these norm diffusion factors was the relative absence of physical force in the imposition of norms. This absence of physical force and the importance of cultural diffusion led me to argue that 'the most important factor shaping the international role of the EU is not what it does or what it says, but what it is' (Manners 2002: 252). As I will now consider through an examination of the interaction of normative political ethos and the development of conflict prevention policy, EU norms of 'sustainable peace' have been a central factor in EU external actions prior to 2003.

NORMATIVE POLITICAL ETHOS AND SUSTAINABLE PEACE IN THE EU

Always overlooked in discussions of Duchêne's civilian power was his reliance on Marion Dönhoff's ideas about transmuting technical nuclear peace into political peace (Duchêne 1972: 47; 1973: 20). Dönhoff's 'second life' after working in the German resistance movement led her to advocate civil activism and collective action based on tolerance, morality, democracy and the idea that 'resistance and moral courage are usually rooted in acts of everyday life' (Mushaben 1999: 20). It is clearly Dönhoff's work which Duchêne draws on when he advocates 'many forms of collective activity which previously had far less influence: cultural example, social movements, pressure groups, economic capacity' (Duchêne 1973: 20), and 'a built-in sense of collective action, which in turn express, however imperfectly, social values of equality, justice and tolerance … [and] the international open society' (Duchêne 1972: 47).

The emphases of Dönhoff and Duchêne on political peace, and the way in which everyday acts and cultural example help to transmute conflict into peace through civil activism and collective action, resonate with other postwar political thinkers and the impact which they had on peace movements across the world. In the European context, ideas regarding the value of the public sphere and the politics of reconciliation became crucial in the post-war rebuilding process, as well as the building of democracies and European integration. Political philosophers such as Hannah Arendt argued that the processes of reconciliation involved the ethos of the public realm (Arendt 1990: 221; 1998: 50). Catherine Guisan-Dickinson suggests that it is the Arendtian 'lost treasures' of American and French revolutionary ethics that have, and should, inform the public political philosophy of the EU (Guisan-Dickinson 2003).

If civil activism, collective action, public sphere and reconciliation are part of a political ethos which *should* inform EU external action, how were these reconcilable with the concerns for preventing violent conflicts such as Yugoslavia and Rwanda in a normative way? From 1995 to 2003, the solution came in the shape of ideas about conflict prevention circulating in the EU and the United Nations (UN) under the term *sustainable peace* (see Manners 2005). The term 'sustainable peace' emphasized the stress the EU placed on addressing the causes, rather than just the symptoms, of conflict and violence. Connie Peck has defined sustainable peace as involving both short-term problem-solving and long-term structural solutions to conflict prevention through the integration of human security concerns and the promotion of good governance (Peck 1998: 15–16). Sustainable peace is not simply about the conjunction of short- and long-term methods but, in line with Arendt, Dönhoff and Duchêne, is informed by the need to build 'indigenous capacity for resolving internal tensions before they lead to violent conflict' (Malloch Brown 2003: 142) that enable a more permanent 'consolidation of peace' (Busumtwi-Sam 2002: 92). In contrast to humanitarian assistance and intervention, the indigenous capacity building of sustainable peace is focused on the rights of ownership of the victims of conflict, rather than charitable acts of the EU (Arendt 1979: 296 in Chandler 2003: 307). Thus, an EU normative commitment to sustainable peace increasingly involved combining short- and long-term conflict prevention with the building of civil capacity that facilitates reconciliation.

The EU sustainable peace initiative came with the Swedish and Finnish foreign ministers suggesting in 1996 that 'increasingly, the need is to prevent conflicts from breaking out and to create the conditions for sustainable peace and security by democratic, political and economic means' (Hjelm-Wallén and Halonen 1996). The EU sought to promote sustainable peace at the UN, for example, in conflict management in Macedonia and Bosnia (Ramaker 1997; Eitel 1998).[2] More importantly, the EU made sustainable peace the aim of its own conflict prevention policies, as seen in the Common Positions and Presidency Statements on Afghanistan, Colombia, South-East Europe, Africa, and Bosnia.[3] Interestingly, both Commissioners Diamantopoulou and Patten argued that sustainable peace depended on the full and equal participation of women in all aspects of the peace-making processes (Diamantopoulou 2003; Patten 2003). The EU advocacy of the principle of sustainable peace contributed to the UN Secretary General's report of June 2001, 'Prevention of Armed Conflict', which pledged the UN to move from 'a culture of reaction to a culture of prevention' (Annan 2001: 9). A broader focus on the nature of sustainable peace and its building-blocks, such as social and economic development, good governance and democratization, the rule of law and respect for human rights, is supplementing the traditional concept of collective security.

It is worth briefly reconsidering an empirical example of the way in which normative power has shaped external actions by looking at the development of EU conflict prevention policy in the context of sustainable peace. A number of surveys of EU conflict prevention policy provide us with a means of assessing the relative consistency and success of EC attempts at preventative diplomacy in the context of short-term problem-solving (see Hill 2001; H. Smith 2002; K. Smith 2003; Kronenberger and Wouters 2004). Five cases in particular illustrate three common points regarding the EU's conflict prevention policy prior to 2003 – the Palestinian–Israeli conflict (Soetendorp 1999; Ginsberg 2001), Central America (H. Smith 1995), South Africa (Holland 1995), Eastern Europe (K. Smith 1999; Miall 2000), and South-Eastern Europe (Ginsberg 2001; Hill 2001; Björkdahl 2005).

Firstly, it is clear that the EC had a long experience of conflict prevention policy with mixed results during the period 1970–93. As suggested above, a number of authors have argued that the EU has played a positive, if not a successful, role in all five of these case studies. Secondly, it is also apparent that although the EC was able to engage in both short-term preventative diplomacy and long-term structural conflict prevention, it was clearly predisposed to and more adept at the latter. This predisposition towards long-term structural conflict prevention clearly reflects the EC's experience in the aftermath of World War Two and was to prove important in shaping peace norms in the 1990s. With the end of the Cold War and the increasing relevance and role of non-governmental organizations (NGOs) in potential and post-conflict situations, the EC emphasis on structural conflict prevention became far more important. These two observations were crucial in contributing to the 'transformative year' in EU conflict prevention policy – 1995. Despite agreement on the Petersburg tasks, the entry into force of the Common Foreign and Security Policy (CFSP), and the initiation of the Balladur Pact in the latter half of 1993, the shocking events of 1994–95 were to shift the culture of conflict prevention in the EU. The combination of atrocities and genocide in Rwanda and Bosnia during this period brought home to Europeans, NGOs, member states and the Commission that preventing violent conflicts must become a priority for the EU's normative power. It is this reflexive factor in the critical reinterpretation and reflection during the 1990s that has become an important characteristic of NPE and the attempts to introduce a sustainable peace policy in 1996.

The transformation of EU conflict prevention policy during 1995 was largely the result of dialogue between the Commission and NGOs with respect to Africa and development policy, as well as south-eastern Europe and post-conflict rebuilding in Bosnia after Dayton. Following the genocide in Rwanda between April and June 1994, the General Affairs Council and Essen European Council in November and December 1994 agreed to a Belgian government suggestion for intensive dialogue with the Organization of African Unity (Coolsaet and Soetendorp 2000). In June 1995 a French Member of the European Parliament, Michel Rocard, following ideas developed in the European Parliament's Forum for the Active Prevention of Conflicts during 1994, proposed that the Commission should establish a 'European Union Analysis Centre for Active Crisis Prevention', an initiative which was to be realized as the Conflict Prevention Network (CPN) in January 1997 (Conflict Prevention Network 2001).[4] These initiatives led to a 'comprehensive policy framework for conflict prevention and peace-building in Africa and beyond' developed in the 'landmark document' on 'Preventative Diplomacy, Conflict Resolution and Peacekeeping in Africa' agreed at the General Affairs Council in December 1995 (McLean and Lilly 2000: 10).

This landmark document on conflict prevention coincided with the agreement on the use of 'conditionality clauses' stating that human rights, democratic principles and the rule of law were 'essential elements' of EU aid and political agreements with third countries. The conditionality clause introduced into the mid-term review of the Lomé IV agreement in 1995 reflected the peace norms developed in relations with the Central and Eastern European Countries (CEECs), in particular the conditionality clauses in co-operation and association agreements since 1992 and the Copenhagen criteria since 1993 (Cremona 1998; K. Smith 1998; Hilpold 2002). Thus, during 1996 both the

Commission and NGOs built on the 1995 shift in conflict prevention norms by developing proposals that explicitly acknowledged the relationships between the structural causes of instability and violence and the need to link both aid and foreign policy together in conflict prevention (European Commission 1996a, 1996b; Rummel 1996a, 1996b). These three years of intensive dialogue and rethinking of conflict prevention finally materialized following leadership from the Netherlands Presidency of the EU in the first half of 1997. The linkage between NGOs and the Dutch government was most clearly demonstrated at the European Conference on Conflict Prevention – a large public gathering of NGOs and national officials held in Amsterdam in February 1997 hosted by the Dutch National Commission for International Co-operation and Sustainable Development in co-operation with the Liaison Committee of Development NGOs to the EU. The output of the conference became 'The Amsterdam Appeal: an Action Plan for European Leaders', with the subsequent creation of the European Platform for Conflict Prevention and Transformation (EPCPT) in September 1997.

This combination of the shift of thinking in the Commission, the Dutch government, the Amsterdam Appeal, and the CPN under the directorship of Reinhardt Rummel, was finally to lead to the Council Common Position on 'Conflict Prevention and Resolution in Africa' and the Resolution on 'Coherence of the EC's Development Co-operation with its Other Policies' from the Amsterdam European Council, both in June 1997. This combination of factors, together with the events in Kosovo during 1999, was to lead to the two crucial reports arguing for the consolidation of the EU's conflict prevention policy – the EPCPT's *Preventing Violent Conflicts*, and Javier Solana and Christopher Patten's *Improving the Coherence and Effectiveness of EU Action in the Field of Conflict Prevention*, both in December 2000 (McLean and Lilly 2000; Björkdahl 2002; Eavis and Kefford 2002).

This brief examination of the way in which EU conflict prevention policy has evolved illustrates the extent to which the close interaction of NGOs, the Commission and Parliament, and reform-minded EU member states led to an emphasis on long-term conflict prevention and transformation, as well as demands for institutional coherence in development aid and external action as part of sustainable peace between 1995 and 2003.

MILITARIZING PROCESSES BEYOND THE CROSSROADS

More active in pursuing our strategic objectives. This applies to the full spectrum of instruments for crisis management and conflict prevention at our disposal, including political, diplomatic, military and civilian, trade and development activities. Active policies are needed to counter the new dynamic threats. We need to develop a strategic culture that fosters early, rapid, and when necessary, robust intervention.

(European Security Strategy 2003: 17)

Like the defence components of the Treaty on European Union of 1991, the 2003 European Security Strategy (ESS) stands as a symbolic signpost at the crossroads of the militarization of the EU. By symbolic signpost, I mean that the processes discussed in this volume have already passed beyond the crossroads of other directions, as such symbols actively constitute our social reality (Manners 2000a: 263). As Gerard Quille argued in his discussion of 'Europe at a crossroads': 'the ESS may be an important first step along the road to an EU strategic culture' (Quille 2004: 429–30). Although many commentators have disagreed about the precise direction of the road marked 'strategic culture', it is clear to me that since the end of 2003 the EU has taken a sharp turn away from the normative path of sustainable peace towards a full spectrum of instruments for robust intervention, as the ESS (above) suggests (see also Duke 2004; Toje 2005).

Here I will consider the way in which the events of 11 September 2001 and 11 March 2004, together with the transatlantic crises created by the US invasion of Iraq, diverted the EU on a road towards militarization led by 'martial potency' and driven by the growth of a Brussels-based military-industrial simplex. I shall discuss EU militarization by briefly considering institutional prioritization, short- and long-term military missions, the Brussels-based trans-national policy 'network', the diverting of the human security agenda both in Brussels and at the UN, all culminating in the development of a military-industrial simplex. I should note that most informed observers identify the most pervasive and corrosive militarization (and securitization) to be occurring in areas other than those considered here, in particular the Commission's security research programme, the militarization of space policy, and the securitization of justice and home affairs, amongst many other areas.

Despite the widespread expectation that 'civilian ESDP missions are more likely than military ones', and that five out of six ongoing European Security and Defence Policy (ESDP) missions are non-military (EUPM, EUPOL Proxima, EUJUST Themis, EUPOL Kinshasa, EUJUST Lex), the extent of institutional prioritization of military structures and frameworks is apparent (see Sangiovanni 2003: 200-1; Keane 2004: 493–4; ICG 2005: 30–2). This prioritization includes the emphasis given to identifying and achieving military capabilities ahead of civilian capabilities, as the Civilian Capabilities Commitment Conference implicitly recognized in November 2004 when it acknowledged that 'shortcomings on issues such as mission and planning support, adequate financing, the ability of the EU to deploy at short notice and procurement needed to be addressed urgently' (Netherlands Presidency 2004: point 19). Prioritization also includes the way in which all aspects of civilian crisis management are framed in terms of subservience to ESDP, such as defining the five non-military missions as ESDP missions, or referring generally to the 'civilian aspects of ESDP'. Similarly, attempts by NGOs and the European Parliament to develop civilian organizations parallel to those in the military sector (such as a European Peacebuilding Agency or a European Civil Peace Corps) are ignored in the drive towards militarization (see Gourlay 2004a;

ICG 2005: 31–2). As the opening quote from the ESS illustrates, in a strategic culture favouring robust intervention, civilian activities appear to be useful only in as far as they are needed to counter new dynamic threats, thus subverting the normative approach of sustainable peace.

Although there has been very little experience of military intervention, it is still possible to take away some lessons from two of the EU's missions – the short-term operation Artemis and the long-term operation EUFOR Althea. In an unfortunate choice of words (mirroring those of George W. Bush just three months earlier) the French Defence Minister Michele Alliot-Marie declared 'mission accomplished' for the EU military operation Artemis in Bunia, Democratic Republic of the Congo in August 2003. As many critics have suggested, 'Artemis was probably possible only *because* its scope was so restricted' which 'merely pushed the problem of violent aggression against civilians beyond the environs of the town, where atrocities continued' (ICG 2005: 46; United Nations Peacekeeping Best Practices Unit 2004: 14). It was probably the case that Alliot-Marie could have announced the mission successful prior to its deployment given the limited mandate that was bound to succeed. Prior to deployment in June 2003, observers both inside and outside the EU had argued that the operation was too limited to achieve even demilitarization in Bunia. Most observers agree, including the EU's advisory agency (the EU-ISS), that Artemis was unable to secure all of Bunia. It allowed massacres to continue in the rest of Ituri province and it also 'skewed the military balance in Ituri', with fighting between armed groups returning to the province in July 2004 (Amnesty International 2003; Faria 2004: 44; ICG 2004: 11; Ulriksen *et al.* 2004: 522). The UN was particularly critical of the fixed nature of Artemis which ensured that the EU 'signalled clearly to all, including the armed belligerents, the transitory nature of the force' and 'risked failure in establishing such a strict exit date' (United Nations Peacekeeping Best Practices Unit 2004: 14, 16). In conclusion, it was the prioritizing of military over civilian operations in Artemis that ultimately undermined any short-term benefits it might have brought: 'the benefits of military efforts may prove to be short lived if they are not immediately accompanied by other complementary measures', such as an integrated police force, urgent reform of the judicial system and support for the Ituri administration (Faria 2004: 51).

If Artemis was 'mission accomplished', then EUFOR Althea may well become 'mission unaccomplishable' as the EU and its Special Representative (Paddy Ashdown) in Bosnia and Herzegovina increasingly deprive local administrations of their political functions (Osland 2004: 556–8; Chandler 2005; ICG 2005: 49–52). From the appointment of Ashdown as the EU Special Representative in March 2002 (as well as the international community's High Representative in May 2002), through the launching of the EU Police Mission in January 2003, to the taking over of the Stabilisation Force (SFOR) by EUFOR in December 2004, the Federation of Bosnia and Herzegovina and the Republika Srpska have been increasingly 'Europeanized'. This Europeanization has involved the EU in state-building the two entities in the direction of a Stabilization and

Association Agreement, and eventual EU membership, without conceding ownership of the process. The prioritization of military objectives over local capacity-building is not without consequences as most independent observers agree that Bosnia and Herzegovinia is now characterized by dependency, helplessness and disillusionment (Osland 2004: 556; ICG 2005: 49). Even the EU-ISS advisory agency has been forced to admit that 'this system of illiberal democracy under international supervision has now become the most serious constraint on the development of an effective state' (Knaus and Cox 2004: 55). These processes of disempowerment by the EU and Ashdown, together with the use of robust force (EUFOR), mean that 'it may already be too late to ensure an owner-driven process', while the EU still 'must prove it can coordinate complex civil and military matters' (Osland 2004: 557; ICG 2005: 52).

These three examples of prioritization of military affairs must be set within the broader context of the role of a Brussels-based transnational policy 'network' which has sought to direct EU militarization beyond the crossroads of 2003 towards a military doctrine of 'preventative engagement', including the 'second pillarization' of civilian crisis management (Bono 2004; Gourlay 2004b: 413; Leonard and Gowan 2004). A number of scholars have identified the ways in which the EU has developed a strategic-cultural discourse of militarization (Cornish and Edwards 2001; Rynning 2003; Bono 2004), but Jocelyn Mawdsley has gone furthest in identifying the 'unusual prevalence of trans-governmentalism within ESDP' (Mawdsley 2005: 15). Mawdsley has closely scrutinized the way in which the limited equipment needs of the Rapid Reaction Force have been quickly expanded into a quantitatively different arms dynamic by the activism of a Brussels-based transnational policy network (Mawdsley and Quille 2003; Mawdsley 2004; also Mawdsley et al. 2004). What seems clear from Mawdsley's scrutiny is the way in which the pre-2001 agreements on the Petersburg tasks and a Rapid Reaction Force were rapidly altered into post-2003 military arrangements for 'preventative engagement' (European Security Strategy 2003: 18) by those who sought to gain from such a sharp turn at the crossroads. In particular, transnational policy institutes themselves see militarization as an opportunity to empower their political role, as well as achieving deeper security and political integration. In this respect, the EU's advisory agency, the EU-ISS, has led the way towards militarization, in particular through encouraging Brussels-based policy centres to see the potential of inter-related security, economic and political logics.

Taken together, such institutes have reached an uneasy agreement on the need to advocate 'preventative engagement' as a European alternative to the US military strategy of 'pre-emptive engagement' – despite the ambiguous nature of the differences between preventative and pre-emptive (Leonard and Gowan 2004: 12–13; Mawdsley 2005: 2). Examples of the transnational networks and policy centres involved in advocacy include the 'Forum Europe' of the New Defence Agenda (NDA), and the joint 'European Security Forum' of the Centre for European Policy Studies (CEPS) and International Institute for Security Studies (sponsored by the German Marshall Fund of the United

States and the US Mission to the European Union). A series of reoccurring names constantly appear at the heart of this transnational policy network, including Javier Solana, Robert Cooper, Chris Patten, Fraser Cameron, Giles Merritt, Nicole Gnesotto, and Burkard Schmitt. The impact of this transnational advocacy appears to be the '*second pillarization*' of EU civilian crisis management where normative practices historically centred on the Commission, with democratic oversight from the Parliament, have been diverted into the Council activities making it 'extremely difficult for national parliaments and European assemblies to scrutinize and influence the policy-making process' (Bono 2004: 451; Gourlay 2004b: 413; Wagner 2006).

The interplay between institutional prioritization, military missions, and a transnational policy network have all contributed to the misdirection of the normative concerns of the human security agenda away from sustainable peace. The focus of all human security concerns has been people-centred freedom from fear and want, which is precisely what the normative principle of sustainable peace has sought to address (Peck 1998: 205–6). Prior to 2003 discussions within the EU on human security, particularly within the context of meeting the UN's Millennium Development Goals, had been focused on the understanding of people-centred freedom from fear and want (see Grimm 2004; Leen 2004).

Despite sixty-three years of development and recognition of the understanding of human development to include freedom from want, Javier Solana's 'study group' on Europe's security capabilities announced in September 2004 that 'A Human Security Doctrine for Europe' refers only to 'freedom for individuals from basic insecurities caused by gross human rights violations' which provide 'seven principles for operations', including 'the appropriate use of force' (Barcelona Report 2004: 5). Prior to Barcelona, in May 2004 Mary Kaldor (group convenor) made clear that 'the Study Group's focus is on physical security, or freedom from fear, more than freedom from want' (Berlin Report 2004: 2). However, the Barcelona Report makes clear that the new European security doctrine prioritizes the appropriate use of force over both freedom from fear and want. This separation of security and development in favour of human rights interventionism is problematic, as Keith Krause argues that 'ideas of security and development cannot be so easily separated, and because the development–security link was not one way' (Krause 2004: 45). Such a turn away from common understandings of human security and the causes of conflict, and towards legitimizing the use of force as part of a responsibility to protect human rights seems a logical strategic direction, but must be understood as part of a broader legitimizing move coming from outside the EU. As critics such as Mirjam van Reisen, Simon Stocker, and Florent Sebban put it: 'the increasing emphasis on security issues, the fight against terrorism and concerns over weapons of mass destruction threaten to overshadow all European foreign policy, leaving little or no room for policies geared towards human security' (2004: 36). The emphasis on human security as a responsibility to protect human rights must be understood within the EU doctrines of 'preventative engagement' and 'effective multilateralism' of the ESS, together with the

EU support for reform of the UN in line with the report of the High Level Panel on 'Threats, Challenges, and Changes' (United Nations High Level Panel 2004; Bono 2005). Led by the ideas of Gareth Evans (former Australian Foreign Minister), as well as Lloyd Axworthy (former Canadian Foreign Minister), the turn from human security towards humanitarian intervention is an attempt to overcome the crisis of the UN caused by the US invasion of Iraq. Whether a doctrine of pre-emption or prevention, after the crossroads of 2003 the EU aim has been to change the UN Charter to allow preventative military intervention under Chapter VII 'Action with Respect to Threats to the Peace' (see Leonard and Gowan 2004: 28-9; Bono 2005).

These five examples of militarization cannot be fully understood without the final factor which turned the EU away from the path of sustainable peace and towards an emphasis on 'martial potency' in 2003 – the role of a European 'military-industrial simplex'. A number of scholars have analysed the way in which the defence industries of EU member states have slowly used European integration as a means and a rationale for armaments co-operation (see Mörth 2003; Mawdsley *et al.* 2004). I use the phrase 'military-industrial simplex' to capture the way in which both the military-armaments lobby and the technology-industrial lobby have worked at the EU level to create a simple but compelling relationship between the need for forces capable of 'robust intervention', the technological and industrial benefits of defence and aerospace research, and the Western European Armaments Group's 1998 'Masterplan for the European Armaments Agency' leading to the creation of the European Defence Agency (EDA) in 2005 (see Mawdsley 2005). This military-industrial simplex was clarified by the Joint Action of the Council of Ministers in July 2004 when it stated that 'the agency will aim at developing defence capabilities in the field of crisis management, promoting and enhancing European armaments co-operation, strengthening the European defence industrial and technological base and creating a competitive European defence equipment market' (Council of the European Union 2004).

CONCLUSION: GREAT POWER OR NORMATIVE POWER BEYOND THE CROSSROADS

> Practical problems of international politics are often described in terms of building a bigger and better state – a European Union, without seeing that such an achievement would leave the problems of interstate politics precisely where they were.
>
> (Wight 1966 in Diez 1997: 287)

Painfully few scholars have heeded Martin Wight's 1966 warning of the consequences of building a bigger and better state (Thomas Diez and Karen Smith are rare exceptions). Yet the conceptual and theoretical consequences for NPE are now more serious than they were forty years ago, as Monnet's warning regarding the temptations of turning the EU into a nineteenth-century great power reminds us. Clearly, the acquisition of better policies, such as martial potency and preventative engagement, like those of great powers, risks making the EU more like bigger states. Thus the militarization of the EU risks making it more like bigger and better great powers, whilst leaving the problems of interstate politics *precisely* where they were. Militarizing the EU does not implicitly increase its power in interstate politics, and, as I have discussed, is increasingly risking its normative power. As the two most obvious expressions of EU normative power have demonstrated in 2004, the willingness of states and societies such as those of Turkey and Russia to accept norms such as 'equality' and 'sustainable development' in the cases of constitutional law and the Kyoto Protocol will change as the EU becomes more like a great power (China, India and the USA, for example). It is unfeasible that either Turkey or Russia would be as receptive to norm diffusion if they believed that EU battlegroups or combat forces would soon be peace-making in Kurdish areas or Chechnya. This is not to say that the acquisition of conflict prevention, peace-keeping and post-conflict reconstruction capacities are a bad thing in the abstract, simply that given the prioritization of military intervention over non-military conciliation, I have little doubt that normative conceptions of the EU are being undermined.

There are a number of factors that lead me to argue that the EU's normative power is being undermined by the unreflexive militarization of the past two years. Firstly, as I have discussed in the previous section, the balances between short-term problem-solving and long-term structural solutions, as well as between freedom from fear and freedom from want, found in the normative policies of sustainable peace, have been lost. Beyond these immediate concerns, the use of military missions in conjunction with civilian ones could present serious future problems for the EU. As the EU acquires more military capability it could become more tempted to use short-term military responses instead of its traditional reliance on long-term structural conflict prevention and transformation. Similarly, the use of EU military personnel in peace-keeping tasks will always run the risk of mission slide into peace-making tasks, particularly where combatants use guerrilla or terrorist tactics. Thirdly, as the recent experiences of Afghanistan and Iraq suggest, in situations where the EU may be seeking to shape post-conflict reconstruction, the mixing of military, political, civilian, and humanitarian agenda is both guaranteed and dangerous. Ultimately, the introduction of EU military forces in theatres and settings where only EU civilian staff once worked risks undermining the EU's peaceful normative power in favour of a more robust, and potentially violent, presence in the lives and minds of receiving populations.

As I suggested at the outset, it is tempting to think that the EU can have-its-cake-and-eat-it-too in militarizing its normative power. But the route to nineteenth-century great power status is not one that need be taken any further if EU military capability is acquired, deployed and analysed in a more reflexive manner. Such reflexivity must involve both reflexive research characterized by interpretation and reflection, and an understanding of the monitored character of social life in order to provide a means of returning to the normative path of sustainable peace as the central norm that guides the external actions of the EU. Within such a broader sustainable peace approach, it is entirely plausible that the EU can engage in most of the Article III-309 tasks ('joint disarmament operations, humanitarian and rescue tasks, military advice and assistance tasks, conflict prevention and peace-keeping tasks') under a UN mandate as part of a wider peace-building solution. However, as I have discussed above, the military tasks ('tasks of combat forces in crisis management, including peace-making and post-conflict stabilization') should only be attempted under a UN mandate, in a critically reflexive context, on a clear, normative basis. Without such fundamental reflection on militarization it is likely that, like Arendt's 'lost treasures', the normative power of the EU will be lost.

Biographical note: Ian Manners is a Senior Lecturer in Political Science, School of Technology and Society, Malmö University, Sweden.

Address for correspondence: Ian Manners, School of Technology and Society, Malmö University, 20506 Malmö, Sweden. email: ian.manners@ts.mah.se

NOTES

1 I am hugely indebted to Jocelyn Mawdsley for inspiration and help in finalizing this article – all the strong points in the fourth section are hers, all the weak ones mine. I am also very grateful to Giovanna Bono, David Chandler, Thomas Diez, Geoffrey Edwards, and an anonymous referee for their help and comments.
2 Jaap Ramaker was Ambassador of the Netherlands to the UN and Tono Eitel was Ambassador of Germany to the UN.
3 Common Position on Objectives Towards Afghanistan, 1998/108/CFSP; Presidency Statement on Peace Talks in Colombia, 6 January 1999; Common Position Concerning the Process on Stability and Good-neighbourliness in South-East Europe, 98/633/CFSP; Common Position Concerning Conflict Prevention, Management and Resolution in Africa, 2004/85/CFSP; Presidency Statement in Response to the Head of the OSCE Mission in Bosnia and Herzegovina, 17 February 2005.
4 European Parliament Resolution A4-0135/1995, 14 June 1995.

REFERENCES

Amnesty International (2003) 'Democratic Republic of Congo, Ituri – How Many More Have to Die?', AI Index: AFR 62/030/2003.
Annan, K. (2001) 'Report of the Secretary-General on Prevention of Armed Conflict', S/2001/574, New York: United Nations.
Arendt, H. (1979) *The Origins of Totalitarianism*, New York: Harvest.
Arendt, H. (1990) *On Revolution*, London: Penguin.
Arendt, H. (1998) *The Human Condition*, 2nd edn, Chicago: University of Chicago Press.
Barcelona Report (2004) 'A Human Security Doctrine for Europe', The Barcelona Report of the Study Group on Europe's Security Capabilities.

Berlin Report (2004) Full Report, Expert Seminar, 'Towards a Global Security Policy for Europe: Tasks and Capabilities', Friedrich Ebert Stiftung, Berlin.

Björkdahl, A. (2002) *From Idea to Norm: Promoting Conflict Resolution*, Lund: Department of Political Science, Lund University.

Björkdahl, A. (2005) 'Norm-maker and norm-taker: exploring the normative influence of the EU in Macedonia', *European Foreign Affairs Review* 10(2): 257–78.

Bono, G. (2004) 'The EU's military doctrine: an assessment', *International Peacekeeping* 11(3): 439–56.

Bono, G. (2005) 'The redefinition of "multilateralism" in the EU and UN crisis management: the return of the Leviathans?'. Paper presented to the British Political Studies Association.

Busumtwi-Sam, J. (2002) 'Sustainable peace and development in Africa', *Studies in Comparative International Development* 37(3): 91–118.

Chandler, D. (2003) 'Rhetoric without responsibility: the attraction of "ethical" foreign policy', *British Journal of Politics and International Relations* 5(3): 295–316.

Chandler, D. (2005) 'From Dayton to Europe', *International Peacekeeping* 12(3): 336–49.

Conflict Prevention Network (2001) *Conflict Prevention Network Project Description*, Berlin and Brussels: Conflict Prevention Network.

Coolsaet, R. and Soetendorp, B. (2000) 'Belgium and the Netherlands', in I. Manners and R. Whitman (eds), *The Foreign Policies of European Union Member States*, Manchester: Manchester University Press, pp. 128–43.

Cornish, P. and Edwards, G. (2001) 'Beyond the EU/NATO dichotomy: the beginnings of a European strategic culture', *International Affairs* 77(3): 587–603.

Cremona, M. (1998) 'The European Union as an international actor: the issues of flexibility and linkage', *European Foreign Affairs Review* 3(1): 67–94.

Diamantopoulou, A. (2003) Address to the European Parliament on the UN Report on Women, War and Peace, Brussels, 20 January.

Diez, T. (1997) 'International ethics and European integration: federal state or network horizon?', *Alternatives* 22(3): 287–312.

Duchêne, F. (1971) 'A new European defense community', *Foreign Affairs* 50(1): 69–82.

Duchêne, F. (1972) 'Europe's role in world peace', in R. Mayne (ed.), *Europe Tomorrow: Sixteen Europeans Look Ahead*, London: Fontana/Collins, pp. 32–47.

Duchêne, F. (1973) 'The European Community and the uncertainties of interdependence', in M. Kohnstamm and W. Hager (eds), *A Nation Writ Large? Foreign-Policy Problems Before the Community*, London: Macmillan, pp. 1–21.

Duke, S. (2004) 'The European Security Strategy in a comparative framework: does it make for secure alliances in a better world?', *European Foreign Affairs Review* 9: 459–81.

Eavis, P. and Kefford, S. (2002) 'Conflict prevention and the European Union: a potential yet to be fully realised', in P. van Tongeren, H. van de Veen and J. Verhoeven (eds), *Searching for Peace in Europe and Eurasia: An Overview of Conflict Prevention and Peacebuilding Activities*, Boulder, CO: Lynne Rienner, pp. 3–14.

Eitel, T. (1998) 'The situation in Bosnia'. Statement to the UN Security Council, 15 June.

Faria, F. (2004) 'Crisis management in Sub-Saharan Africa: the role of the European Union', EU-ISS Occasional Paper 51.

Ginsberg, R. (2001) *The European Union in International Politics: Baptism by Fire*, Lanham, MD: Rowman & Littlefield.

Gourlay, C. (2004a) *Feasibility Study on the European Civil Peace Corps*, Brussels: International Security Information Service.

Gourlay, C. (2004b) 'European Union procedures and resources for crisis management', *International Peacekeeping* 11(3): 404–21.

Grimm, S. (2004) 'Human Security – Placing Development at the Heart of the EU's External Relations', Briefing Document for Dóchas, Ireland.

Guisan-Dickinson, C. (2003) 'The European Union's identity and the politics of recon-
  ciliation'. Paper presented to EUSA, Nashville, USA.
Hill, C. (2001) 'The EU's capacity for conflict prevention', *European Foreign Affairs
  Review* 6(3): 315–33.
Hilpold, P. (2002) 'EU development cooperation at a crossroads: the Cotonou
  Agreement of 23 June 2000 and the principle of good governance', *European
  Foreign Affairs Review* 7(1): 53–72.
Hjelm-Wallén, L. and Halonen, T. (1996) 'Swedish–Finnish initiative on EU conflict
  management capability'. Joint articles in *Dagens Nyheter* (Sweden) and *Helsingin
  Sanomat* (Finland), 21 April.
Holland, M. (1995) 'Bridging the capability–expectations gap: a case study of
  CFSP joint action on South Africa', *Journal of Common Market Studies* 33(4):
  556–72.
International Crisis Group (2004) 'Maintaining Momentum in the Congo: the Ituri
  Problem', ICG Africa Report 84, Nairobi/Brussels.
International Crisis Group (2005) 'EU Crisis Response Capability Revisited', Europe
  Report 160.
Keane, R. (2004) 'The Solana process in Serbia and Montenegro: coherence in EU
  foreign policy', *International Peacekeeping* 11(3): 491–507.
Knaus, G. and Cox, M. (2004) 'Bosnia and Herzegovina: Europeanisation by decree?',
  in J. Batt (ed.), *The Western Balkans: Moving On*, Chaillot Paper 70, Paris: EU-ISS,
  pp. 55–68.
Krause, K. (2004) 'Is human security "more than just a good idea"?', in M. Brzoska and
  P. Croll (eds), *Promoting Security: But How and For Whom?*, Bonn Centre for
  Conversion Brief 30.
Kronenberger, V. and Wouters, J. (eds) (2004) *The European Union and Conflict Pre-
  vention Policy and Legal Aspects*, Cambridge: Cambridge University Press.
Leen, M. (2004) 'The European Union, HIV/AIDS and Human Security', Briefing
  Document for Dóchas, Ireland.
Leonard, M. and Gowan, R. (2004) *Global Europe: Implementing the European Security
  Strategy*, London: Foreign Policy Centre.
Malloch Brown, M. (2003) 'Democratic governance: towards a framework for sustain-
  able peace', *Global Governance* 9(2): 141–6.
Manners, I. (2000a) *Substance and Symbolism: An Anatomy of Cooperation in the New
  Europe*, Aldershot: Ashgate.
Manners, I. (2000b) 'Normative power Europe: a contradiction in terms?', Copenhagen
  Peace Research Institute, Working Paper 38.
Manners, I. (2002) 'Normative power Europe: a contradiction in terms?', *Journal of
  Common Market Studies* 40(2): 235–58.
Manners, I. (2003) 'Europaian studies', *Journal of Contemporary European Studies*
  11(1): 67–83.
Manners, I. (2005) 'The value of peace', in M. Aziz and S. Millns (eds), *Values in the
  Constitution of Europe*, London: Dartmouth.
Mawdsley, J. (2004) 'The Commission moves into defence research', *European Security
  Review* 22, International Security Information Service.
Mawdsley, J. (2005) 'Creating a European security policy: transgovernmentalism or the
  development of transnational policy communities?'. Paper presented to the British
  Political Studies Association.
Mawdsley, J. and Quille, G. (2003) 'Equipping the Rapid Reaction Force: options
  for and constraints on a European defence equipment strategy', Bonn International
  Centre for Conversion Paper 33.
Mawdsley, J., Martinelli, M. and Remacle, E. (eds) (2004) *Europe and the Global Arma-
  ment Agenda: Security, Trade and Accountability*, Baden-Baden: Nomos.

McLean, A. and Lilly, D. (eds) (2000) *Preventing Violent Conflict: Opportunities for the Swedish and Belgian Presidencies of the European Union*, Utrecht: European Platform for Conflict Prevention and Transformation.

Miall, H. (2000) 'Preventing potential conflicts: assessing the impact of "light" and "deep" conflict prevention in Central and Eastern Europe and the Balkans', in M. Lund and G. Rasamoelina (eds), *The Impact of Conflict Prevention Policy: Cases, Measures and Assessments*, SWP-Conflict Prevention Network Yearbook 1999/2000, Baden-Baden: Nomos, pp. 23–45.

Monnet, J. (1962) 'A ferment of change', *Journal of Common Market Studies* 1(1): 203–11, reprinted in B. Nelsen and A. Stubb (eds), *The European Union: Readings on the Theory and Practice of European Integration*, 3rd edn, Basingstoke: Palgrave, pp. 19–26.

Mushaben, J.M. (1999) 'Collective memory divided and reunited: mothers, daughters and the Fascist experience in Germany', *History and Memory* 11(1): 7–40.

Mörth, U. (2003) *Organizing European Co-operation. The Case of Armaments*, Lanham, MD: Rowman & Littlefield.

Osland, K. (2004) 'The EU police mission in Bosnia and Herzegovina', *International Peacekeeping* 11(3): 544–60.

Patten, C. (2003) 'The role of women in conflict resolution'. Speech to the World Women Lawyers Conference, 30 June.

Peck, C. (1998) *Sustainable Peace: The Role of the UN and Regional Organizations in Preventing Conflict*, Lanham, MD: Rowman & Littlefield.

Quille, G. (2004) 'The European security strategy: a framework for EU security interests?', *International Peacekeeping* 11(3): 422–38.

Ramaker, J. (1997) 'Crafting a sustainable peace: supporting conflict prevention, conflict management and conflict resolution'. Statement to the UN Parliamentary Forum, 9 October.

van Reisen, M., Stocker, S. and Sebban, F. (2004) 'European Union security concerns vs. human security aspirations', in *Social Watch Annual Report 2004*.

Rummel, R. (1996a) 'Conflict prevention: the need for a CFSP strategy', in *Conflict Prevention: A Challenge for the European Union*, London: Oxfam and Saferworld.

Rummel, R. (1996b) *Common Foreign and Security Policy and Conflict Prevention: Priorities for the Intergovernmental Conference*, London: Saferworld and International Alert.

Rynning, S. (2003) 'The European Union: towards a strategic culture?', *Security Dialogue* 34(4): 479–96.

Sangiovanni, M.E. (2003) 'Why a common security and defence policy is bad for Europe', *Survival* 45(3): 193–206.

Smith, H. (1995) *European Union Foreign Policy in Central America*, Basingstoke: Macmillan.

Smith, H. (2002) *European Union Foreign Policy: What It Is and What It Does*, London: Pluto.

Smith, K.E. (1998) 'The use of political conditionality in the EU's relations with third countries: how effective?', *European Foreign Affairs Review* 3(2): 253–74.

Smith, K.E. (1999) *The Making of EU Foreign Policy: The Case of Eastern Europe*, Basingstoke: Macmillan.

Smith, K.E. (2003) *European Union Foreign Policy in a Changing World*, Cambridge: Polity Press.

Soetendorp, B. (1999) *Foreign Policy in the European Union: Theory, History and Practice*, London: Longman.

Solana, J. and Patten, C. (2000) *Improving the Coherence and Effectiveness of EU Action in the Field of Conflict Prevention*. Report presented to the Nice European Council, December.

Spivak, G.C. (1999) *A Critique of Postcolonial Reason: Toward a History of the Vanishing Present*, Cambridge, MA: Harvard University Press.

Toje, A. (2005) 'The 2003 European Union security strategy: a critical appraisal', *European Foreign Affairs Review* 10: 117–33.

Wagner, W. (2006) 'The democratic control of military power Europe', *Journal of European Public Policy* 13(2): 200–16.

Wight, M. (1966) 'Why is there no international theory?', in H. Butterfield and M. Wight (eds), *Diplomatic Investigations*, London: Allen & Unwin, pp. 17–34.

Ulriksen, S., Gourlay, C. and Mace, C. (2004) 'Operation *Artemis*: the shape of things to come?', *International Peacekeeping* 11(3): 508–25.

Official documents

Council of the European Union (2004) General Affairs and External Relations, 2597. Council Meeting, Brussels Press Release, 11105/04 (Presse 216).

European Commission (1996a) 'Linking relief, rehabilitation and development', Commission Policy Paper, Brussels.

European Commission (1996b) 'The European Union and the Issue of Conflicts in Africa: Peace-Building, Conflict Prevention and Beyond', Communication from the Commission to the Council (SEC (96) 332).

European Security Strategy (2003) 'A Secure Europe in a Better World', Brussels: European Council, 12 December.

Netherlands Presidency (2004) 'European Security and Defence Policy Report', endorsed by the European Council, December.

United Nations High Level Panel (2004) *A More Secure World: Our Shared Responsibility*, New York: United Nations.

United Nations Peacekeeping Best Practices Unit (2004) *Operation Artemis: The Lessons of the Interim Emergency Multinational Force*, New York: United Nations.

The democratic control of military power Europe[1]

Wolfgang Wagner

INTRODUCTION

Since 2003, the European Union (EU) has been an active player in military crisis management: the EU has led military missions in Bosnia, Macedonia and the Bunia region in Northern Congo with up to some 7,000 troops in Bosnia and 2,000 in Bunia. The development of a European Security and Defence Policy (ESDP) has raised concerns over the EU's identity as a 'civilian power'. Most prevalent, of course, have been concerns over a gradual replacement of civilian policy instruments (such as aid, diplomacy, or sanctions) by military force (cf., for example, Smith 2000). Less attention has been paid to the repercussions of the ESDP for civil–military relations and the democratic control of security and defence policy.

To be sure, civilian control of the ESDP has never been challenged. In contrast, civil–military relations in the EU have followed the democratic role model:[2] the newly established Military Committee (MC, composed of chiefs of defence, represented by military representatives) and Military Staff (MS, composed of seconded experts from the member states) are clearly subordinate to the Political and Security Committe (PSC, consisting of senior diplomats at ambassador level) and the foreign ministers in the General Affairs and External Relations Council (GAERC). The defence ministers have not even been granted a Council configuration of their own. Instead, they have only been able to meet at the fringes of the GAERC.

However, a new generation of scholars working on civil–military relations in democracies have been less concerned with 'the threat of praetorian military intervention in domestic politics and the resultant need to enforce civilian executive control of the military' (Cottey *et al.* 2002: 31). Instead they plead for a reconceptualization 'in terms of democratic governance of the defense and security sector' (Cottey *et al.* 2002: 32) and for particular attention to be paid 'to the role of parliaments in providing oversight of the armed forces, defense policy, and the executive's control of the military and the wider civil society debate on armed forces and defense' (Cottey *et al.* 2002: 39).

This article argues that the ESDP, though not challenging civilian control of the military, does warrant concerns about the democratic control of defence policy in Europe. The lack of attention to this problematique is surprising for at least three reasons: first, the democratic control of foreign, security and defence policy has frequently been regarded as a defining moment of a civilian power (cf., for example, Stavridis 2001 and Smith 2004). This is closely related to a second reason, namely that democracy has been celebrated as a cause for peace in large parts of the peace research community. According to the 'democratic peace', 'the participatory nature of the states' political institutions constrains leaders because the populations who must bear the costs of war may be unwilling to do so if the costs are high or the policy fails' (Siverson 1995: 482; cf. also Russett 1993; Russett and Oneal 2001). Thus, the literature on the democratic peace provides the theoretical foundation of why the democratic control of security and defence policy is indeed an important feature of a civilian power. Third, the deficiencies of the EU as a democracy have been subject to a lively debate but this debate has focused almost exclusively on issues of the first pillar of the EU (for an excellent overview of that debate cf. Hix 2005: ch. 6).

This article focuses on the implications of the ESDP for the democratic control of security and defence policy. It argues that the Europeanization of defence politics leads to a democratic deficit. Because the democratic control of security and defence policy can be considered an essential element of a civilian power, this aggravates concerns about the future of the 'civilian power Europe'.

Space constraints do not allow a comprehensive discussion of the manifold aspects of democratic control of security and defence politics (for a more comprehensive discussion of the democratic legitimacy of the ESDP, cf. Wagner 2005). The second section argues, however, that the parliamentary control of deployment decisions is a key aspect of democratic control and may therefore serve as a proxy for the problem at large. The third section then demonstrates that national parliaments' capacity to control executive decisions to use military force has been weakened by the ESDP. The fourth section sketches problems and options of parliamentary control at the European level. It discusses the competencies of the European Parliament and the 'Interim European Security and Defence Assembly' as well as further options to strengthen transnational parliamentary control. Finally, the concluding section presents an assessment of the damage done to the EU as a civilian power by the emerging democratic deficit.

PARLIAMENTARY CONTROL OF DEPLOYMENT DECISIONS

Security and defence politics impacts on citizens' lives in many ways: recruitment policy determines how much (if any) time young men must spend as conscripts, and the defence budget influences how much the government can dedicate to social policy, etc. The most tremendous impact, however, results from decisions on the actual deployment of troops in military missions because, in addition to their political and fiscal repercussions, citizens' lives are then put at risk. Since the end of the Cold War, the importance of deployment decisions has grown because 'peace support operations' have become more common as a number of violent conflicts have increased the demand for such missions. At the same time, the United Nations (UN) Security Council has been blocked less frequently by one of the veto powers. In 2003, the then fifteen member states of the EU had deployed some 55,000 troops in international peace support operations (Giegerich and Wallace 2004: 169). From the perspective of democratic control, deployment decisions can therefore be regarded as the most important aspect of contemporary security and defence policy.

In the literature on the democratic peace, regular free elections are considered the most important mechanism to hold executives accountable. According to Morgan and Campbell, 'leaders who have to stand for popular election should be expected to take public attitudes into account when making decisions' (1991: 190). Democracies are considered to be less war-prone because 'leaders of democratic states typically experience high political costs from fighting wars – always from losing them, and often despite winning them' (Russett and Oneal 2001: 54). In addition to free elections, Morgan and Campbell have identified the 'nature of political competition' and 'the degree to which the leader must share decision-making power' as further mechanisms to constrain political leaders. These latter mechanisms are of particular importance where deployments below the threshold of war are concerned because they are less likely to have an impact on citizens' electoral decisions (especially if they are carried out early in the election cycle). In such cases, 'parliaments are the central locus of accountability for any governmental decision-making concerning the use of force' (Hänggi 2004: 11; cf. also Morgan and Campbell 1991: 191). As elected representatives of the people, the articulation of popular interests and concerns has been a prominent task of members of parliament.

Hans Born and Heiner Hänggi have distinguished three dimensions of parliamentary power in security and defence politics: 'authority' refers to 'the power which Parliament uses to hold government accountable' and which is 'derived from the constitutional and legal framework as well as customary practices'.

'Ability' denotes the resources such as specialized committees, budget and staff which are necessary to make efficient use of the authority conferred upon parliament. Finally, 'attitude' refers to the 'willingness to hold the executive to account' which, among other things, depends on the extent to which legislative–executive relations are characterized by party discipline (all quotes from Born 2004: 209–11). Although each of these factors has had an influence on the effectiveness of parliamentary accountability, Born and Hänggi conclude that 'the strongest means of parliamentary oversight by far is ... the constitutional or legal right to approve or reject such use of force' (Hänggi 2004: 14). In contrast, budget and staff are certainly indispensable to make use of legal authority but they *reflect* rather than cause legal powers.

Therefore, in discussing the democratic control of security and defence policy, this article focuses on parliament's control of deployment decisions.

THE ESDP AND THE WEAKENING OF NATIONAL DEMOCRACY

This section argues that the ESDP tends to undermine parliamentary control of deployment decisions at the national level. The general claim that a democratic deficit results from a Europeanization of policy-making has of course been well established. However, this claim has been almost exclusively substantiated with case studies from the EU's first pillar where member state governments may even be outvoted in Council under qualified majority voting. The first part of this section demonstrates that the integration of military structures in particular brings about a similar effect. The second part then adds an important caveat, namely that this tendency to undermine parliamentary control is very uneven across the member states because member countries differ vastly as regards their parliaments' competencies in security and defence policy. In the third part of this section, Germany's decision to participate in the military enforcement of the no-fly zone over Bosnia in 1993 serves as an illustration.

The difficult parliamentary control of deploying integrated military structures

Particularly since the Danish voters' rejection of the Maastricht Treaty in 1992, scholars of EU politics have been concerned with a democratic deficit in European politics. Andrew Moravcsik and Klaus Dieter Wolf in particular have pointed to this 'dark side of intergovernmental cooperation' (Wolf 1999: 334), i.e. that 'international cooperation tends to redistribute domestic political resources toward executives' (Moravcsik 1994: 7). According to Moravcsik, a loss of control over the executive results from four causal mechanisms: first, international co-operation enhances the executive's control over the domestic agenda because the international agenda has been 'cartelized' between national leaders. Second, once *international* agreement has been reached, it 'may be costly, sometimes prohibitively so, for national parliaments, publics or officials to reject, amend or block ratification of and compliance with decisions reached by national executives in international fora' (Moravcsik 1994: 11). Third, international co-operation gives executives privileged access to information about the political constraints of other governments and about the technical consequences of alternative policies. Finally, executives can impose an initial ideological 'frame' on an issue which is difficult for domestic groups to challenge.

This general trend of privileging the executive in the process of Europeanization is exacerbated in security and defence policy by the integration of military forces on an international level.[3] If forces have been integrated, any state's decision against its participation in a mission de facto frustrates the entire deployment because other states' forces cannot work effectively without the missing state's contribution. As a consequence, states whose forces have been integrated on an international level may come under heavy peer pressure from those states that advocate the use of joint forces.

Since the end of the Cold War, EU member states have faced strong incentives to integrate their military forces. First of all, shrinking defence budgets in all member states have made their efficient spending more pressing. Member states have therefore been more prepared to participate in joint armaments projects and to engage in role specialization in order to obtain more value for money (Schmitt 2003). Furthermore, the integration of military forces has been promoted for political reasons. With the common threat to Western European security disappearing, experts and decision-makers across Europe have been concerned about a renationalization of security and defence policies. The integration of military structures has been a powerful instrument to give credibility to the commitment to prevent a renationalization of defence policies.

An uneven democratic deficit

The degree to which a Europeanization of security and defence policy undermines parliamentary control at the national level not only depends on the degree to which military forces have been integrated but also on the level of parliamentary control over security and defence policy in the first place. Among the EU member states, there have been huge differences as regards parliaments' competencies in security and defence policy.[4] In former colonial powers, for example, governments are usually allowed to deploy troops without the consent of parliament (Born and Urscheler 2004: 64f.). Thus, the governments in France and the United Kingdom decided to participate in North Atlantic Treaty Organization (NATO) air strikes against Serbian targets in 1999 without having consulted parliament. In a similar vein, no parliamentary approval is required in Spain, Belgium and Greece.

In contrast, the consent of parliament prior to any deployment of troops has been required in Germany, Austria, Denmark, Sweden, Ireland, and many of the new member states from Central and Eastern Europe. In Hungary, even two-thirds of the Members of Parliament must vote in favour of a deployment. In Italy and the Netherlands, governments have regarded parliamentary approval as indispensable although there has been no constitutional requirement to do so. However, in some of these countries, the deployment law provides for exceptions from and modifications of the general rule of parliamentary approval. In Austria, parliament has delegated its right to approve or disapprove of military deployments to a standing committee ('Hauptausschuss') which has participated in the exercise of various executive tasks. Moreover, the government may deploy troops without parliamentary approval if urgency does not allow for it. In this case, a debate must be held within fifteen days. In case parliament does not endorse the deployment, the respective troops have to be ordered back.

Yet another exemption from general parliamentary approval can be found in Sweden: here, the government may deploy troops without consulting parliament if the deployment takes place within the framework of multilateral security institutions. In particular, deployments based on a 'standby agreement' as provided by article 43 of the UN Charter do not require the consent of the Riksdag. Similarly, deployments based on international agreements that have been endorsed by parliament are exempted from further approval. In Ireland, there has been still another exemption from general parliamentary approval for deployments consisting of less than twelve armed soldiers.

This brief survey of deployment law underlines the differences among EU member states with regard to parliament's role in security and defence policy. As a consequence, the 'dark side of international co-operation' can be felt in the EU member states to very different degrees.

Parliamentary accountability versus alliance solidarity: the case of Germany

As the EU has only begun to assume a role in peace support operations, it has not yet experienced severe conflicts between the demands of military integration, on the one hand, and parliamentary control, on the other hand. In this section, therefore, the case of Germany in NATO will serve as an illustration. Of course, NATO differs from the EU in many respects, most importantly as regards the dominant role of the US which retains a fully-fledged unilateral military capability. At the same time, however, NATO and the EU resemble each other in one important respect of relevance here, i.e. in having developed a strong sense of common identity and solidarity. As a consequence, NATO as well as EU members tend to include their fellow members' concerns in their definition of security interests (Risse-Kappen 1995; Risse 2001; Sjursen 2004). Moreover, the case of NATO's Airborne Warning and Control System (AWACS) fleet comes very close to what the EU envisions in terms of military integration and role specialization. Thus, conflicts very similar to that experienced by Germany in NATO are likely to arise in the EU, especially if it realizes the 'Headline Goal 2010' which provides for the creation of multinational, integrated 'battle groups'.

Germany is particularly suited to illustrate the conflicting demands of military integration and parliamentary control. As a consequence of two world wars and the atrocities of the Wehrmacht, Germany has been a champion of both multilateralism and antimilitarism (among many others, see Anderson and Goodman 1993; Berger 1998). Since the fierce debate over rearmament in the 1950s, a reluctance to use military force and a commitment to multilateralism became prime pillars of post-war German security policy. However, since the end of the Cold War and the growing number of peace support operations out of area, tensions between these two principles have mounted.

Right after the Cold War, a participation of the Bundeswehr in out of area missions was widely opposed in Germany. Indeed, the German government refrained from sending the Bundeswehr to the Persian Gulf in 1990–91. At the time of the Gulf crisis of 1990–91, German politicians were eager to demonstrate the country's peacefulness and were 'surprised that the USA and Israel, among others, condemned Germany for not contributing militarily against Iraq' (Philippi 2001: 51). German decision-makers had to realize that its NATO partners now expected Germany as an ally to make a substantial contribution to non-article 5 operations (Baumann 2001: 166). Moreover, they realized that 'similar behaviour in a future conflict would probably result in a crisis with its major allies' (Philippi 2001: 51). From then on, German governments aimed at overcoming the antimilitarist culture as an obstacle to the deployment of the Bundeswehr out of area. For this purpose, 'reliability as an ally' and 'alliance solidarity' became prominent arguments in the German debate over out of area missions (cf. Schwab-Trapp 2002). These arguments were buttressed by references to integrated force structures of which the Bundeswehr had been part. References to Germany's participation in NATO's AWACS illustrate this point: AWACS has been designed to recognize enemy aircraft over a given territory, most importantly in the event of an attack (defensive function). In addition, it may help to identify and select targets for air strikes (offensive function). In 1993, NATO offered its AWACS fleet to enforce the no-fly zone over Bosnia which the UN Security Council had agreed on. The German government's decision not to withdraw Bundeswehr personnel from AWACS met considerable criticism from the opposition and even from within the governing coalition. Thus, in early 1993, the Federal Constitutional Court (FCC) had to give a preliminary ruling on whether the participation of the Bundeswehr violated the German constitution as the opposition argued.[5]

With a narrow margin of 5:3 votes, the FCC endorsed the government's decision to have the Bundeswehr participate in AWACS's mission over Bosnia. Concerns about alliance solidarity and reliability played a decisive role in the judgment. The Court noted that the Bundeswehr made up for around 30 per cent of AWACS's personnel. As a consequence, a withdrawal of German soldiers at the very moment of this mission would endanger the enforcement of the no-fly zone over Bosnia. Furthermore, 'allies and European neighbours would inevitably lose trust in German policy; the resulting damage would be irreparable.'[6] Thus, the fact that the Bundeswehr participated in an integrated military structure played a decisive role in legitimizing Germany's first combat (in contrast to humanitarian or peace-keeping) mission out of area. Since then, the scope of Germany's contribution to out of area missions has grown continually (cf. for an overview Baumann and Hellmann 2001).

In the main judgment of July 1994, the FCC affirmed the principle that any deployment of the Bundeswehr must obtain parliamentary approval in advance. According to the FCC, the use of the armed forces is not within the executive's sole discretion but as a 'parliamentary army' part of the democratic constitutional order. However, the principle of advance parliamentary approval is circumscribed in two cases: 'The participation of the Bundestag in a specific decision to deploy troops that constitutional law requires must not compromise Germany's ability to defend itself (*Wehrfähigkeit*) and to make alliance commitments (*Bündnisfähigkeit*)' (author's translation).

Since the FCC's ruling, the Bundestag has dealt with more than thirty deployments of the Bundeswehr (including the prolongation and extension of missions) (Meyer 2004: 19–20). However, this practice has again come under pressure since NATO's Prague summit decided to set up a multinational 'Response Force' that could be deployed for the most demanding peace support missions within a few days. The deployment of the NATO Response Force (NRF) was simulated at an informal NATO summit in Colorado Springs in October 2003. It soon became clear that a rapid deployment could be endangered by the required advance approval of the German parliament. As with AWACS, German troops would play an essential role in the NRF. In contrast to AWACS, however, even a belated 'green light' would possibly cause problems. As a consequence, German Defence Minister Struck immediately launched a debate about a reform of Germany's parliamentary proviso. Struck's suggestion was supported by his American colleague, Donald Rumsfeld, who urged NATO members 'to bring NATO's decision-making structures up to date so that NATO military commanders can take decisive action against fast-moving threats in the 21st century'.[7]

To be sure, the conflict between the democratic control of the armed forces and the demands of alliance politics is nowhere likely to be as intense as in Germany where both demanding standards of parliamentary control and multinational integration were designed to prevent a resurgence of militarism. However, similar though possibly less intense conflicts are likely to occur in other states with traditionally high levels of parliamentary control as well. Moreover, the EU might become the prime forum for such conflicts to the extent that the ESDP steps into NATO's footprints. In particular, the project of EU 'battle groups', i.e. small, integrated multinational forces to be deployed at short notice, is likely to result in conflicts very similar to those over the NRF. Moreover, the EU comprises a couple of member states that remained aloof from military alliances during the Cold War. As the brief survey of member states' standards above demonstrated, many of these states (e.g. Austria, Ireland and Sweden) have had high standards of parliamentary control similar to those in Germany.

PROSPECTS OF PARLIAMENTARY CONTROL AT THE EUROPEAN LEVEL

The emerging democratic deficit at the national level has led to calls to compensate for the weakening of national parliaments with a strengthening of supranational or transnational parliamentary institutions. This section therefore explores the prospects of redressing the democratic deficit at the European level. It begins with a discussion of the competencies of the European Parliament (EP), then proceeds to analyse the merits of the 'Interim European Security and Defence Assembly', and finally presents some further options for transnational parliamentary collaboration.

The limited powers of the European Parliament

The member states have only hesitantly endowed the EP with competencies in foreign, security and defence policy. In fact, the establishment of European Political Cooperation outside the Treaty Establishing the European Community and the establishment of the Common Foreign and Security Policy as a distinct pillar of the EU was primarily driven by a desire to keep the supranational institutions' competencies limited.

While the EP has established itself as an actor in foreign and security policy, the ESDP has remained aloof from the EP's involvement. Article 21 of the Treaty on European Union (TEU) which obliges the Presidency to consult the EP 'on the main aspects and the basic choices of the common foreign and security policy' and to 'ensure that the views of the European Parliament are duly taken into consideration' does not even mention the ESDP explicitly. However, this wording has not prevented the Presidency and the Council from extending consultations informally to the realm of the ESDP (Mammonas 2003: 5; Gourlay 2004: 188f.). One member of the EP's foreign affairs committee even observed that the High Representative, Solana, and the Commissioner for External Affairs, Chris Patten, discussed external affairs with the committee more frequently than their national counterparts with national parliaments. As these habits underline, the scope of article 21 should be extended to security and defence policy. Indeed, the constitutional treaty suggests a respective rewording. According to article I-40 (8), 'The European Parliament shall be regularly consulted on the main aspects and basic choices of the common security and defence policy. It shall be kept informed of how it evolves.'

Over the last couple of years, the EP has begun to redress the lack of resources devoted to the ESDP (cf. Brok and Gresch 2004). Whereas its foreign affairs committee devoted a considerable part of its resources to the enlargement process during the fifth parliamentary term (1999–2004), the current committee has established a subcommittee on security and defence which is a clear indicator of future priorities. Since 2002, an interinstitutional agreement gives the Council the possibility of sharing classified documents with a small committee of the EP. As Catriona Gourlay has pointed out, this 'agreement does not, however, confer rights on the parliament to receive access to classified information but rather gives the Council the right to share classified information where it is appropriate and possible in the light of the nature and the content of the information' (Gourlay 2004: 190). Furthermore, the EP has endeavoured to cultivate good relations with NATO's Parliamentary Assembly (PA). Since 2001, the EP has sent a delegation to the PA's sessions. Moreover, there have been joint sessions of EP and PA committees. In doing so, the EP has demonstrated its ability to foster relations with those NATO countries that are not members of the EU. Drawing on the three factors determining the effectiveness of parliamentary oversight, one can conclude that the EP has now begun to enhance its ability to use its legal powers. Notwithstanding these improvements, however, the EP's overall powers in security and defence policy are still rather limited. Most importantly, the member state governments have no obligation to even consult the EP before deciding on the deployment of troops. As regards this crucial aspect of defence politics, the EP can therefore hardly compensate for the weakening of parliamentary control at the national level.

The 'Interim European Security and Defence Assembly'

The transfer of operational tasks from the Western European Union (WEU) to the EU has led to the odd situation that a further supra- or rather transnational parliament has been involved in European Security and Defence Policy: the WEU's Parliamentary Assembly. Because the WEU's mutual defence commitment exceeds that of NATO, members of the WEU preferred not to dissolve the WEU but only to transfer its operational tasks to the EU. The decision not to dissolve the WEU Treaty also implied that its article IX, according to which the Council of the WEU submits an annual report to the WEU Parliamentary Assembly, remained valid. At the time, some urged the Parliamentary Assembly to dissolve itself. Instead, the parliamentarians, who are not elected directly but nominated from national parliaments, decided to rename it the 'Interim European Security and Defence Assembly' and to continue their work.

The 'Interim European Security and Defence Assembly' may even claim several comparative advantages over the EP in scrutinizing the ESDP: First, the interim assembly's composition of national deputies fits the ESDP's intergovernmental structure well. After all, national governments will retain prime responsibility for the foreseeable future. Thus, it appears appropriate to delegate democratic control of the ESDP to national parliamentarians in a transnational institution. Second, the interim assembly assembles deputies from twenty-eight members of the 'WEU family' (as the assembly's homepage puts it). In addition to twenty-three EU members (i.e. all EU states except Malta and Cyprus), this includes Bulgaria, Romania, Turkey, Iceland and Norway which are members of NATO but not of the EU and whose appropriate involvement in the ESDP has been heavily contested (cf. Missiroli 2002). Thus, the interim assembly could contribute to good relations between the EU and European NATO members on a parliamentary level.

These advantages of giving the interim assembly a prominent role in the democratic control of the ESDP are balanced by several disadvantages. Firstly, the members of national parliaments currently participating in the WEU/interim assembly do not always belong to the defence and foreign affairs committees in their respective parliaments, since they usually also participate in the Council of Europe Assembly. However, most importantly, a second chamber for the democratic control of the ESDP adds further complexity to the institutional system of the EU. Such an increase in complexity would conflict with transparent and clear-cut lines of accountability which are a prerequisite of democratic legitimacy. Moreover, an institutional separation of the ESDP and other issues of external relations seems artificial and difficult to maintain. At a time when the EU's 'double executive' in external affairs begins to merge in order to increase policy coherence, as suggested in the draft Constitutional Treaty, it seems odd to create a 'double legislative' to supervise external policies. What is more, turf battles between the EP and the interim assembly are inevitable.

As a result, the interim assembly has been more and more marginalized in European security and defence politics and is likely to suffer from a further loss of attention when the EP dedicates more resources to the ESDP. As a consequence, the interim assembly's capacities to compensate the emerging democratic deficit on a national level have been very limited and are likely to decline even further.

Options for transparliamentary control of the ESDP

As the previous paragraphs made clear, neither the EP nor the interim assembly has been granted sufficient competencies to compensate for the democratic deficit that the Europeanization of defence politics has brought about at the national level. Since the EP has reinforced its ability to monitor the ESDP at a *supra*national level, the main challenge ahead lies in improving the *trans*national scrutiny of the ESDP, particularly as the interim assembly has been increasingly marginalized.

Ultimately, it is the national parliaments themselves which have to decide how to organize an exchange of information and points of views. After all, the success of inter-parliamentary co-operation depends first of all on delegates' efforts and commitment. Four options can be suggested for discussion.

First, of course, a new institution could be established. The latest proposal in this vein was submitted to the 'Constitutional Convention'. Its President, Valéry Giscard d'Estaing, proposed a 'Congress of European Peoples', composed of members of the European and the national parliaments, that would meet on a regular, possibly annual, basis. However, the proposal was suspected of intentionally weakening the EP. Mainly for this reason, it did not find a majority among the delegates in the convention and was dropped from the final version of the Treaty for a European Constitution.

Second, inter-parliamentary co-operation in security and defence policy could be organized by the EP (Gourlay and Tappert 2004). Such an endeavour could build upon inter-parliamentary co-operation on issues of the European Community's first pillar (for an overview cf. Maurer 2003). Here, joint sessions of EP committees with their national counterparts have served to exchange information and views. Moreover, joint committee sessions have given members of national parliaments the opportunity to address EU officials directly. So far, this instrument has hardly been used in foreign, security and defence policy. However, the new subcommittee on security and defence may choose to make inter-parliamentary co-operation a priority of its work.

Third, the 'Conference of Community and European Affairs Committees of Parliaments of the European Union' (COSAC) could make security and defence policy a new focus of its work. What makes the COSAC an interesting institution to build on is that it has not been a creation of the member state governments but an example of parliamentary self-organization resulting from an initiative of the then President of the French Assemblé National, Fabius. Thus, it has been a successful and visible expression of national parliaments' desire and capacity to strengthen inter-parliamentary co-operation. Since 1989, national European affairs committees as well as the EP each delegate six deputies to the COSAC meetings which take place twice a year before the meeting of the European Council. The COSAC has so far focused almost exclusively on institutional questions. In contrast, issues of security and defence have played only a marginal role (Mittag 2003: 97). The COSAC's focus would be easy to change, however, exactly because it has been an exercise in parliamentary self-organization and does not depend on intergovernmental conferences to change its statute. In order to give security and defence policy a more prominent role, the COSAC would have to give members of national parliaments' foreign affairs and defence committees access to the COSAC. This, of course, requires the members of the European affairs committees to share some of their powers. Moreover, member parliaments' delegations should become more representative of the party pluralism in national parliaments (Hilger 2002). It remains to be seen whether this turns out to be a significant obstacle to making the COSAC the centre of multi-level parliamentary control in security and defence policy.

Finally, efforts to organize inter-parliamentary co-operation in security and defence could of course build upon the interim assembly whose merits have been discussed above. As mentioned above, however, the EP tends to regard the interim assembly more as a competitor than a collaborator. The interim assembly could, however, seek stronger ties with the COSAC. For example, the interim assembly could aim at becoming some kind of COSAC security and defence chamber.

Taken together, the responsibility for democratic legitimacy should not be left to national parliaments alone. Because the Europeanization of security and defence policy tends to weaken national parliaments *vis-à-vis* their executives, a multi-level system of parliamentary control seems most appropriate. In addition to national parliaments' tasks, such a system would include a strong EP and some form of inter-parliamentary co-operation comprising both the European and the national parliaments. As regards the EP, the constitutional treaty would contribute to an enhanced supranational input legitimacy. Although the EP would not acquire competencies akin to those in common market legislation, its competencies in foreign policy would be explicitly extended to security and defence policy. As regards inter-parliamentary co-operation, several institutional venues appear possible, and it is up to the members of national parliaments in particular to organize co-operation.

CONCLUSION

The analysis of parliamentary control of deployment decisions has pointed to a democratic deficit in the EU's security and defence policy. To be sure, other dimensions of democracy may suffer less and some (e.g. transparency and openness of decision-making) may even gain from a Europeanization of security and defence politics. In terms of the dimension of parliamentary control on which this paper has focused, however, a democratic deficit has emerged.

At first glance, this should not come as a surprise as EU politics has become familiar with the notion of a democratic deficit ever since European integration went beyond the establishment of a free trade area. However, it seems worthwhile noting some differences between the democratic deficit in the first pillar and the one in the ESDP: first, the extent of the democratic deficit depends on the traditional level of parliamentary control of security and defence politics in the member states. As a consequence, the democratic deficit differs widely across the member states. Second, the impact of security and defence policy may, of course, be much more noticeable than many domestic issue areas. After all, security and defence policy does imply the possibility of sending citizens to a battlefield. As a consequence, a severe policy failure (such as high casualties in a EU-led military mission) may not only damage support for and legitimacy of the ESDP but of the EU as a whole (see below).

From the normative viewpoint which has inspired much of the civilian power literature, the democratic deficit in the ESDP must appear alarming as the democratic control of security and defence policy has frequently been counted among the defining features of a civilian power. More specifically, the democratic deficit in security and defence politics may damage the EU as a civilian (and civilizing) power in several ways: first, following the core claim of democratic peace research, a mounting democratic deficit in EU security and defence policy may ease the use of force since institutional constraints have been weakened.[8] As the example of Germany has illustrated above, opposition against the use of force is easier to overcome for executives if security and defence politics have been internationalized.

Second, the democratic deficit in the ESDP may damage the legitimacy of EU-led military missions. If input legitimacy for the deployment of armed forces via parliamentary debate and approval has been weakened, a mission's legitimacy becomes largely dependent on its output. As a consequence, any failure (e.g. high casualties) may severely damage support for the EU's defence policy or even the EU in general.

Third, the ability of the EU to lead by virtuous example – a central feature of the EU's normative power (Manners 2002: 244) – may be compromised. If the EU continues to regard the spread of democracy (and, by extension, the democratic control of security and defence policy) as an instrument to promote peace, its own democratic deficit would render it vulnerable.

Given these negative consequences of the ESDP for the EU as a civilian power, the EU should make more efforts to improve parliamentary control of the ESDP at the supranational and transnational level.

Biographical note: Wolfgang Wagner is a Research Fellow at the Peace Research Institute Frankfurt (PRIF), Germany.

Address for correspondence: Wolfgang Wagner, Peace Research Institute Frankfurt (PRIF), Leimenrode 29, D-60322 Frankfurt/Main, Germany. email: wwagner@hsfk.de

NOTES

1 I have benefited from discussions at the CIDEL workshop in Oslo in October 2004, at the EUSA conference in Austin in March 2005, and at a seminar at the University of Oslo in April 2005. In particular I would like to thank Helene Sjursen, Michael Bothe, Erik O. Eriksen, Carlos Closa, Matthias Dembinski, Anna Geis and Knud Erik Jørgensen.

2 On civil–military relations cf. the classical work by Huntington (1957) as well as Feaver (2003).

3 Respective concerns have been voiced, among others, by Hummel (2003) and by Bono (2004). Matthias Koenig-Archibugi has even argued that the disentanglement from parliamentary control has been an important driving force for EU governments to advocate a Europeanization of foreign, security and defence policy (cf. Koenig-Archibugi 2004).

4 A good overview has been given in the Assembly of the Western European Union, the Interim European Security and Defence Assembly, National Parliamentary Scrutiny of Intervention Abroad by Armed Forces Engaged in International Missions: The Current Position in Law (Doc. A/1762), Paris, 2001. This report treats all then EU members except for Ireland and Austria. Parliamentary competencies in Denmark, France, Germany, Sweden, the United Kingdom and Poland are further treated in Mittag (2003). See also Siedschlag (2002).

5 After a previous preliminary ruling on German participation in monitoring a maritime embargo against Yugoslavia and a further preliminary ruling on the Bundeswehr's participation in the United Nations Operation in Somalia (UNOSOM) II, the main ruling was made in July 1994 (BverfG E [decisions of the Federal Constitutional Court] vol. 90, 286, II, pp. 286–394). However, we will focus on the preliminary 'AWACS' ruling because it was part of the decision-making process on Germany's first combat mission.

6 BverfG E vol. 88, 173, II, p.183, author's translation.

7 US Department of Defense, News Transcript, Press Conference with Secretary Donald H. Rumsfeld and NATO Secretary-General Lord Robertson; Wednesday, 8 October 2003.

8 This concern may turn out to be the least important, however, because the integration of military forces not only weakens parliamentary control at the national

level but at the same time creates new institutional constraints at the international level (cf. also Dembinski *et al.* 2004). Just as a single state faces growing difficulties to *block* the collective use of integrated forces (as Germany experienced with regard to AWACS), it has become equally difficult for a single state to *trigger* the collective use of integrated forces. Thus, states that have engaged in role specialization and the integration of military forces may soon find themselves in a 'joint decision trap' (Scharpf 1988): they are no longer capable of deciding on the use of their military individually because key capabilities (such as long-range airlift) have effectively been 'communitarized'. At the same time, a joint decision on the use of force can only be achieved after each member to an integrated structure has given its consent.

REFERENCES

Anderson, J.J. and Goodman, J.B. (1993) 'Mars or Minerva? A united Germany in a post-Cold War Europe', in R.O. Keohane, J.S. Nye and S. Hoffmann (eds), *After the Cold War. International Institutions and State Strategies in Europe, 1989–1991*, Cambridge, MA: Harvard University Press, pp. 23–62.

Baumann, R. (2001) 'German security policy within NATO', in V. Rittberger (ed.), *German Foreign Policy since Unification. Theories and Case Studies*, Manchester: Manchester University Press, pp. 141–84.

Baumann, R. and Hellmann, G. (2001) 'Germany and the use of force: "total war", the "culture of restraint", and the quest for normality', *German Politics* 10(1): 61–82.

Berger, T.U. (1998) *Cultures of Antimilitarism: National Security in Germany and Japan*, Baltimore: Johns Hopkins University Press.

Bono, G. (2004) 'The European Union as an international security actor. Challenges for democratic accountability', in H. Born and H. Hänggi (eds), *The 'Double Democratic Deficit'. Parliamentary Accountability and the Use of Force under International Auspices*, Aldershot: Ashgate, pp. 163–81.

Born, H. (2004) 'The use of force under international auspices: strengthening parliamentary accountability', in H. Born and H. Hänggi (eds), *The 'Double Democratic Deficit'. Parliamentary Accountability and the Use of Force under International Auspices*, Aldershot: Ashgate, pp. 203–15.

Born, H. and Urscheler, M. (2004) 'Parliamentary accountability of multinational peace support operations: a comparative perspective', in H. Born and H. Hänggi (eds), *The 'Double Democratic Deficit'. Parliamentary Accountability and the Use of Force under International Auspices*, Aldershot: Ashgate, pp. 53–72.

Brok, E. and Gresch, N. (2004) Untitled contribution in N. Gnesotto (ed.), *EU Security and Defense Policy. The First Five Years*, Paris: EU Institute for Security Studies, pp. 179–88.

Cottey, A., Edmunds, T. and Forster, A. (2002) 'The second generation problematic: rethinking democracy and civil–military relations', *Armed Forces and Society* 29(1): 31–56.

Dembinski, M., Hasenclever, A. and Wagner, W. (2004) 'Towards an executive peace? The ambivalent effect of inter-democratic institutions on democracy, peace, and war', *International Politics* Special Issue 41(4): 543–64.

Feaver, P. (2003) *Armed Servants. Agency, Oversight, and Civil–Military Relations*, Cambridge, MA: Harvard University Press.

Giegerich, B. and Wallace, W. (2004) 'Not such a soft power. The external deployment of European forces', *Survival* 46(2): 163–82.

Gourlay, C. (2004) 'Parliamentary accountability and ESDP: the national and the European level', in H. Born and H. Hänggi (eds), *The 'Double Democratic Deficit'. Parliamentary Accountability and the Use of Force under International Auspices*, Aldershot: Ashgate, pp. 183–200.

Gourlay, C. and Tappert, M. (2004) 'Revising the European Parliament's scrutiny of foreign affairs and defence', *European Security Review* 21: 3–5.

Hänggi, H. (2004) 'The use of force under international auspices: parliamentary accountability and "democratic deficits"', in H. Born and H. Hänggi (eds), *The 'Double Democratic Deficit'. Parliamentary Accountability and the Use of Force under International Auspices*, Aldershot: Ashgate, pp. 3–16.

Hilger, M. (2002) 'Défense européenne et contrôle démocratique: une tâche pour la Convention sur l'avenir de l'Europe', *Politique Étrangère* 67(2): 455–70.

Hix, S. (2005) *The Political System of the European Union*, 2nd edn, Basingstoke: Palgrave.

Hummel, H. (2003) 'Die Europäische Union und der "Demokratische Frieden": Zur parlamentarischen Kontrolle der Europäischen Sicherheits- und Verteidigungspolitik', in P. Schlotter (ed.), *Europa – Macht – Frieden? Zur Politik der 'Zivilmacht Europa'*, Baden-Baden: Nomos, pp. 159–78.

Huntington, S. (1957) *The Soldier and the State. The Theory and Politics of Civil–Military Relations*, Cambridge: Cambridge University Press.

Koenig-Archibugi, M. (2004) 'International governance as new raison d'état? The case of the EU Common Foreign and Security Policy', *European Journal of International Relations* 10(2): 147–88.

Mammonas, D. (2003) 'The parliamentarisation of the ESDP as an answer to global challenges?'. Paper presented at the meeting of the International Studies Association in Budapest, June.

Manners, I. (2002) 'Normative power Europe: a contradiction in terms?', *Journal of Common Market Studies* 40(2): 235–58.

Maurer, A. (2003) 'Die Konferenz der Europa-Ausschüsse (COSAC) und der Konvent: Schwächung oder Stärkung der demokratischen Legitimation in der EU', in R. Geiger (ed.), *Neuere Probleme der parlamentarischen Legitimation im Bereich der auswärtigen Gewalt*, Baden-Baden: Nomos, pp. 187–227.

Meyer, B. (2004) *Von der Entscheidungsmündigkeit zur Entscheidungsmüdigkeit? Nach zehn Jahren Parlamentsvorbehalt für Bundeswehreinsätze naht ein Beteiligungsgesetz*, HSFK-Report 4, Frankfurt a. M.: Peace Research Institute Frankfurt.

Missiroli, A. (2002) 'Turkey and EU–NATO cooperation in crisis management: no Turkish delight for ESDP', *Security Dialogue* 33(1): 9–26.

Mittag, J. (2003) 'The parliamentary dimension of CFSP/ESDP. Options for the European convention', Brussels/Cologne.

Moravcsik, A. (1994) 'Why the European Community strengthens the state: domestic politics and international institutions', Center for European Studies Working Paper Series 52, Cambridge, MA: Center for European Studies.

Morgan, T.C. and Campbell, S.H. (1991) 'Domestic structure, decisional constraints, and war: so why can't democracies fight?', *Journal of Conflict Resolution* 35(2): 187–211.

Philippi, N. (2001) 'Civilian power and war: the German debate about out-of-area operations 1990–99', in S. Harnisch and H.W. Maull (eds), *Germany as a Civilian Power? The Foreign Policy of the Berlin Republic*, Manchester: Manchester University Press, pp. 49–67.

Risse, T. (2001) 'A European identity? Europeanization and the evolution of nation-state identities', in M.G. Cowles, J. Caporaso and T. Risse (eds), *Transforming Europe. Europeanization and Domestic Change*, Ithaca, NY: Cornell University Press, pp. 198–216.

Risse-Kappen, T. (1995) *Cooperation among Democracies. The European Influence on U.S. Foreign Policy*, Princeton, NJ: Princeton University Press.

Russett, B. (1993) *Grasping the Democratic Peace. Principles for a Post-Cold War World*, Princeton, NJ: Princeton University Press.

Russett, B. and Oneal, J.R. (2001) *Triangulating Peace: Democracy, Interdependence, and International Organizations*, New York: Norton.

Scharpf, F. (1988) 'The joint decision trap. Lessons from German federalism and European integration', *Public Administration* 66(3): 239–78.

Schmitt, B. (2003) *The European Union and Armaments. Getting a Bigger Bang for the Euro*, Chaillot Paper 63, Paris: EU Institute for Security Studies.

Schwab-Trapp, M. (2002) *Kriegsdiskurse: die politische Kultur des Krieges im Wandel 1991–1999*, Opladen: Leske & Budrich.

Siedschlag, A. (2002) 'Nationale Entscheidungsprozesse bei Streitkräfteeinsätzen im Rahmen der Petersberg-Aufgaben der EU – Deutschland, Frankreich, Grossbritannien, Italien, Schweden', in E. Reiter, R. Rummel and P. Schmidt (eds), *Europas ferne Streitmacht. Chancen und Schwierigkeiten der Europäichen Union beim der ESVP*, Forschungen zur Sicherheitspolitik 6, Hamburg: Mittler, pp. 222–32.

Siverson, R.M. (1995) 'Democracies and war participation: in defense of the institutional constraint argument', *European Journal of International Relations* 1(4): 481–89.

Sjursen, H. (2004) 'Security and defence', in W. Carlsnaes, H. Sjursen and B. White (eds), *Contemporary European Foreign Policy*, London: Sage, pp. 59–74.

Smith, K. (2000) 'The end of civilian power EU: a welcome demise or cause for concern?', *International Spectator* 35(2): 11–28.

Smith, K. (2004) 'Still "civilian power EU?"'. Paper presented at the CIDEL Workshop 'From Civilian to Military Power: The European Union at a Crossroads?', Oslo, 22–23 October.

Stavridis, S. (2001) 'Why the "militarising" of the European Union is strengthening the concept of a "civilian power Europe"', Working Paper RSC 2001/17, Florence: EUI.

Wagner, W. (2005) 'The democratic legitimacy of European Security and Defence Policy', Occasional Paper 57, Paris: Institute for Security Studies.

Wolf, K.D. (1999) 'The new raison d'état as a problem for democracy in world society', *European Journal for International Relations* 5(3): 333–63.

'Normative' power Europe: a realist critique

Adrian Hyde-Price

INTRODUCTION

Since the end of the Cold War, liberal and idealist notions have shaped much of the discourse of European Studies and International Relations. Particularly influential have been conceptions of the European Union (EU) as a 'civilian' or 'normative' power, committed to 'civilizing' international relations as part of a wider transformation of international society (Duchêne 1972; Hill 1990; Manners 2002). Such liberal-idealist views regard the EU as a novel and uniquely benign entity in international politics which serves as the harbinger of a Kantian *foedus pacificum*. Central to such liberal-idealist arguments is the claim that the apparent weakness of the Union as an international actor – its lack of coercive instruments and its consequent reliance on declaratory politics and 'soft power' – in fact constitute the very sources of its strength. Such arguments fit comfortably with a view prevalent in European policy-making circles that while Europeans may not come 'from Venus' (Kagan 2003), nonetheless there is a distinctive 'European' approach to international politics that favours diplomacy, persuasion, negotiation and compromise, in contrast to the rather more martial (and 'Martian') American approach which is more prone to using military coercion.

This article offers an alternative theoretical account of the EU as an international actor. It differs sharply from liberal-idealist concepts of 'civilian' and 'normative' power which seek to explain the international role of the EU from the perspective of actor-based ontologies and interpretivist epistemologies. The problems with such liberal-idealist approaches are threefold. First, they are reductionist in that they seek to 'explain international outcomes through elements and combinations of elements located at national or subnational levels' (Waltz 1979: 60). Second, they suffer from liberal-idealism's perennial weakness, namely 'the almost total neglect of power' (Carr 2001: cv). As Hedley Bull noted, the civilian power concept was a contradiction in terms because 'the power of influence exerted by the European Community and other such civilian actors was conditional upon a strategic environment provided by the military power of states, which they did not control' (Bull 1982: 151). Third, they are explicitly normative, in that they regard civilian and normative power as a 'good thing'. The problem here is that when the object of study is seen as embodying the core values one believes in, it is difficult to achieve any critical distance. In contrast to such reductionist and explicitly normative approaches, this article presents a systems level analysis rooted in the structural realist tradition of International Relations. Neorealism is one of the most sophisticated and influential theories of international politics, yet there have been few attempts to apply it to the EU's foreign, security and defence policy. European integration, and the Common Foreign and Security Policy (CFSP)/European Security and Defence Policy (ESDP) in particular, are 'hard cases' for neorealist theory (Waltz 1979: 123), which tends to emphasize the obstacles to co-operation within a self-help system. Nonetheless, whilst structural realism cannot explain the fine-grain of European foreign and security co-operation, it has considerable explanatory power in elucidating the nature of the EU as an international actor and the underlying dynamics of the CFSP/ESDP.

NEOREALISM AND THE STUDY OF THE CFSP/ESDP

For much of the last two decades, neorealism has been the single most influential paradigm in International Relations. It is therefore something of an anomaly that it has had so little impact on the study of EU foreign and security policy co-operation. The reasons for this are fourfold.

To begin with, neorealists themselves tend to downplay the significance of institutionalized multilateral co-operation because of the emphasis they place on the problems of achieving 'co-operation under anarchy'. Hence 'realists have not produced comprehensive theory-informed empirical studies in this area' (Jørgensen 2004: 38). Second, neorealism is widely perceived to be state-centric, overly preoccupied with hard power (particularly military power) and focused on the 'high politics' of international security (Keohane and Nye 1977: 23–4). For these reasons, it is seen as having little to offer the study of an atypical international actor which is not a state, possesses limited coercive power resources and which is primarily concerned with 'low politics'. Third, neorealism is often presented in highly jaundiced terms in order to set up a 'straw-man' with which to demonstrate the sophistication of other approaches and theories. This means that few in the field are aware of neorealism's explanatory power and theoretical sophistication. Finally, many scholars working on EU foreign and security policy empathize closely with the object of their research. Consequently, they are instinctively hostile to an approach that questions many of the normative and liberal claims that surround the 'European' project.

Structural realism cannot provide a full and comprehensive explanation of European foreign and security policy. A full theoretical account of the CFSP/ ESDP requires both an analysis of the domestic dimensions of interest-articulation and decision-making as well as systemic influences. However, as there is still no adequate theory that combines these two levels, students of European affairs will need to work with different theories for different purposes. This article concentrates on the international level because the effects of structure of the international system on the EU have been largely overlooked or misunderstood (see Waltz 1979: 174). The claim advanced here is that neorealist theory can shed considerable light on the systemic pressures that 'shape and shove' EU member states' international behaviour. In so doing, neorealism can open up space for a more informed and balanced debate on the EU as a foreign and security policy actor. Systemic theory can offer insights into the international role of the EU that reductionist theories miss. Structural realism offers not only a series of specific criticisms of the 'civilian' and 'normative' power concepts, but – more importantly – an alternative theoretical understanding of the CFSP/ESDP based on an analysis of the structural distribution of power.

The CFSP/ESDP is clearly a 'hard case' for neorealism. Neorealism emphasizes the problems of co-operating under anarchy given concerns with relative gains, and suggests that international institutions have little impact on the behaviour of states, especially the major powers (Mearsheimer 1995). Yet the EU has undoubtedly emerged as an important element of Europe's security architecture, and neorealists need to account for such institutionalized multilateral co-operation (Grieco 1997).

Before outlining the key features of a neorealist analysis of the CFSP/ESDP, a brief sketch of the main tenets of neorealist theory is required. This is because neorealism is not a monolithic and homogenized body of thought, but a diverse and vibrant intellectual tradition with a number of distinct approaches within it – most notably, offensive and defensive realism. It is also important to note that explanatory theory is, by definition, parsimonious and deductive. It seeks to explain, not describe. This necessarily involves abstraction and simplification. Consequently, explanatory theory is not necessarily 'realistic' in the sense of being descriptively accurate. 'Explanatory power', Waltz notes, 'is gained by moving away from "reality", not by staying close to it. A full description would be of least explanatory power; an elegant theory, of most' (Waltz 1979: 7). Theoretical analysis involves searching for underlying trends and patterns of behaviour. It seeks to explain the regularities and repetitions of behaviour, not specific events, individual cases or unexpected developments. In short, theory is an 'organisation of a domain', which 'indicates that some factors are more important than others, and specifies the relations among them' (Waltz 1995: 71).

KEY TENETS OF NEOREALISM

Neorealist analyses are based on a set of assumptions, from which a series of general propositions are inferred. These can be used to generate more specific empirical hypotheses for testing.

Core assumptions

International systems are anarchic
Structural realism depicts the international system as anarchic – a domain without a sovereign. For this reason, it is also a self-help system: states must look to their own security and survival in what is a competitive realm. Security competition is pervasive, and although war is a relatively rare occurrence, there is always the risk that security competition could lead to war given the anarchic nature of international politics. Most importantly, neorealism suggests that the primary roots of conflict and war lie not in the domestic character of individual states or regimes, or in human nature, but in the structure and dynamics of the international system (Waltz 1959).

States are the primary international actors
Realists, like Marxists, emphasize the importance of groups, not individuals, in human history (Carr 2001: 91). International politics is the realm of competition between rival political groups, the most important of which is the state. The state is not the only international actor, but it is by far the most important, and it is states, especially powerful ones, which set the context and establish the rules for other actors, including the EU (Waltz 1979: 94). The EU is not a sovereign actor in its own right, but acts as a vehicle for the collective interests of its member states.

States are functionally similar
In hierarchical systems, units become functionally differentiated. In anarchic systems, however, units remain functionally similar. They exhibit similar institutional features and are socialized into the international system through a combination of competition and imitation (Waltz 1979: 128). Functional similarity also means that all states – particularly great powers – seek to maintain a balanced portfolio of power capabilities. One consequence of this is that all great powers have some offensive military capability, 'which gives them the wherewithal to hurt and possibly destroy each other' (Mearsheimer 2001: 30).

States are rational, unitary actors

For the purposes of the theory, neorealism assumes that states are unitary actors capable of acting strategically on the basis of rational calculation of the costs and benefits of alternative courses of action. Clearly, this is not descriptively true. Since Allison's (1971) pioneering work, it is common knowledge that all states are characterized by institutional polyphony, and that rationality is 'bounded'. However, explaining the regularities and repetitions of international politics involves abstracting and simplifying domestic political processes. States, it is assumed, 'are able not just to perceive systemic-level constraints but also to formulate and to execute measures in response to them' (Grieco 1997: 166). As Keohane notes, the rationality assumption is the crucial link between system structure and actor behaviour, 'which enables the theorist to predict that leaders will respond to the incentives and constraints imposed by their environment' (Keohane 1986: 167).

Propositions

On the basis of these four assumptions, a set of five propositions can be inferred about the dynamics of the international system and the motive-forces driving states' interaction with other states.

Security competition in a self-help system

International anarchy, coupled with the constant shadow of war and conflict, generates pervasive security competition in what remains a self-help system. States must rely for their survival and security on their own resources, or on those of their allies (Walt 1987). The level of security competition varies according to the structural distribution of power in the system, but it can never be eradicated. Fear is pervasive, and trust is a scarce commodity. In this context, co-operation is difficult – though not impossible – to achieve, and those institutions that are created have no independent power or autonomy. 'They are based on the self-interested calculations of the great powers, and they have no independent effect on state behaviour' (Mearsheimer 1995: 334). Consequently, the EU should be seen as an intervening variable which matters only at the margins of European security.

Security and power maximization

In anarchic self-help systems, security is the primary concern of states. Security is best assured by maximizing power so as to be able to eliminate or neutralize all potential rivals and establishing hegemony over one's region (Kissinger 1957: 144; Mearsheimer 2001: 33–4). At the very least, states must seek to preserve their power relative to their potential enemies and competitors: if they can strengthen their position relative to others, so much the better. Realism assumes that states are rational actors, and thus will not aggressively pursue power maximization strategies if doing so risks undermining their security by, for example, generating hostile alliances or pre-emptive strikes. When power maximization strategies are counterproductive, states will focus on security maximization until more favourable opportunities present themselves. For long periods of time, therefore, states can act more like 'defensive positionalists' (Grieco 1997: 167) rather than power maximizers; they will only seek to maximize their power if the benefits outweigh the costs (Snyder 2002: 172).

Relative gains

Neorealism assumes that states focus on relative gains, and argues that this places limits on co-operative enterprises. States are concerned about their position in the international system relative to their main rivals and potential enemies, and will therefore only engage in co-operation if they benefit as much or more than other major powers. This is particularly the case with major powers; small powers can be more concerned with absolute gains. Nonetheless, realists recognize that, under some conditions, concerns with relative gains are relaxed. This tends to occur in conditions when security competition is muted or weak, and when states do not face an immediate interstate threat: 'Absolute gains become more important as competition lessens' (Waltz 1979: 195). Even in this context, however, major powers remain concerned about relative gains, and rarely rest content with absolute gains for long (Grieco 1993: 323).

Milieu shaping

States, especially great powers, have an interest in the stability of their external environment. Consequently they pursue what Arnold Wolfers termed 'milieu goals' (1962: 73–5). All states face common problems (Waltz 1979: 209): the issue, however, is how the required governance of the international system can be achieved in the absence of a central authority. Who will incur the costs of addressing common problems given concerns about relative gains? How can the 'free-rider' problem be overcome? Will major powers allow any one of their number to take the lead in addressing common problems if in doing so it thereby accrues political or other benefits? Regional governance tasks are more likely to be undertaken by great powers, because they have a greater stake in the stability of their region, and because they have the capabilities to take on special responsibilities (Waltz 1979: 198). From a realist perspective, therefore, EU external policy co-operation constitutes a collective attempt at milieu shaping, driven primarily by the Union's largest powers.

Second-order concerns

States are not motivated purely by security and power maximization concerns. They also pursue a range of ethical concerns reflecting their distinct political values – from protecting the environment to international human rights. But these are always 'second-order' concerns: they rank below national security and other fundamental national interests in importance, and when push comes to shove, states will sacrifice them if they clash with their core national interests or conflict with balance-of-power logic (Mearsheimer 2001: 46–7). Over the last decade, the EU has increasingly come to serve as the institutional repository for the 'second-order' concerns of its member states. Member states explicitly see the EU as a 'force for good' in the world (EU Institute for Security Studies 2003), committed to furthering shared European political values such as democracy, multilateralism and human rights. Commitment to an 'ethical' foreign policy may lead EU member states to intervene in parts of the world where the great powers have no significant strategic interests (such as parts of Africa). It has already led the EU to advocate the end of capital punishment (Manners 2002) – a policy which has no impact on the balance of power and minimal impact on trade promotion. But, realists would argue, member states will only allow the EU to act as the repository for shared ethical concerns as long as this does not conflict with their core national interests. The example of economic relations with Putin's Russia, or of arms sales to China, underscores the limits of the concept of Europe as a 'normative power'.

STRUCTURAL REALISM AND FOREIGN POLICY ANALYSIS

Neorealism presents a much bleaker view of international politics than that offered by the dominant liberal-idealist approach exemplified by Duchêne (1972) and Manners (2002). Nonetheless, its emphasis on the structural distribution of power – rather than on human nature, regime type or ideational factors – provides a powerful analytical tool capable of shedding light on the dynamics of EU foreign, security and defence co-operation. Structural realism cannot explain all aspects of European affairs, and certainly not the nuances and intricacies of EU politics. However, it can explain both the Cold War origins and post-Cold War development of the European Political Co-operation (EPC) and CFSP.

   Neorealism is sometimes portrayed as a determinist theory. This is incorrect. The theory does not suggest that states are like prisoners trapped in an iron cage of structural forces (Mearsheimer 2001: 12). But neither do they enjoy free will to construct their own future. The structural distribution of power in the international system provides rewards for certain patterns of behaviour and punishes others. It 'shapes and shoves' state behaviour, but it does not determine it. As Waltz has argued, 'international political theory deals with the pressures of structure on states and not with how states will respond to the pressures' (Waltz 2000: 27). How states respond to structural pressures depends on a range of domestic political factors, including decision-making competence, ideology and sectional interests. Moreover, in some contexts structural pressures are indeterminate, leaving states considerable scope to shape their own future. At all times, skilful diplomacy and virtuoso statecraft can counter the shaping and shoving of structural constraints (Gilpin 1986: 312; Waltz 1986: 344–5).

   In general, however, states face a limited range of options in an anarchical self-help system. Very powerful states (like the USA today) clearly enjoy greater room for manoeuvre than others. Paradoxically, however, strategic options are more constrained for great powers than small states. Great powers face three main options: balancing, buck-passing and bandwagoning. Small states also have the option of 'hiding' or seeking to 'transcend' the international system (see Schroeder 1995). Thus although international political theory cannot predict the precise foreign and security policies of EU member states, it would suggest that their approach to the CFSP/ESDP will fall within the following range of options:

- *Balancing:* Member states might seek to use the EU to balance against the dominant global power, the USA, by, for example, playing the 'China card' or cultivating close relations with Russia. For Waltz, balancing is the most likely outcome that international political theory would predict (Waltz 1979: 128);
- *Buck-passing* (Christensen and Snyder 1990): EU member states might be tempted to leave the USA to deal with security threats in the Middle East or the Asia-Pacific region (Taiwan, North Korea), allowing them to focus on trade and economic issues;
- *Bandwagoning:* EU member states could align with the strongest power in the system in order to gain influence or other coveted values. Randall Schweller argues that 'bandwagoning for rewards is actually the dominant tendency for states – particularly revisionist states – seeking to increase, not just preserve, their core values and to improve their position in the system' (Schweller 1994: 87; see also Labs 1992).

BIPOLARITY

Having considered the main tenets of neorealism, let us now examine how they can explain the origins and development of European security and defence policy. European integration is today frequently portrayed as an explicit 'peace project' designed to overcome the animosities of war and lay the foundations for a stable peace. From a realist perspective, the pertinent question is why the post-war European Coal and Steel Community (ECSC)/European Economic Community (EEC) was successful, whilst cognate projects inspired by liberal-idealist notions (notably the League of Nations and the Locarno Treaties) failed after the First World War. The answer can be found in the structure of power. Realists argue that the crucial permissive condition that made the post-1945 integration process succeed was bipolarity.

International political theory suggests that co-operation is easier to achieve in bipolar systems than in multipolar ones (Waltz 1979: 167–70). When the structure of power in Europe was multipolar, the continent's great powers found themselves, more often than not, embroiled in intense and unrelenting competition for power and wealth. Relations between them were driven by concerns over relative gains and the balance of power. In the wake of the Second World War, however, this changed dramatically. The international system became bipolar, and Europe's major powers became security consumers. In this context, concerns about relative gains were relaxed and security competition between them waned. Co-operation to tackle shared 'milieu goals' was consequently easier to achieve.

Co-operation in Western Europe took place under the security umbrella provided by the USA and institutionalized in the North Atlantic Treaty Organization (NATO). The USA actively encouraged West European co-operation, not least through the provision of Marshall Aid, which was predicated on regional economic co-operation. Because their security was guaranteed by NATO and the US nuclear umbrella, West European democracies were able to devote considerably more resources to 'welfare' than to 'warfare'. As a security consumer, for example, West Germany was able to focus on becoming a successful *Handelsstaat* ('trading nation'), and to profile itself as a 'civilian power' (Maull 1993). Franco–German *rapprochement* was crucial to the success of post-war integration, but this was only possible given the reassuring presence of the American 'pacifier' (Joffe 1984).

The bipolar structure of power, coupled with nuclear deterrence, also had important consequences for domestic developments. Most importantly, it created the conditions in which nationalism could be tamed and tentative multiple identities begin to blossom. Much of the extreme nationalism that had developed in the late nineteenth and early twentieth centuries was a response to the structural pressures of multipolarity, which generated intense security competition. Bipolarity and nuclear weapons removed the imperative for this sort of political preparation for total war. Nationalist passions were gradually tamed in post-war Western Europe.

The essential point to note in all of this is that it was the bipolar distribution of power that created the permissive conditions for the European integration process.

> Politics among European states became different in quality after World War II because the international system changed from a multipolar to a bipolar one. The limited progress made in economic and other ways toward the unity of Western Europe cannot be understood without considering the effects that followed from the changed structure of international politics.
>
> (Waltz 1979: 71)

Bipolarity did not mean the end of conflicts of interest between West European states, only that these conflicts were resolved peacefully. 'Conflicts of interest remain, but not the expectation that someone will use force to resolve them' (Waltz 1979: 71).

The achievement of novel, albeit limited, forms of economic and political co-operation in the context of bipolarity does not mean that the EEC constituted a new form of power as Duchêne claimed (1972: 43–4), or that the nature of international politics had fundamentally changed (Nye 1990). The EEC was not a new actor wielding a new form of civilian power, but rather a vehicle for co-operation on a limited range of second-order issues driven by its largest powers, a development facilitated by the bipolar structure of power.

One development of significance was the emergence of a limited form of foreign policy co-ordination in the shape of European Political Co-operation. EPC emerged as a response to the perceived need for common approaches to milieu shaping, and provided a forum for limited policy co-ordination towards the

Middle East, the Conference on Security and Co-operation in Europe (CSCE) and the United Nations. As realists would expect, however, the process was driven by its largest participating states and few would dispute that its impact on international politics was, at best, marginal.

THE EU AND THE END OF THE COLD WAR

The events of 1989–91 constituted a watershed in international politics, resulting in a major realignment of global and regional power relations. With the disintegration of the old bipolar structure of power, new systemic pressures on state behaviour began to assert themselves (Hyde-Price 1991). The full implications of this structural transformation were not immediately apparent, and there was considerable lag in foreign policy behaviour as the major powers responded only slowly and incrementally to changes in the incentive structure afforded by the international system. The 1990s thus constituted an interregnum, as great powers relearnt old roles or learnt new ones.

In Europe, the epicentre of structural change, the demise of Cold War bipolarity had three immediate consequences for the EU. First, there was broad agreement that a united Germany should be embedded in an 'ever closer union' in order to address concerns of its neighbours and allies arising from the shift in relative power capabilities. This was one of the main integrationist impulses behind the Maastricht Treaty on European Union (TEU). Second, the TEU gave renewed energy to the task of completing the economic agenda of the 1980s in order to compete globally with America and Japan. Third, with the end of the bipolar European order, EU member states – particularly Germany – were faced with the prospect of political instability and economic crisis in the post-communist lands to their east. The new democracies of East Central Europe all sought to 'return to Europe' by joining the EU, a prospect not immediately welcome to many member states (Hyde-Price 1996). In this context, the EU acquired a significant new role: projecting stability into Central and Eastern Europe.

As noted above, all states have an interest in the stability of their external milieu. The problem is how the necessary governance tasks can be fulfilled in a self-help system. Few EU member states – and even fewer in East Central Europe – were happy to see Germany take on a special responsibility for the management of *Mitteleuropa* alone – the historical precedents were too unsettling. At the same time Germany itself was stretched dealing with unification, and was therefore keen to share the burdens of the 'triple transformation' in the East. Consequently, a consensus quickly emerged that the EU should act as a collective vehicle for 'milieu shaping' in the East, focusing on the provision of 'soft' security governance. The 'hard' security guarantees sought by the post-communist democracies of East Central Europe were to be provided by NATO and the USA. The EU was to address the economic, social and political aspects of transformation through providing guidance, advice and economic incentives.

In so doing, the EU was used by its most influential member states as an instrument for collectively exercising hegemonic power, shaping its 'near abroad' in ways amenable to the long-term strategic and economic interests of its member states. The instruments employed by the EU in order to shape its milieu were based both on 'soft power' (i.e. diplomatic persuasion, negotiation and compromise) and 'hard power'. The latter involved coercive economic state-craft, primarily in the form of 'conditionality clauses', in order to impose its vision of political and economic order on the post-communist democracies (Smith 2003). This illustrates that in its dealings with its 'near abroad', the EU does not act as a 'normative power' whose international role is shaped not by 'what it does or what it says, but what it is' (Manners 2002: 252). Rather, the EU serves as an instrument of collective hegemony, shaping its external milieu through using power in a variety of forms: political partnership or ostracism; economic carrots and sticks; the promise of membership or the threat of exclusion. The EU acts as a 'civilizing power' only in the sense that it is used by its most powerful member states to impose their common values and norms on the post-communist East.

As an instrument for collective milieu shaping, the EU faced its severest test in the Balkans. Crises often serve to lay bare the stark realities of power relations which can otherwise remain obscure during more placid times, and in this respect, the tragic wars of Yugoslav succession were no exception. 'This is the hour of Europe', Jacques Poos announced at the onset of the crisis (Gow 1997: 48, 50). But hubris was followed by tragedy, as the soft power of 'civilian power' Europe failed to make any significant impact on the warring parties. The violent breakup of Yugoslavia was important in four respects. First, it presented EU member states with difficult questions about managing the fall-out from the conflict. Who would take the lead and bear the costs of tackling the common problems of spill-over and regional instability? After the EU's failure, Britain and France took up the burden, although with little real enthusiasm. Second, the USA, basking in its 'unipolar moment', chose not to involve itself in Balkan affairs for most of the early 1990s. When it did engage, at Dayton and in Kosovo, it did so in ways that unsettled many Europeans. Third, the crisis underlined the limitations of soft power and the need for the EU to have credible military forces to back up its diplomacy if it wished to engage in effective coalitional crisis management. Fourth, it exposed the illusory character of many of the claims made for the EU as an international actor. The CFSP was effectively sidelined as Europe's great powers worked through the Contact Group, in a classic example of 'concert diplomacy' (Gow 1997: 260–1; Holbrooke 1999: 114–17). Finally, the Balkans provided the stage where a number of European states relearnt their old great power roles. The prime example of this is Germany, which shed its *Zivilmacht* reservations about an 'out-of-area' role for the Bundeswehr and assumed the responsibilities that great power status entailed. By the end of the decade, the German government was actively articulating and pursuing its national interests, and had taken part in offensive military operations against a sovereign state without an explicit UN Security Council mandate (Hyde-Price 2000).

Events in the Balkans also played a catalytic role in the launch of the ESDP, a development with potentially far-reaching implications for the EU's role as a collective hegemon. Clearly, a number of domestic and international factors contributed to the emergence of the ESDP. In terms of the structural distribution of power, however, two developments were crucial to the ESDP initiative: the preponderance of US power globally ('unipolarity') and balanced multipolarity in Europe. The ESDP is thus the product of the conflux of these two systemic pressures: global unipolarity and regional multipolarity.

UNIPOLARITY

With the breakup of the USSR, the US was left as the only remaining superpower. 'Unipolarity' is the phrase that has been widely employed as a means of capturing conceptually the uniquely powerful position of the USA in global politics. With the disintegration of its only significant strategic competitor, America is now the only great power with a global power projection capability (Posen 2003). Its power is not just military, but economic, scientific, technological and cultural. In addition, it enjoys substantial reserves of 'soft power' (Nye 1990), although these have been eroded since the start of the 'war on terror'.

The concept of unipolarity is, of course, not unproblematical. The international system remains anarchic, not hierarchic. The US is not a global hegemon: it exercises hegemonic power in the Western hemisphere, but it does not dominate all regions of the world. This is primarily because of the 'stopping power of water' (Mearsheimer 2001: 44). The main concern of regional hegemons like the USA is not to strive relentlessly for global hegemony, but rather 'to prevent great powers in other regions from duplicating their feat' (Mearsheimer 2001: 41). This largely accounts for the ambivalence found in Washington towards the European integration process: while the USA would welcome a more cohesive and effective ally with which to 'burden-share', there is concern that a more integrated Europe would be less willing to acquiesce to US leadership.

As the most powerful state in the international system by far, the USA enjoys the luxury of much greater room for manoeuvre in global affairs. It can choose where and when to intervene, and can afford to wait on events before having to act. As Waltz notes (1979: 194), 'greater power permits wider ranges of action, while leaving the outcomes of action uncertain'. It also means that the more powerful 'enjoy wider margins of safety in dealing with the less powerful and have more to say about which games will be played and how'. Whereas weak states 'operate on narrow margins' and cannot afford flawed policies or inopportune acts,

> strong states can be inattentive; they can afford not to learn; they can do the same dumb things over again. More sensibly, they can react slowly and wait to see whether the apparently threatening acts of others are truly so.

(Waltz 1979: 195)

At the same time, strong states without a significant competitor can go off in search of dragons to slay (in Iraq, for example).

> Close competition subordinates ideology to interest; states that enjoy a margin of power over their closest competitors are led to pay undue attention to minor dangers and to pursue fancies abroad that reach beyond the fulfilment of interests narrowly defined in terms of security.
>
> (Waltz 1979: 205)

The consequence of unipolarity for transatlantic relations was that the USA could afford to pay less attention to the concerns of its European allies and devoted less time to alliance management. It could use power for its own narrowly defined national interests, not those of its allies. Thus in the early 1990s when European attention was focused on the Balkans, that of the US was directed towards the Middle East and East Asia. Indeed, Secretary of State James Baker famously dismissed calls for US intervention in Bosnia on the grounds that 'we don't have a dog in this fight' (Holbrooke 1999: 27).

From a European perspective, therefore, unipolarity seemed to make US foreign policy more unreliable and capricious, if not arbitrary and high-handed. America appeared to be indifferent to some threats (such as those in the Balkans) whilst pursuing 'fancies abroad' (in Cuba, Iraq and Iran). Worries about US capriciousness and unreliability were clearly felt more acutely in places like France, Belgium and Luxembourg, but even traditional 'Atlanticist' powers like Britain, Germany and the Netherlands increasingly worried about the long-term implications of unipolarity for transatlantic relations (Layne 2003: 27). The consequence of this was that by the late 1990s a consensus had emerged between the 'big three' that they needed other options (Posen 2004: 10). In particular, they needed the option of addressing regional crises in their 'backyard' on their own terms and with their own resources.

MULTIPOLAR EUROPE

If the capriciousness and unreliability of US unipolarity provided the exogenous stimulus to the ESDP, it was the very different regional structure of power in Europe that made security and defence co-operation feasible. If power had been distributed in a highly asymmetrical manner between the great powers of Europe such that one or more of them constituted a potential regional hegemon (a configuration of power known as 'unbalanced multipolarity'), then EU military co-operation would be far harder to achieve. As it is, post-Cold War Europe is characterized by *balanced multipolarity*. In balanced multipolarity, the levels of fear and suspicion between major powers are greater than in bipolar systems, but less than in unbalanced multipolar systems (Mearsheimer 2001: 44–5). Europe for much of the nineteenth century was characterized by balanced multipolarity, and as the example of the Concert of Europe demonstrates, in this context great power co-operation to manage common security problems is possible (Kissinger 1957: 315).

Bipolar Europe has evolved into a system of balanced multipolarity with five great powers: the USA, Russia, Germany, France and Britain. Despite America's global power, Europe is not characterized by 'unipolarity'; the USA is, at best, *primus inter pares*, not a regional hegemon. Russia is much weakened after the collapse of the Soviet Union, and is now separated from Central Europe by a belt of independent states in Eastern Europe. Germany is the largest and economically strongest EU member state, but its relative power advantage over France and Britain is not so marked that it can make a realistic bid for regional hegemony (in part, because of the ongoing costs of unification and its deep-seated structural economic problems, as well as its lack of nuclear weapons). In short, as the bipolar distribution of power has gradually waned, a system of balanced multipolarity has emerged, and Europe's former great powers have begun to relearn their old roles.

In the context of balanced multipolarity, security competition in Europe remains muted, as it was throughout the 1990s (Mearsheimer 2001: 361). Because no great power can make a credible bid for hegemony, their strategic behaviour is characterized more by security, rather than power, maximization. At the same time, concerns over relative gains are also less pronounced than in contexts of intense security competition, thereby increasing the prospects for co-operation. The lack of a major external security threat, coupled with balanced multipolarity, means that there is little need for mass conscript armies. Most European countries have now abandoned or watered down conscription, which has further facilitated the 'taming' of nationalism and the emergence of multiple 'European' identities. The break in the centuries-old connection between citizenship and military service is an important 'second image' development of great consequence, but its causes can be traced back to structural changes at the systemic level.

The emergence of slimmed-down professional armed forces in Europe in place of mass conscript armies reflects a shift away from collective or national territorial defence towards expeditionary warfare and power projection. This is an important consequence of balanced multipolarity and a lessening of great power security competition. European armies are now less focused on preparing to fight high-intensity full-spectrum wars of national survival, and are now being restructured for military crisis management, peace support operations and humanitarian intervention. This represents a shift away from what Thomas Schelling termed 'brute force' towards coercion and the discriminate use of force (Schelling 1966: 2–3). The ESDP needs to be seen in this context: it is not a 'European army' designed for collective territorial defence; rather, it is an instrument for coalitional coercive diplomacy. The ESDP can thus be seen as the response of EU member states to the uncertainties of US security policy in the context of global unipolarity. As realism would predict, the process has been driven by the 'Big Three', and remains firmly intergovernmental. The ESDP is not about collective European territorial defence, and the European Rapid Reaction Corps is not a 'European army'. The ESDP is a collective instrument for coalitional coercive diplomacy and military crisis management by EU member states, as defined by the Petersberg Tasks and the European Security Strategy (EU Institute for Security Studies 2003). It establishes an institutional and procedural framework for limited security co-operation in order to collectively shape the Union's external milieu, using military coercion to back up its diplomacy. The ESDP thus represents the EU's response to the failures of 'civilian power' Europe in the Balkans, and is a development made possible by the twin structural dynamics of a unipolar world and a multipolar Europe.

THE FUTURE OF EUROPEAN SECURITY AND DEFENCE POLICY

Although structural realism does not advance strong claims to predictive ability, an analysis of the global and regional structural distribution of power does suggest some broad conclusions about the future of European security and defence co-operation. First and foremost, structural realism would suggest that Europe's great powers will continue to jealously guard their sovereign rights to pursue their own foreign and security policy priorities. Consequently, the CFSP/ESDP is destined to remain firmly intergovernmental. Co-operation in the second pillar will remain limited to a set of 'second-order' concerns agreed on the basis of the lowest common denominator. Multipolarity will also set limits to the scope and ambition of EU foreign and security policy. Although security competition is muted in Europe at present, realists would expect it to grow as power relationships change, as they inevitably will. The conflict between Russia and EU member states over the Ukrainian presidential election in the autumn of 2004 may well presage intensifying security competition in Central and Eastern Europe.

Second, if the EU is to have an international role beyond milieu shaping in its 'new neighbourhood' and act as the institutional repository of the shared second-order ethical concerns of its member states, the responsibility for giving direction and substance to 'EU' foreign and security policy will have to be vested in the hands of the Union's largest powers. In this respect, the 'EU3' policy towards Iran may be a harbinger of things to come. It builds on the experience of the Contact Group in the Balkans, and offers an opportunity for Europeans to demonstrate a less confrontational and belligerent approach to foreign policy than that emanating from Washington. Whether 'European' diplomacy will succeed where American threats have failed is another question. There is no doubt, however, that it represents a crucial test-case for European foreign and security policy, and that it fits realist expectations about the role of great powers in the management of international affairs.

Third, transatlantic relations are likely to experience further 'continental drift' as the USA loses interest in, and reduces its military commitment to, Europe, and as EU member states seek to provide themselves with options for autonomous military crisis management. Deteriorating transatlantic relations might act as a catalyst for a more cohesive EU with a sharper and more effective international role. However, if great power security competition increases in a multipolar Europe, EU member states are likely to pursue a variety of strategies towards America, from balancing to bandwagoning. The divisions between 'old' and 'new' Europe that emerged during the Iraq crisis of 2002–03 are suggestive of the patterns of relations that could emerge, with some states allying with the USA and others pursuing a *Kleineuropa* ('small Europe') option of integration between a select group of 'core' states. European international politics in the early twenty-first century are thus likely to be characterized by shifting coalitions of great and middle powers.

This will open up space for skilful statecraft to either exploit structural pressures or to buck them. The structure of the international system – global unipolarity and balanced multipolarity in Europe – sets a range of potential options available to states, and provides incentives for particular foreign policy strategies, but it does not predetermine particular outcomes. 'Thinking in terms of systems dynamics does not replace unit-level analysis nor end the search for sequences of cause and effect', Waltz argues. What it does do is 'change the conduct of the search and add a dimension to it' (Waltz 1986: 344). That great diplomatic virtuoso, Otto von Bismarck, once declared that: 'A statesman cannot create anything himself. He must wait and listen until he hears the steps of God sounding through events; then leap up and grasp the hem of his garment' (Taylor 1955: 115). Henry Kissinger expressed the same idea more prosaically: 'The test of a statesman', he wrote, 'is his ability to recognize the real relationship of forces and to make this knowledge serve his ends' (Kissinger 1957: 325). The ESDP will undoubtedly continue to be 'shaped and shoved' by structural pressures, but its future will also depend very much on the ability of European leaders to hear God's footsteps sounding through events and 'then leap up and grasp the hem of his garment'.

Biographical note: Adrian Hyde-Price is Professor of Politics and International Relations and Head of Department in the Department of Politics and International Relations, University of Leicester, UK.

Address for correspondence: Adrian Hyde-Price, Department of Politics and International Relations, University of Leicester, Leicester LE1 7RH, UK. Tel: +44 116 252 2795. Fax: +44 116 252 5082. email: agvhp1@le.ac.uk

REFERENCES

Allison, G. (1971) *Essence of Decision: Explaining the Cuban Missile Crisis*, Boston: Little Brown.
Bull, H. (1982) 'Civilian power Europe: a contradiction in terms?', *Journal of Common Market Studies* 21(2): 149–82.
Carr, E.H. (2001) *The Twenty Years' Crisis: An Introduction to the Study of International Relations*, 2nd edn, New York: Palgrave.
Christensen, T. and Snyder, G. (1990) 'Chain gangs and passed bucks: predicting alliance patterns in multipolarity', *International Organization* 44(2): 137–68.
Duchêne, F. (1972) 'Europe's role in world peace', in R. Mayne (ed.), *Europe Tomorrow: Sixteen Europeans Look Ahead*, London: Fontana, pp. 32–47.

EU Institute for Security Studies (2003) *A Secure Europe in a Better World. European Security Strategy*, Brussels: EU Institute for Security Studies.

Gilpin, R. (1986) 'The richness of the tradition of political realism', in R. Keohane (ed.), *Realism and Its Critics*, New York: Columbia University Press, pp. 301–21.

Gow, J. (1997) *The Triumph of the Lack of Will. International Diplomacy and the Yugoslav War*, London: Hurst & Company.

Grieco, J. (1993) 'Understanding the problem of international cooperation: the limits of neo-liberal institutionalism and the future of realist theory', in D. Baldwin (ed.), *Neorealism and Neoliberalism*, New York: Columbia University Press, pp. 301–39.

Grieco, J. (1997) 'Realist international theory and the study of world politics', in M. Doyle and J. Ikenberry (eds), *New Thinking in International Relations Theory*, Boulder, CO: Westview Press, pp.163–201.

Hill, C. (1990) *European Foreign Policy: Power Bloc, Civilian Model – or Flop?*, Boulder, CO: Westview Press.

Holbrooke, R. (1999) *To End a War*, rev. edn, New York: The Modern Library.

Hyde-Price, A. (1991) *European Security Beyond the Cold War: Four Scenarios for the Year 2010*, London: Sage.

Hyde-Price, A. (1996) *The International Politics of East Central Europe*, Manchester: Manchester University Press.

Hyde-Price, A. (2000) *Germany and European Order: Enlarging NATO and the European Union*, Manchester: Manchester University Press.

Joffe, J. (1984) 'Europe's American pacifier', *Foreign Affairs* 54: 64–82.

Jørgensen, K. (2004) 'European foreign policy: conceptualising the domain', in W. Carlsneas, H. Sjursen and B. White (eds), *Contemporary European Foreign Policy*, London: Sage, pp. 32–56.

Kagan, R. (2003) *Paradise and Power. America and Europe in the New World Order*, London: Atlantic Books.

Keohane, R. (1986) 'Theory of world politics: structural realism and beyond', in R. Keohane (ed.), *Realism and Its Critics*, New York: Columbia University Press, pp. 158–203.

Keohane, R. and Nye, J. (1977) *Power and Interdependence: World Politics in Transition*, Boston: Little Brown.

Kissinger, H. (1957) *A World Restored: Europe After Napoleon*, Boston: Houghton Mifflin.

Labs, E. (1992) 'Do weak states bandwagon?', *Security Studies* 1(3): 383–416.

Layne, C. (2003) 'America as European hegemon', *National Interest* 72: 17–30.

Manners, I. (2002) 'Normative power Europe: a contradiction in terms?', *Journal of Common Market Studies* 40(2): 235–58.

Maull, H. (1993) 'Civilian power: the concept and its relevance for security issues', in L. Babic and B. Huldt (eds), *Mapping the Unknown: Towards a New World Order*, Stockholm: Swedish Institute of International Affairs, pp. 115–31.

Mearsheimer, J. (1995) 'The false promise of international institutions', in M. Brown, S. Lynn-Jones and S. Miller (eds), *The Perils of Anarchy. Contemporary Realism and International Security*, Cambridge, MA: MIT Press, pp. 332–76.

Mearsheimer, J. (2001) *The Tragedy of Great Power Politics*, New York: W.W. Norton & Co.

Nye, J. (1990) *Bound to Lead*, New York: Basic Books.

Posen, B. (2003) 'Command of the commons: the military foundation of US hegemony', *International Security* 28(1): 5–46.

Posen, B. (2004) 'ESDP and the structure of world power', *International Spectator* 39(1): 5–17.

Schelling, T. (1966) *Arms and Influence*, New Haven: Yale University Press.

Schroeder, P. (1995) 'Historical reality vs. neo-realist theory', in M. Brown, S. Lynn-Jones and S. Miller (eds), *The Perils of Anarchy. Contemporary Realism and International Security*, Cambridge, MA: MIT Press, pp. 421–61.

Schweller, R. (1994) 'Bandwagoning for profit: bringing the revisionist state back in', *International Security* 19(1): 72–107.

Smith, K. (2003) *European Union Foreign Policy in a Changing World*, Cambridge: Polity Press.

Snyder, G. (2002) 'Mearsheimer's world – offensive realism and the struggle for security', *International Security* 27(1): 149–73.

Taylor, A.J.P. (1955) *Bismarck: The Man and the Statesman*, London: Penguin.

Walt, S. (1987) *The Origin of Alliances*, Ithaca, NY: Cornell University Press.

Waltz, K. (1959) *Man, the State and War: A Theoretical Analysis*, New York: Columbia University Press.

Waltz, K. (1979) *Theory of International Politics*, New York: McGraw-Hill.

Waltz, K. (1986) 'Reflections on *Theory of International Politics*: a response to my critics', in R. Keohane (ed.), *Realism and Its Critics*, New York: Columbia University Press, pp. 322–46.

Waltz, K. (1995) 'Realist thought and neorealist theory', in C. Kegley (ed.), *Controversies in International Relations Theory. Realism and the Neoliberal Challenge*, New York: St Martin's Press, pp. 67–82.

Waltz, K. (2000) 'Structural realism after the Cold War', *International Security* 25(1): 5–41.

Wolfers, A. (1962) *Discord and Collaboration: Essays in International Politics*, Baltimore: Johns Hopkins University Press.

The EU as a 'normative' power: how can this be?

Helene Sjursen[1]

INTRODUCTION

The idea that the European Union (EU) should be conceptualized as a 'civilian', 'normative', 'civilizing' or 'ethical' power in the international system has proved to be a fruitful avenue for research. This is so in particular because it has brought the research agenda on European foreign policy a step forward from the at times sterile discussion on whether the EU 'actually' has a foreign policy or not. However, conceptualizing the EU's international role in such a way also raises a number of questions and provokes debate. The conception of the EU as a 'normative', 'civilian', etc. power is contested. Indeed, the fact that it corresponds very closely to the EU's own description of its international role could be enough to set the alarm bells ringing. Nevertheless, there might be some validity to such conceptualizations of the EU. Hence, rather than being rejected outright, they should be examined more closely. A number of empirical observations regarding issues such as the EU's policy of democracy promotion, its introduction of human rights clauses in trade agreements, the emphasis on encouraging regional co-operation and its focus on strengthening international institutions could very well indicate that there is something distinctive about the EU's foreign policy, at least in comparison with what we tend to think of as the foreign policies of great powers, that requires attention. However, the above conceptualizations lack sufficient precision and they do not provide any criteria or assessment standards that would make it possible to qualify, substantiate or reject their implicit claim that the EU is a 'force for good'.

In fact it is difficult to find a single consistent definition of 'normative', 'civilian', 'ethical', 'civilizing' power Europe. Yet, the literature taken as a whole has certain common themes that refer to the EU's distinctiveness and normativity. According to Ian Manners whose article, together with François Duchêne's (1972) conception of the EU as a 'civilian power', has become a core reference in this literature: 'the central component of normative power Europe is that the EU exists as being different to pre-existing political forms, and that this particular difference *predisposes it to act in a normative way*' (Manners 2002: 242; my emphasis). Yet, how, if at all, can we know, as it is implied, that 'acting in a normative way' is a 'good thing'? The 'normative power argument' needs to be further specified, scrutinized and accounted for. This is so regardless of whether we want to further substantiate, modify or, in the end, reject it. Consequently, the questions asked in this article are, if the EU were to be a 'normative', 'civilian' or 'civilizing' power, what might be its core identifying features – how do we know a 'normative' or 'civilizing' power when we see it? And furthermore, would such features set the EU apart from other actors in the international system?

An important aim is to be explicit about a possible standard that might be used to assess claims about the EU's normative dimension. It is only if such standards and criteria are explicitly indicated that it is possible to criticize them. And further, it is only by presenting clear definitions of what 'normative' power is, and consequently also what it is not, that we can realistically hope to say something about the empirical relevance of the argument. In order to do so, we need a theory that takes the putative normative dimension seriously but that also gives us the tools to be critical. We need an approach that considers norms to have a rational basis.

The article is organized in three sections. In each section a particular feature that might be used to identify a 'normative' power is discussed. The questions of the general 'fit' of this feature with the EU and of the extent to which this can be said to be a feature that is particular to the Union, are also raised, although the main aim is not to systematically test the empirical relevance of the 'normative power' argument. In the last section of the article I suggest that a core distinguishing feature of a 'normative' power might be that it seeks to overcome power politics through a strengthening not only of international but cosmopolitan law, emphasizing the rights of the individuals in the international system.

'NORMATIVE' POWER AS 'CIVILIAN' POWER

The lack of military instruments is often mentioned as important to the EU's 'normative' power.[2] Is this then the core feature that allows us to identify not only a civilian but also a 'civilizing' power, as well as to highlight the distinctiveness of European 'normative' power? This argument has its roots in François Duchêne's (1972) conception of the EU, and has attracted attention not only within the rather limited community of academics interested in the EU's external policies, but also in the broader policy debate, as the writings of Robert Kagan (2003) testify to. Arguing that the Europeans come from Venus and the Americans from Mars, Kagan establishes a contrast between the (in his view 'realistic') US, which relies on military power and subscribes to a perspective on international relations consistent with a so-called Hobbesian war of all against all, and the EU's 'Kantian' approach, focusing on 'soft', civilian means.

Although Kagan's pamphlet has received more attention than the academic writings on the topic, similar arguments about what characterizes the EU's international role are found in the academic literature. Thus Menon et al. argue that the EU is:

> a pioneer in long term interstate peace building, a pioneer actor through trial and error and thus designing options for peaceful governance. In this vision, the EU is one of the most formidable machines for managing differences peacefully ever invented.
>
> (Menon et al. 2004: 11)

Karen Smith also considers this to be the core feature of the EU's international role: 'the EU still clearly prefers positive civilian to coercive military measures' (Smith 2000; 2003: 111). The emphasis is on the panoply of civilian instruments that the EU, in contrast to, for example, the North Atlantic Treaty Organization (NATO), has at its disposal, and that puts it in the unique position of being able both to contribute to prevent conflict from erupting and to manage the aftermath of conflict.

However, given that the EU is now developing military capabilities, where does this leave the argument? Are the conceptions of the EU as 'civilian' power and 'civilizing'/'normative' power inextricably linked together? With military means at its disposal, the EU would be able to make credible threats. It would not need to pay too much attention to other actors' interests, perspectives, or arguments in order to get its way. The option of 'going alone' and/or imposing its own interests or values would be a more realistic one than what it has been so far.

From Kagan's perspective Kantian Europe is only 'Kantian' by necessity, not by choice. Consequently, one would expect the EU to pursue a different approach if it were to obtain military capabilities. However, there is a twin problem with this expectation. Firstly, it relies on a perspective on the international system that makes it impossible to consider an alternative understanding of the EU's international role to that of 'Kantian by necessity'. It is Kagan's view of international relations – the world outside Europe – as essentially ruled by the 'laws of the jungle', where might is right, that leads him to the conclusion that if the EU could, it would be a 'Hobbesian' rather than a 'Kantian' power. The structures or characteristics of the system would make it inevitable. Kagan presents this 'Hobbesian' perspective as a description of 'reality' and as such it is contested and contestable. Even realists stress that this perspective on the international system can only be a theoretical assumption and not a full description of the 'real world' (Hyde-Price 2006). A second problem with Kagan's expectations is that he does not have a conceptual apparatus that allows him to investigate the, at least theoretical, possibility that things might develop differently. In order to do this, a conception of actors rationally assessing not only what kind of action might be most beneficial to them, but also what might be the 'right' or the 'appropriate' course of action in a particular setting is needed. As I shall argue later in the article, this is a weakness that many realist analyses seem to share.

In fact, the claim that the EU is a 'civilian' and thus 'civilizing' power by necessity must be problematized. If we consider the EU's Security Strategy (ESS), where the so-called 'new threats' to European security are reviewed and analysed, it becomes clear that the use of military force is still not considered the first option (European Council 2003; Bailes 2005). Rather, the ESS seems to continue the tradition of 'civilian power' in the sense that it argues not only that the 'new threats' are not purely military, as they were considered to be during the Cold War, but also that most of them cannot be tackled by military means. Economic instruments are stressed as important to ensure reconstruction and so is civilian crisis management. Trade and development policies are highlighted as powerful tools to promote reform and ensure stability. And assistance programmes, conditionality and targeted trade measures are underlined as important elements in the EU's Security Strategy. Such initiatives are part of what the ESS defines as 'pre-emptive engagement' – aimed at ensuring 'a world which is seen as offering justice and opportunity for everyone' (European Council 2003; see also Schröder 2005). Consequently, the EU does not seem to have abandoned the belief in civilian instruments even though its potential ability to do so if it wishes to is increasing.

'Soft' versus 'hard' instruments – a false debate?

However, one thing is to argue that even with military capabilities at its disposal, the EU tends to favour civilian instruments. Another is to argue that the availability of military force is by definition alien to a concept of 'normative' or 'civilizing' power. Karen Smith (2000, 2004) considers this to be the case, while Manners' answer is that these things should be kept separate. Yet his reasons for keeping them separate are that he is not interested in capabilities but in 'normative power of an ideational nature' and that the EU's ability to 'shape conceptions of "normal" in international affairs needs to be given much greater attention' (Manners 2002: 239). The main point for him then seems to be to highlight an additional dimension to the EU's international role.[3] However, does this really tackle the potential difficulty of one dimension of the EU's international role undermining another, i.e. of 'military EU' coming back to haunt the putative ideational nature of the EU's 'normative' power? And further, what are the mechanisms at play that trigger this ability of the EU to 'shape conceptions of normal'? What is the 'power mechanism' in normative power?

Arguably we cannot from the outset say that the ability to threaten to use military force would be contrary to a 'civilizing' or 'normative' power.

What if important norms are clearly and systematically broken? Would this not provoke a responsibility to react rather than to look the other way? It may also be that the threat of the use of force is required in order to appear credible to third parties when seeking to promote particular norms. The criticisms of the EU's role in the crises in former Yugoslavia, for example, suggest that, for a putative 'normative' power, the *in*capacity to act is considered by many to be as problematic as the capacity to act (Gow 1997; Hyde-Price 2006). Most importantly, perhaps, civilian instruments, although often referred to as 'soft' instruments, are not necessarily benign and neither are they necessarily non-coercive. Economic sanctions can cause serious harm, and what is more, their effects are often indiscriminate. They may hit civilians and in particular children very hard. So the use of non-military instruments cannot on its own be enough to identify a polity as a 'normative' power.

PROMOTING NORMS NOT SELF-INTEREST?

If 'civilian' power is not a sufficient or satisfactory criterion for identifying a 'normative' or 'civilizing' power, can the claim that the EU, in its external policies, promotes norms and values rather than, or in addition to, its own particular interests do the trick? There is a general sense that the EU's external policies are not solely derived from a desire to promote its own interests, but must be seen as moved also by a certain understanding of what 'ought' to be done (Rosencrance 1998; Whitman 1998; Manners 2002; Aggestam 2004). The argument has perhaps been forwarded most systematically with regard to the EU's enlargement policies, although here the literature differs with regard to what type of norms can explain the EU's policies (Sjursen 2002).

Not all agree with this way of understanding the EU's international role though. Amongst the sceptics is Richard Youngs (2004) who has sought to demonstrate that EU human rights policies, for example, actually rest on strategic considerations and can be explained as the outcome of rational utility calculations. However, Youngs does not even make it plausible that the EU's policy has come about as a result of self-interested calculations. He observes that the EU's approach to human rights in third countries is inspired by a 'gradualist philosophy' seeking controlled change in target states. Yet, rather than provide evidence for his argument that self-interest is 'at the bottom' of the EU's human rights policy, this points to (normative) considerations of how best to promote human rights norms in third countries having been at play. One might add that even if Youngs had demonstrated that the policy was triggered by strategic considerations, it would not necessarily topple the 'normative' power argument, given that the norms diffused may very well be considered valid and legitimate even though the motives of the EU for diffusing such norms are self-regarding (Eriksen 2006).

Knud Erik Jørgensen and Katie Laatikainen, also sceptical of the 'normative' power argument, observe that 'the EU's self-image is characterised by a curious blindness to own interests. Instead, the Union tends to present itself as a force for goodness in international society' (Jørgensen and Laatikainen 2004: 15). Their argument appears to be that what the EU 'really' does is to play down its own interests, and that this needs to be better explained. Furthermore, they find it difficult to see the emphasis on values and norms as something that is particular to the EU. There is indeed little doubt that not only the US but also the former Soviet Union could be described as 'normative' or 'civilizing' powers.

US 'normative' power

Although the emphasis on ideals and moral principles has varied over time and also in accordance with the holder of the Presidential office, there is a long tradition of seeing the foreign policy of the US as having important normative undertones, as well as having a particular focus on human rights and democratic principles (cf. Cox *et al.* 2000). This is so, for example, in the US' relations with Eastern Europe where, at the end of the First World War, President Woodrow Wilson's Fourteen Points achieved status as a basic charter for freedom among the European peoples. Human rights are also considered to have been crucial to Jimmy Carter's foreign policy in the 1970s. Even Ronald Reagan's foreign policy must be seen as inspired by a sense of moral conviction and not only by realpolitik (Dallek 1984: 129–30; Sjursen 2003). Yet the EU is often described as a 'normative' power *in contrast* to the US (Lucarelli 2004). How can this be?

The example of the US is instructive not only because it demonstrates that an emphasis on the diffusion of norms, values and ideas is a characteristic that is not particular to the EU's foreign policy. It also alerts us to the fact that efforts to justify foreign policy with reference to norms often lead to suspicions of hypocrisy and hidden agendas. As Lundestad argues, the US' 'normative' foreign policy provokes profound scepticism:

> Most European observers have been rather sceptical about the American claim to uniqueness, particularly as it usually implied American superiority. To many Europeans, what was unique about America was its uncanny ability to make the most inspiring idealism coincide almost perfectly with rather ordinary national objectives.
>
> (Lundestad 1990: 41)

This scepticism in many ways echoes Youngs' (2004) doubts about the normative dimension to the EU's foreign policy. In both cases what troubles the observers is that they consider normative arguments to have been made for strategic purposes, to promote particular interests. The problem with this interpretation is that it risks becoming a self-fulfilling prophecy, unless the analyst has an alternative conception of political processes available that would allow her to consider the theoretical possibility that references to norms can be something other than hypocritical (Sjursen 2004).

Norms, coercion and missionary politics

The scepticism is not, however, only of the above realist variant, where the underlying assumption is that there is no alternative to an understanding of foreign policy as one where states have certain fundamental interests that they pursue systematically in the international system. US 'normative' power also provokes scepticism owing to the methods or instruments employed in order to ensure respect for its convictions. US idealism is linked to norms and principles being imposed through force. The element of 'power politics' does not disappear even if diffusion of norms is what is apparently at stake. As already noted, Reagan's policy for instance, may be seen to have been inspired by a deep-rooted conviction that the values promoted by the US were ultimately beneficial to the rest of the world. However, defending such values was interpreted as a national mission, which followed logically from the US' status as a superpower (Sjursen 2003). Reagan's ideals were pursued in accordance with the premises of power politics (see, for example, Meese 1992).

Furthermore, the US is often criticized for seeking to impose its norms without regard for the particular context in which they are to be inserted (Davis 1974: 378; Coker 1989: 44). Here the point seems to be that a policy that focuses exclusively on the abstract validity of norms is problematic. The importance of contextual knowledge such as historical conditions, geopolitical characteristics, and the realities of power or particular interest is underlined. Such contextual knowledge may contribute to answer the question of what is the most appropriate solution to a particular policy dilemma in situations where different normative priorities collide. Is it possible then that a distinguishing mark of the US' 'normative' approach has in certain periods been an explicit priority given to 'moral imperatives' – and a desire to avoid the moral ambiguity that almost inevitably arises when you move from abstract principles to practical policy (Sjursen 2003)? If this is so, it might mean that there is after all a contrast between the 'normative' power of the US and that of the EU, both with regard to the instruments used and the approach chosen.

It remains nevertheless that the example of the US makes it clear that in order to pinpoint a 'normative' power, as well as to distinguish European 'normative' power from the normative dimension that is part of the foreign policies also of other actors in the international system, it is not enough simply to argue that it has to do with promoting norms and values and not only strategic interests in the international system. In fact, the scepticism pointed to with regard to the policies of the US confirms that norms, values and ideas are not benign, and, furthermore, that the conceptions of the EU as a 'normative', 'civilian' or 'civilizing' power are normatively biased. They imply that the actor defined by these concepts is actually a 'force for the good' to use Jørgensen and Laatikainen's (2004) expression. Yet, how can we actually know that this is the case?

The concepts of 'normative', 'ethical' or 'civilizing' power are too indiscriminate. We need a conceptual apparatus that allows us to distinguish what might be normatively acceptable, i.e. what might be a legitimate pursuit of norms, from a pursuit of norms that is not considered to be so. Otherwise, how do we know that 'normative power' Europe is not simply an expression of Eurocentric imperialism? And how do we know if it is only because the EU is less powerful than the US that the scepticism towards its 'normative' power so far is less strong?

A 'predisposition to act in a normative way'?

As noted in the introduction, most authors argue that the 'normative', 'ideational' or 'civilizing' power of the EU is linked to the core characteristics of the organization – which 'predisposes it to act in a normative way' (Manners 2002: 242; also Duchêne 1972; Whitman 1998). Yet what is it about this organization that 'predisposes' it to act in such a way? Three features are identified by Manners as important in this regard: the EU's historical context; its characteristic as a hybrid polity; and its political–legal constitution (Manners 2002: 240). More concretely, he refers to the fact that in the context of the end of the Second World War Europeans were committed to pool sovereignty in order to curb nationalism; that the EU is a new type of entity that combines supranationalism and international forms of governance; and finally that its constitutional norms, which embody the principles of democracy, rule of law, social justice and respect for human rights condition its international identity. Yet, questions remain: are these characteristics of the EU on their own enough to demonstrate that 'the EU is not simply promoting its own norms in a similar manner to historical empires and contemporary powers' (Manners 2002: 240)? Can we reasonably expect, based on this description of the EU, that it continues to 'act in a normative way' and to do so consistently? What is the mechanism that allows us to account for such expectations of consistency? And – again – how do we know if 'acting in a normative way' is actually a 'good thing'?

It would seem that in order for the 'normative' power argument to become a plausible hypothesis, and thus in order for it to be possible to identify 'normative powers', further theoretical underpinnings are necessary. We must at least be able to account for why it is reasonable to expect that a polity such as the EU would not pursue an external policy that breaks with internal principles (i.e. why is it that its organizational characteristics 'predispose it to act in a normative way'), as well as be able to discriminate between different types of norms and their legitimacy and validity (as we cannot de facto assume that 'acting in a normative way' is necessarily a good thing).

Theoretical underpinnings

First of all we need a conception of human agency that allows us to account for normative behaviour as a 'rational' choice. According to the theory of communicative action, actors are considered rational when they are able to justify and explain their actions in relation to intersubjectively valid norms, i.e. norms that cannot be reasonably rejected in a rational debate. It pertains to the idea that not only empirical evidence but also the norms themselves have to be critically assessed and justified (Eriksen and Weigård 1997: 228; Lose 2001: 185). This concept provides a starting point, as it allows for claims regarding the importance and relevance of normative conviction in foreign policy to be taken seriously. Without this, analyses are predetermined to conclude that such claims are simply, as Lundestad (1990) argues, a cover for particular interests, or an expression of particularistic values. A 'normative' power would simply be a hypocrite without this conception. Such theoretical conceptions do not preclude the possibility of hypocrisy; however, they leave it open to empirical studies to reveal what would be the best way of understanding a particular policy-initiative.

However, one thing is to conceive of actors that may act in accordance with normative convictions and not only with reference to particular interests. Quite another is to know whether this leads the actor to do the right thing from a prin-cipled point of view, and another one again to know whether it is the right thing to do in a particular or concrete context or situation. According to discourse ethics, it is possible to come to agreement on, or realize, or identify, a prin-ciple of universalization, indicating which norm may be considered valid. This is a norm that meets the condition that: '*All* affected can accept the con-sequences and the side effects its *general* observance can be anticipated to have for *everyone's* interest (and the consequences are preferred to those of known alternative possibilities for regulation)' (Habermas 1990: 65). This principle requires all parties to view the issue from the perspective of the other parties involved. In order to identify the EU as a 'normative' or 'civilizing' power, the question would then be whether or not its external action relies on norms that may be tested and found to be in accordance with this principle: does the EU, in its external action, refer to reasons that can be expected to gain approval in a free and open debate in which all those affected are heard?

However, as noted, it is one thing to be able to justify a norm with reference to the principle of universalization. Another is to know if the norm is correct in a particular context. What is the right action in a given situation is not necessarily self-evident. Different universal norms may collide in a concrete situation or a particular context: 'The test of universalisability can be used to rule out certain norms of action if it turns out that they are not universalisable' (Eriksen and Weigård 2003: 80). However, in a given context we often face several universa-lizable norms that have conflicting content and that would point us in different directions. In order to solve this dilemma, a distinction has been made between a discourse of justification and a discourse of application. According to the latter, 'the question is rather *if* a particular rule should be followed in the present cir-cumstances, and in case of yes, how this should be done' (Eriksen and Weigård 2003: 80; cf. Günther 1993). As noted earlier with regard to the US, a possible hypothesis would be that the EU's and the US' approaches to normative issues are linked, or have at various times in history been linked, to different views of how to handle the tension between different abstract norms. Whereas the US appears less concerned with the particular context in which universal principles are to be pursued and implemented, the EU appears, if we are to believe, for example, Youngs (2004), concerned with adapting to the context in which such principles are to be introduced.

The above is not enough to close the door to suspicions and accusations of hypocrisy – or to suspicions that actors use norms to justify pursuing particular interests. Neither does it solve concerns about inconsistency in the application and pursuit of norms. However, it gives us some basic building blocks that might allow us to theoretically account for claims about the EU, or other actors, being 'normative' or 'civilian' powers. Furthermore, it gives us some tools to start distinguishing between different claims and establishes a core principle suggesting how to evaluate different initiatives, how to know whether to 'act in a normative way' can be considered legitimate or not. Finally, it provides us with the theoretical tools that would allow us to account for why it might make sense to expect, as the normative power argument appears to do, consistency between the internal and external standards of a polity such as the EU. In a communicative process, or a process of reason-giving:

> Verbal statements raise expectations of consistency between claims and their correctness and between words and actions. In certain situations double standards and cognitive dissonance will be problematic. Under certain conditions deliberation compels actors to explain and justify their preferences to critical interlocutors and revise them when criticized.
>
> (Eriksen *et al.* 2005: 238)

As the EU's constitutional norms embody the principles of democracy, rule of law and respect for human rights, some of these conditions are in place in the EU. Consequently, living by double standards becomes a problem. The point is not only then that the Common Foreign and Security Policy (CFSP) may form a sphere in which deliberation about foreign policy takes place in a manner where the member states have to justify their positions and viewpoints to each other (Mitzen 2006). The EU may also create expectations from third parties that it lives up to the standards it has identified and committed itself to.

SELF-BINDING THROUGH LAW

The principle of universalization may allow us to establish the necessary distinctions that make it possible to assess the legitimacy of initiatives in particular cases. However, it is perhaps not a sufficiently strong indicator of 'normative' power. A stronger indicator, which would at the same time alleviate suspicions of hypocrisy and ensure consistency in the application and pursuit of norms, might be linked to what kind of legal principles the EU relies on in its external initiatives. There is always a risk that actors will follow their own interests even if they know that this may harm others, or suspect that others do so, even if they say the opposite. In order to avoid such risks, common rules are necessary. The law functions as a system of action that makes it possible to implement moral duties or commitments.

To 'act in a normative way' would then be to act in accordance with legal principles.[4] This would also mean that it would not matter so much if particular interests coincided with legal obligations, as long as legal commitments would be respected also when the opposite was the case. The pursuit of norms would be legitimate in the sense that it would be consistent with agreed legal norms. If coercion were used, it would be so only in consistence with existing legal arrangements and in order to uphold the respect for such arrangements.

Multilateralism

Such a perspective would fit with the EU's strong emphasis on international law and multilateralism. Multilateralism is at the core of the ESS, which commits the EU to work for 'an effective multilateral system' (European Council 2003). The EU's objective is thus described as to develop a stronger international society, well-functioning international institutions and a rule-based international order. Membership in key international institutions is to be encouraged and regional organizations are considered important in the effort to strengthen global governance. The cornerstone of a law-based international order is, according to the ESS, the United Nations. Its role must be strengthened; it must be equipped to fulfil its responsibilities and to act effectively.

However, is a commitment to multilateralism enough in order for us to identify the EU as a 'normative' power? And is it enough to distinguish the EU from other 'normative' powers? Following Ruggie, what is distinctive about multilateralism is its qualitative dimension: 'it coordinates national policies in groups of three or more states ... on the basis of certain principles of ordering relations among those states' (Ruggie 1992: 567). It is these principles of conduct, and not the particular interests of the states or the 'strategic exigencies' of a specific situation, that specify what is the appropriate conduct. In this way Ruggie rules out the possibility that the state with most resources at its disposal can on this basis alone legitimately expect to have the final word in any given situation within a multilateral setting. So far, an emphasis on multilateralism appears to fit with the concept of 'normative' or 'civilian' power and to give us an indicator of what a 'normative' power might be.

However, a core feature of multilateralism is the principle of sovereignty. In fact, Ruggie shows that the earliest multilateral arrangements were designed to cope with the international consequences of this principle, such as the need to ensure the possession of territory and the exclusion of others from it. A core element of the solutions found was that the same rule would apply to all states irrespective of their size, domestic political regime or material resources. So this ensures equality before the law and alleviates the concern that the most powerful only seek to impose their own interests or values in the name of normative concerns. However, the onus is on the rights of states and the equality of *states* before the law. Consequently, not all the norms that the EU claims to promote have legal backing in a multilateral system. This is so in particular with regard to human rights, which is a core principle of the EU's external policy

(Smith 2003; Menéndez 2004; Lerch and Schwellnus 2006). Although the emphasis on human rights as an important international principle has developed in multilateral settings, human rights do at the same time challenge the core of multilateralism. Discussions in the context of the reforms of the United Nations testify to this. The principle of human rights breaks with the principle of external sovereignty (Eriksen 2006).

Unless the principles of human rights also become positive legal rights that can be enforced, it is difficult to avoid the fact that the most powerful only use a 'moral' foreign policy for their own interest and that even when they don't, they are still suspected of doing so (Eriksen 2003). In turn this leads to arbitrariness, as human rights are not, in practice, universal principles applied to all. Such arbitrariness is also visible in the EU's foreign and security policy (Smith 2003). In order to overcome this problem, all international relations would have to be subordinated to a common judicial order that would transform the parameters of power politics and redefine the concept of sovereignty. Human rights would then be 'rights which have to be implemented in a legal sense' (Habermas 1999: 270). The international order would need to move from an exclusive emphasis on the rights of sovereign states within a multilateral order to the rights of individuals in a cosmopolitan order.

A second reason why a focus on promoting multilateralism might not be enough in order for us to define 'normative' power Europe is that a multilateral arrangement is vulnerable. The vulnerability is linked to the absence of the possibility of sanctions within a multilateral system – the absence of the mutual commitment of all the member states to be legally bound by the principles of multilateralism. Mutually binding legal arrangements connected to sanctions may actually be what is required in order to ensure that actors comply. The legal commitment in multilateralism is weaker than this. There may be a general expectation of consultation, equality and non-hierarchical decision-making processes following from multilateralism; and when states break with these mutually accepted norms, they may provoke strong reactions. However, the possibility of sanctioning the norm-breaker is limited. Multilateralism is to a large extent dependent on the benevolence of the member states and in particular the benevolence of the most powerful states within the system. This means that multilateralism does not really ensure an equal commitment of all parties to adhere to overarching laws. It does not fit with modern law.

Finally, one might add that an emphasis on multilateralism as the core defining feature of 'normative' power does not make the EU unique or particular in the international context, even though to promote the principles of multilateralism in the current international context may look like an uphill struggle. A number of states in the international system subscribe to, and seek to promote and protect, multilateralism as a core principle of international affairs.

The (im-)possibility of cosmopolitan law?

Many will, however, consider that multilateralism is as good as it can get (Brown 1999). Some would argue that this is due to inherent cultural differences that make it impossible to come to a rational agreement on universally acceptable norms. Others would rather emphasize the inherent characteristics of the international system leading to insurmountable practical difficulties in establishing cosmopolitan law, which would ensure the rights not only of states but also the fundamental rights of citizens. The former seems to be the position of Diez (2004), who suggests that the 'normative' power argument should be understood as a practice of constructing a European identity. With 'identity' as the beginning and the end point, it is difficult to come to the conclusion that a 'normative' power can be anything but a 'force for the good' in the sense of an enterprise that is bound to impose particularistic conceptions on others. From an identity perspective, actor rationality is linked to a particular context, and the possibility of coming to a rational agreement beyond different cultural contexts or identities is limited. Claims to universality are seen as expressions of a particular conception of what is 'good'. In the words of Diez: 'The standards of the self are not simply seen as superior but of universal validity, with the consequence that the other should be convinced or otherwise brought to accept the principles of the self' (Diez 2004: 10). Consequently, the best option is recognition of the other as different – and non-interference is the logical, and only acceptable, corollary. This is preferable according to Diez because 'it reduces the possibility to legitimise harmful interference with the other' (Diez 2004: 11). However, if this is so, the conclusion regarding 'normative' power EU is given in advance: contrary to what Manners argues, 'normative' power cannot be anything other than the EU promoting its own norms in a similar manner to historical empires and contemporary powers, that is, if 'normative', power Europe aims to 'shape conceptions of what is normal' (Manners 2002: 239).

Not all agree. Axel Honneth writes that although a critique of the universalism of human rights finds advocates in growing numbers, it 'belongs to the antiquated heritage of the counter-Enlightenment' (Honneth 1997: 167). He further rejects the claim that 'the moral obligations of universalism are too great a burden both for individual subjects and for nations' (Honneth 1997: 167). He argues that the character of the moral relationship between nations and civil actors has changed and that owing to the spread of democracy, civil society plays an increasingly independent role also in international affairs. Increased transparency and access to information pressure governments to provide reasons for their policies. A number of organizations and movements promote the realization of human rights across state borders. Consequently, the transformation of power politics is already under way, according to Honneth.

In line with this, the distinction between values and rights, or higher order norms, must be highlighted. Whereas it would not be reasonable to expect transcultural agreement about values, the same is not necessarily the case with regard to higher order norms such as 'equality, freedom, solidarity, self-realisation and human dignity' (Eriksen and Weigård 2003: 138). Values or conceptions of what is good may vary according to cultural or social contexts. They are particular, for example, to a specific community or a specific collective identity. If the EU defines itself, and thinks of itself, as a 'force for the good', this risks being a subjective definition linked to a particular European understanding and defined in a particular European cultural context. It may not match what is defined as 'good' or 'valuable' in other parts of the world, conditioned by other cultural or social norms. So the EU's 'normative' power might simply be an expression of Euro-centric cultural imperialism. To establish what is right, fair or just, on the other hand, can be kept separate from this, hence the principle of universalization:

> The question of fairness does not refer to an axiological value, but to a moral norm – a deontological principle. It is concerned with what we are obliged to do when our actions have consequences for others. Rights then refer to higher order principles and claim universal validity.
>
> (Eriksen and Weigård 2003: 134–5)

It could be then that the core feature of a 'normative' or 'civilizing' power would be that it acts in order to transform the parameters of power politics through a focus on the international legal system, rather than to write itself into the existing international system through an emphasis on multilateralism. As the international system is still one in which legal procedures for protecting human rights are weak, the question would be to what extent the EU's arguments for human rights were presented only with regard to particular actors or cases or whether they were also part of a broader effort to transform their legal status in international law. Furthermore, one might expect that a 'normative' power would develop standards, mechanisms and policy instruments that might ensure that its own policies are consistent with such principles; the crucial point being that it would bind itself and not only others to common legal principles. Indicators suggesting that this would fit with the role of the EU are, for example, the EU's support for the International Criminal Court (ICC), the fact that a human rights clause has been standard content of all trade agreements with third countries since 1992, as well as the incorporation of the Charter in the Constitutional Treaty (Menéndez 2004).

CONCLUSION

In this article I have discussed what might be the distinguishing features of a 'normative', 'civilian', 'ethical' or 'civilizing' power, as well as their potential fit with the EU as we know it. I have suggested that the argument that the EU is not only a 'civilian' power (in the sense that it does not possess military capabilities) but that it is (also) a 'civilizing' or 'normative' power within the international system needs to be further specified and that explicit criteria for assessing if the EU's putative pursuit of norms is legitimate are necessary. Without such criteria we are simply left to trust the assessment of the analyst and her – personal – assessment of whether or not the EU is, has been, or is moving in the direction of, a 'normative' power.

In this context a main challenge is to identify what kinds of norms are necessary to achieve intersubjective agreement. Are some norms of a more universal character than others, in the sense that they may be considered principles having intersubjective transcultural validity? This is important in order to know if the putative normative dimension to European foreign policy is only a form of cultural imperialism or if it can be expected to be acceptable across cultural and political boundaries. But the core challenge is to establish a criterion for what might be legitimate action in the international system.

I have suggested that a strong indicator of the EU as a 'normative' or 'civilizing' power would be linked to what kind of legal principles its external policy is based upon. But what kind of quality is required for such law at the international level? Pointing to the distinction between multilateralism and cosmopolitanism, I have proposed that a focus on strengthening the cosmopolitan dimension to international law would be a strong indicator for a 'normative' or 'civilizing' power. This would also be consistent with the suggestion that one might think of a 'normative' power as one that breaks with what we understand by the 'traditional' foreign policy practice of great powers. In this sense, a 'normative' power would be one that seeks to overcome power politics through a strengthening of not only international but cosmopolitan law, emphasizing the rights of individuals and not only the rights of states to sovereign equality. It would be a power that is willing to bind itself, and not only others, to common rules. However, on this issue there is a potential tension in the EU's external policy between its emphasis on multilateralism, which rests on external sovereignty, and on human rights, as core principles in its foreign policy orientation. Thus, based on this standard, it is not altogether straightforward to conclude that the EU is a 'normative' power.

Biographical note: Helene Sjursen is Senior Researcher at ARENA – Centre for European Studies, University of Oslo, Norway.

Address for correspondence: Helene Sjursen, ARENA – Centre for European Studies, University of Oslo, PO Box 1143 Blindern, N–0317 Oslo, Norway. Tel: +47 22 85 49 58. Fax: +47 22 85 78 32. email: helene.sjursen@arena.uio.no

NOTES

1 Many thanks to Lars Blichner, Erik O. Eriksen, John Erik Fossum, Agustín José Menéndez, Anne Elizabeth Stie, Knud Erik Jørgensen and an anonymous referee for comments on this article. The research conducted for the article was supported by a grant from the Norwegian Ministry of Defence. An earlier version was presented at EUSA, Austin, Texas, March 2005.
2 The member states do, of course, have military capabilities; however, these capabilities have, until very recently, not been available to the EU itself.
3 However, recently he appears to have changed his view on this (Manners 2006).
4 The argument is based on the assumption that modern law is premised on human rights. For further discussions of the relationship between law and morality, see Apel (1997) and Habermas (1997).

REFERENCES

Aggestam, L. (2004) 'A European foreign policy? Role conceptions and the politics of identity in Britain, France and Germany'. Doctoral dissertation, Department of Political Science, Stockholm University.

Apel, K.-O. (1997) 'Kant's "Towards Perpetual Peace" as historical prognosis from the point of view of moral duty', in J. Bohman and M. Lutz-Bachmann (eds), *Perpetual Peace. Essays on Kant's Cosmopolitan Ideal*, Cambridge, MA: MIT Press, pp. 79–110.

Bailes, A. (2005) 'The European Security Strategy: an evolutionary history'. SIPRI Policy Paper 10, Stockholm: Stockholm International Peace Research Institute.

Brown, C. (1999) 'Universal human rights: a critique', in T. Dunne and N.J. Wheeler (eds), *Human Rights in Global Politics*, Cambridge: Cambridge University Press, pp. 103–27.

Coker, C. (1989) *Reflexions on American Foreign Policy since 1945*, London: Pinter.

Cox, M., Ikenberry, G.J. and Inoguchi, T. (eds) (2000) *American Democracy Promotion: Impulses, Strategies and Impacts*, Oxford: Oxford University Press.

Dallek, R. (1984) *Ronald Reagan: The Politics of Symbolism*, Cambridge, MA: Harvard University Press.

Davis, L. (1974) *The Cold War Begins: Soviet American Conflict Over Eastern Europe*, Princeton, NJ: Princeton University Press.

Diez, T. (2004) 'Constructing the self and changing others: problematising the concept of "Normative power Europe"'. Paper presented at the Millennium Conference 'Facets of Power in International Relations', London School of Economics and Political Science, London, 30–31 October.

Duchêne, F. (1972) 'Europe's role in world peace', in R. Mayne (ed.), *Europe Tomorrow: Sixteen Europeans Look Ahead*, London: Fontana, pp. 32–47.

Eriksen, E.O. (2003) 'Why a constitutionalised Bill of Rights?', in E.O. Eriksen, J.E. Fossum and A.J. Ménendez (eds), *The Chartering of Europe*, Baden-Baden: Nomos, pp. 48–70.

Eriksen, E.O. (2006) 'The EU – a cosmopolitan polity?', *Journal of European Public Policy* 13(2): 252–69.

Eriksen, E.O. and Weigård, J. (1997) 'Conceptualizing politics: strategic or communicative action?', *Scandinavian Political Studies* 20(3): 219–41.

Eriksen, E.O. and Weigård, J. (2003) *Understanding Habermas*, London: Continuum.

Eriksen, E.O., Fossum, J.E. and Sjursen, H. (2005) 'Widening or reconstituting the EU?', in E.O. Eriksen (ed.), *Making the European Polity. Reflexive Integration in the EU*, London: Routledge, pp. 237–52.

Gow, J. (1997) *The Triumph of the Lack of Will. International Diplomacy and the Yugoslav War*, London: Hurst & Co.

Günther, K. (1993) *The Sense of Appropriateness*, Albany: State University of New York Press.

Habermas, J. (1990) *Moral Consciousness and Communicative Action*, Cambridge: Polity Press.

Habermas, J. (1997) 'Kant's idea of perpetual peace, with the benefit of two hundred years' hindsight', in J. Bohman and M. Lutz-Bachmann (eds), *Perpetual Peace. Essays on Kant's Cosmopolitan Ideal*, Cambridge, MA: MIT Press, pp. 113–53.

Habermas, J. (1999) 'Bestiality and humanity: a war on the border between legality and morality', *Constellations* 6(3): 263–72.

Honneth, A. (1997) 'Is universalism a moral trap? The presuppositions and limits of a politics of human rights', in J. Bohman and M. Lutz-Bachmann (eds), *Perpetual Peace. Essays on Kant's Cosmopolitan Ideal*, Cambridge, MA: MIT Press, pp. 155–78.

Hyde-Price, A. (2006) '"Normative" power Europe: a realist critique', *Journal of European Public Policy* 13(2): 217–34.

Jørgensen, K.E. and Laatikainen, K.V. (2004) 'The EU and the UN: multilateralism in a new key?'. Paper presented at the Second Pan-European Conference on EU Politics, 'Implications of a Wider Europe: Politics, Institutions and Diversity', Bologna, 24–26 June.

Kagan, R. (2003) *Of Paradise and Power. America and Europe in the New World Order*, New York: Knopf.

Lerch, M. and Schwellnus, G. (2006) 'Normative by nature? The role of coherence in justifying the EU's external human rights policy', *Journal of European Public Policy* 13(2): 304–21.

Lose, L. (2001) 'Communicative action and the world of diplomacy', in K. Fierke and K.E. Jørgensen (eds), *Constructing International Relations*, New York: Sharpe, pp. 179–200.

Lucarelli, S. (2004) 'EU foreign policy between telos and identity. A normative reading of the transatlantic divide'. Paper presented at the Second Pan-European Conference on EU Politics, 'Implications of a Wider Europe: Politics, Institutions and Diversity', Bologna, 24–26 June.

Lundestad, G. (1990) *The American 'Empire'*, Oslo: Universitetsforlaget.

Manners, I. (2002) 'Normative power Europe: a contradiction in terms?', *Journal of Common Market Studies* 40(2): 235–58.

Manners, I. (2006) 'Normative power Europe reconsidered: beyond the crossroads', *Journal of European Public Policy* 13(2): 182–99.

Meese, E. (1992) *With Reagan: The Inside Story*, Washington, DC: Regnery Gateway.

Menéndez, A.J. (2004) 'Human rights: the European Charter of Fundamental Rights', in W. Carlsneas, H. Sjursen and B. White (eds), *Contemporary European Foreign Policy*, London: Sage, pp. 239–51.

Menon, A., Nicolaïdis, K. and Walsh, J. (2004) 'In defence of Europe – a response to Kagan', *Journal of European Affairs* 2(3): 5–14.

Mitzen, J. (2006) 'Anchoring Europe's civilizing identity: habits, capabilities and ontological security', *Journal of European Public Policy* 13(2): 270–85.

Rosecrance, R. (1998) 'The European Union: a new type of international actor', in J. Zielonka (ed.), *Paradoxes of European Foreign Policy*, The Hague: Kluwer Law International, pp. 15–23.

Ruggie, J.G. (1992) 'Multilateralism: the anatomy of an institution', *International Organization* 46(3): 561–98.

Schröder, G. (2005) Speech on the 41st Munich Conference on Security Policy, 2 December.

Sjursen, H. (2002) 'Why expand? The question of legitimacy and justification in the EU's enlargement policy', *Journal of Common Market Studies* 40(3): 491–513.

Sjursen, H. (2003) *The United States, Western Europe and the Polish Crisis: International Relations in the Second Cold War*, London: Palgrave Macmillan.

Sjursen, H. (2004) 'Changes to European security in a communicative perspective', *Cooperation and Conflict* 39(2): 107–28.

Smith, K.E. (2000) 'The end of civilian power EU: a welcome demise or cause for concern?', *International Spectator* 35(2): 11–28.

Smith, K.E. (2003) *European Union Foreign Policy in a Changing World*, Cambridge: Polity Press.

Smith, K.E. (2004) 'Still "civilian power EU"?'. Paper presented at the CIDEL Workshop, 'From Civilian to Military Power: The European Union at a Crossroads?', Oslo, 22–23 October.

Youngs, R. (2004) 'Normative dynamics and strategic interests in the EU's external identity', *Journal of Common Market Studies* 42(2): 415–35.

Whitman, R. (1998) *From Civilian Power to Superpower? The International Identity of the European Union*, Basingstoke: Macmillan.

Official documents

European Council (2003) *A Secure Europe in a Better World: European Security Strategy*, Brussels, 12 December.

The EU – a cosmopolitan polity?

Erik Oddvar Eriksen

INTRODUCTION

The European Union (EU) has for a long time been described as a 'civilian power' (Duchêne 1972).[1] It has been reluctant to use coercive means in order to solve conflicts and achieve its goals. This has been an integral part of its identity from the very start of European Political Cooperation (EPC) in the 1970s. It is contended that present efforts to establish military capability will endanger the 'civilian' aspects of the EU (cf. Manners 2006). The enhanced military capability at the European level through peace-keeping and conflict-preventing missions will make the EU an actor like other actors in the world system. But is coercion foreign to a 'humanitarian polity'? Can absence of coercive means be the defining characteristic of a normatively justifiable political entity?

I would like to address this problem from a Kantian perspective which, unlike what is often believed, implies the need for coercive means because only with the threat of sanctions can the law compel compliance. From this perspective the defining characteristic of a 'civilian power' cannot be the absence of coercive means and merely the pursuance of honourable goals, but rather whether it respects basic humanitarian principles. Every organized community acts on their interests and on preferences that may be good or bad in ethical terms. The propensity to act on honourable motives cannot itself represent the criteria for judging the polity's normative quality because they may very well be arbitrary. A policy based on good intentions may very well neglect others' interests or values or fail to give them due consideration. A robust criterion can only be derived from the constraints set by 'international law', here taken to mean *the cosmopolitan law of the people* which depicts a possible community based on certain universal principles (Kant 1797: 172). From this perspective, it is only by subjecting its actions to a higher ranking law – to human rights and criteria of justice – that the EU can qualify in normative terms.

I suggest as a criterion of a legitimate foreign policy that the EU does not aspire to become a world organization – a world state – but subscribes to the principles of human rights, democracy and rule of law also for dealing with international affairs, hence underscoring the cosmopolitan law of the people.[2] In such a perspective the borders of the EU are to be drawn both with regard to what is required for the Union itself in order to be a self-sustainable and well-functioning democratic entity and with regard to the support and further development of similar regional associations in the rest of the world – that is, with regard to the viability of the Organization for African Unity (OAU), Mercado Común del Sur (MERCOSUR), the Association of South East Asian Nations (ASEAN), etc. In this perspective, the borders of the EU should be drawn with regard to functional requirements both for itself and for other regions, all within the framework of a democratized, rights-enforcing United Nations (UN).

The aim of this article is to establish this criterion, its theoretical and institutional underpinnings, and provisionally assess whether the EU in fact complies with it. The quest for institutional underpinning pertains to the problem of the present world order regarding human rights politics: as long as human rights are not properly institutionalized, when they exist merely as moral rights, they can be used at will. Human rights politics can easily become imperialistic in the name of morality and the risk of *arbitrariness* is inevitable as some may continue to violate human rights with impunity. What is at stake with human rights protection and the institutionalization of human rights beyond the nation state is the sovereignty of the modern state as laid down in the Westphalian order in 1648.

The question of theoretical underpinning pertains to how such an order can be conceived in action theoretical terms. A cosmopolitan order is one where actors subject their actions to the constraints of a higher ranking law and we need an approach that does not rule out this as a logical possibility. An extended conception of agent rationality – actors can act out of a sense of justice – expands the range of possible options available at the international level. This makes possible an analysis where material as well as ideal factors play a role in international politics.

I start by addressing the institutional questions and explore the tension between democracy and human rights and the quest for a law-based supranational order. I ask whether the recent constitutional development of the Union can help to reduce the tension between human rights and democracy. In addition to submitting national practices to supranational review, the EU has incorporated human rights as a horizontal clause in all its external relations. In order to assess compliance I address the allegation that this is merely 'cheap talk'. I give some examples of why this is not always necessarily so, and bolster this by a theoretical perspective that allows for ideal factors to play a role as opposed to 'realist' approaches that rule out such a possibility. Lastly I address the dangers involved in cosmopolitanism with regard to unchecked power, and see the EU as a regional entity to bar against such a circumstance.

COSMOPOLITAN LAW OF THE CITIZENS

The Westphalian principle of state sovereignty is a principle that has protected the most odious regimes. It was only when Hitler's Germany attacked Poland that World War II broke out, not when the persecution of Jews started. This directs us to the limitations of nationally founded and confined democracy. While human rights are universal and refer to humanity as such, democracy refers to a particular community of legal consociates who come together to make binding collective decisions. The validity of the laws is derived from the decision-making processes of a sovereign community. The propensity to adopt rights, then, depends on the quality of the political process in a particular community. But such processes often fail to respect the rights and liberties of their citizens as well as other states' legitimate interests. Even though the contradiction between rights and democracy is, in principle, a false one – since there can be no democracy without the protection of individual rights, and since rights are not valid unless they have been democratically enacted – in empirical terms there is a contradiction as democracy is only institutionalized at the level of the nation state. States are geared towards self-maintenance as the primary responsibility of the decision-makers is their own constituency. The state is so to say limited by the people: 'The individual may say for himself: "Fiat justitia, pereat mundus (Let justice be done, even if the world perish)," but the state has no right to say so in the name of those who are in its care' (Morgenthau 1993: 12). Hence, democracies may be *illiberal*. To resolve the tension between human rights and democracy the authors of the law must at the same time be its addressees. This is the core principle of cosmopolitan democracy. Here the inhabitants would see themselves as citizens of the world and not merely of their native countries. According to cosmopolitans, the urgent task is to domesticate the existing state of nature between countries by means of human rights, the transformation of international law into a law of global citizens (cf. Held 1995, 2002; Archibugi 2003a; Falk and Strauss 2003).

In the last decades we have witnessed a significant development of rights and law enforcement beyond the nation state. Human rights are institutionalized in international courts, in tribunals and increasingly also in politico-judicial bodies over and above the state that controls resources for enforcing norm compliance. Examples are the international criminal tribunals for Rwanda and the former Yugoslavia, the International Criminal Court, the UN and the EU. In addition, European states have incorporated the European Convention for the Protection of Human Rights and Fundamental Freedoms (ECHR) and many of its protocols into their domestic legal systems. Thus legal developments over the last century have been remarkable and one of their main thrusts has been to protect human rights (Fassbender 1998; Habermas 2004). Today, almost nobody can be treated as a stranger devoid of rights. These rights are no longer only present in international declarations and proclamations. Increasingly they are entrenched in power-wielding systems of action and in the actual policies pursued. Aggressors can now be tried for crimes against humanity, and offensive wars are criminalized. Sometimes human rights protection trumps state sovereignty. The North Atlantic Treaty Organization (NATO) war against Serbia in 1999 to protect an innocent population was formally illegal according to the UN Charter, but was declared legitimate by the Independent International Commission on Kosovo 2000.

But human rights politics is often power politics in disguise. 'The concept of humanity is an especially useful ideological instrument of imperialist expansion' (Schmitt 1996: 54). That is, as long as human rights are not positivized and law is not made equally binding on each of the member states, human rights politics easily degenerate into empty universalistic rhetoric. Some states may continue to violate human rights with impunity, and some may use them for self-serving purposes. Human rights are ensured by non-democratic bodies such as courts and tribunals or, what is more often the case, enforced by the US and its allies. Hence, the need for a democratic law-based supranational order.

PEACE THROUGH LAW

From the Enlightenment stems the trust in written constitutions and judicial review as a means to civilize relations among men as well as among nations. In Europe we have witnessed a strong development towards the abolishment of force through right, to talk as does Hans Kelsen. But what is the role of force in such an order? In the Kantian perspective the coerciveness of the law is intrinsically linked to equal liberties for all – it is to ensure compliance with such as this that a polity can legitimately use force. Also in external relations conflicts between states should be settled as legal disputes by an impartial and powerful third party. 'The problem of establishing a perfect civil constitution is subordinate to the problem of a law-governed external relationship with other states, and cannot be solved unless the latter is also solved' (Kant 1784: 47). A constitution is a system of rights that constitutes the legal medium, and hence is authorized to enforce norms. It is a means for compelling compliance but it cannot itself establish the required legitimacy. The authority of the law stems from the fact that it is made by the people and hence claims to be just, and that it is made binding on every part to the same degree and amount.

'The legitimacy of the laws, then, paradoxically also stems from the very fact that they are obligatory and coercive' (Eriksen 2004: 49).

Further, law is a functional complement to politics and morality as it stabilizes behavioural expectations and solves the collective action problem. Pure agreements do not warrant collective action nor the delegation of sovereignty. There may be reasons to oppose even a rational agreement, and nobody is obliged to comply unless all others also comply. Owing to weakness of will and as long as citizens are not reassured that the violation of norms will not be left unsanctioned, general and spontaneous compliance is endangered. Thus, without the threat of force there will be no political association. The medium of law stabilizes behavioural expectation in two ways. First, it alleviates *co-ordination problems* by signalling which rule to follow in practical situations (Luhmann 1995: 136). In this way it is also a functional complement to morality as the latter, owing to the indeterminacy of norms, cannot tell what should be done in particular contexts. Many justified norms may apply, but which is the correct one in this particular situation cannot be inferred from the bare existence of moral agreements. Even angels need 'a system of laws in order to know the right thing to do' (Honoré 1993: 3).

Secondly, the sanctioning of non-compliance and defecting makes it less risky for actors to act in a morally adequate manner. People may comply with the law out of self-interest because it is costly not to do so. However, law is not merely a constraint on morality. In fact, law is enabling such while it makes it possible for actors to behave correctly without personal losses. By sanctioning non-compliance and preventing violence, law-based orders make it possible for its members to act in accordance with their own conscience, out of a sense of duty or justice (Apel 1998: 755). The point is that the law binds the others' will and thereby makes it possible for the individual to act morally without being in a 'sucker' position (cf. Axelrod 1990: 8).

Law-based sanctions are in short supply in international affairs, and at present there are no European prisons, no European army and no European police corps. This is a problem as we are instructed by our moral reason to act when states 'fail', when genocide and ethnic cleansing take place: when faced with crimes against humanity and when all other options are exhausted, the international society should be enabled to act, even with military force. Human rights are universal – they appeal to humanity as such, to the interests of irreplaceable human beings and exhibit a categorical structure – and they have a strong moral content: 'Human dignity shall be respected at all costs!' Collectives do not make the same strong claim – 'they do not feel pain'. Thus borders of states have merely derivative status in a cosmopolitan perspective (Beitz 1979: 182).

As an answer to the perceived 'capability–expectations gap' (Hill 1998), and the crises of the former Yugoslavia, the so-called *rapid-reaction mechanism* was established in 2001 designed to permit the Union to respond in an 'efficient and flexible manner to situations of urgency or crisis or to the emergence of crisis'.[3] The crisis of Kosovo 1999 and the perceived problems of the EU to cope with security issues after 11 September have led to a push for a more able security policy (Dannreuther 2004). *The European Security Strategy*, which is analysed in several of the contributions in this issue, was adopted by the European Council, 12–13 December 2003. The question is whether this strategy will be pursued in line with cosmopolitan law. I return to this. First we need to establish whether the EU is internally consistent; that is, willing to bring human rights to bear on member states' self-determination.

CHARTERING EUROPE

In 2000 the fourteen other member states imposed sanctions on Austria for letting Haider's Freedom Party into government. While it was the member states that decided to impose sanctions against Austria, the EU itself has now established procedures to ensure that breaches of fundamental principles are sanctioned. The Treaty of Nice amended Article 7 of the Treaty on European Union (TEU), which specifies the concrete procedures to follow in case of a 'clear risk of a serious breach' on the part of one member state. Moreover, when the Treaty of Nice comes into force, a qualified majority vote will be enough to take action against the recalcitrant member state. This development of rights protection and polity-building was carried further by the decision to frame a Charter of Fundamental Rights at the Cologne European Council (3–4 June 1999). In October 1999, at the Tampere European Council, it was decided to establish a sixty-two-member Convention to draft the Charter. A convention, which is an assembly with constitutional overtones set up to handle the most fundamental questions of the political order, is supposed to conduct its affairs in a deliberative manner. Forty-six of the members were parliamentarians – thirty members of the member state parliaments and sixteen members of the European Parliament (EP). It was led by a Praesidium of five. This was the first time that the EP was represented in the same manner as the member state governments and the national parliaments in a process of a constitutional nature.

At the December 2000 Summit in Nice the Charter was solemnly proclaimed. The eventual incorporation into the Treaties was to be decided by the 'next' intergovernmental conference (IGC). All articles on the rights of EU citizens in the TEU have now been collected in one document of fifty-four articles, inspired by the ECHR (without replacing it), the Social Charters adopted by the Council of Europe and by the Community and the case law of the European Court of Justice (ECJ). The Charter adds to the fundamental rights of Union citizens by expressing the principles of humanism and democracy.

The Charter contains provisions on civil, political, social and economic rights. Put together, these are intended to ensure the dignity of the person, to safeguard essential freedoms, to provide a European citizenship, to ensure equality, to foster solidarity, and to provide for justice. The number and range of rights listed are comprehensive. The Charter enumerates several 'rights to solidarity' – social rights – even though the realization of these is not within the actual competence of the Union. They nevertheless constitute vital reasons for exceptions to market freedoms (Menéndez 2003: 192). In addition to provisions which most charters and bills of rights hold and which pertain to such clauses as the right to life, security and dignity, there are numerous articles that seek to respond directly to contemporary issues and challenges of globalized risk societies. But why did the Charter come about in the first place?

PREDICTABILITY AND SECURITY

The Charter enhances the *legal certainty* of the citizens of Europe as everybody can claim protection for the same interests and concerns. The principle of legal certainty is currently secured only in a limited sense at the Community level. The citizen cannot be sure what rights she really is entitled to. The founding treaties of the European Community (EC) contained no reference to fundamental rights. As integration deepened, and as the Community came to have more far-reaching effects on the daily lives of citizens, the need for explicit mention of fundamental rights was recognized. They came to the fore in 1964 when the ECJ set out the doctrine of supremacy of EC law over national law. This was objected to by Italy and Germany because EC law, in contrast to their national constitutions, did not protect human rights. As the EU is not itself a signatory to the ECHR the Community is not bound by it in the same way as the subscribing member states.

Another source of initiative for making a charter of fundamental rights is the argument that the EU, which is 'a staunch defender of human rights externally', 'lacks a fully-fledged human rights policy'. '[T]he Union can only achieve the leadership role to which it aspires through the example it sets' (Alston and Weiler 1999: 4–5). It is difficult to be a champion of cosmopolitan law and urge others to institutionalize human rights when one is not prepared to do so oneself. When basic institutions are lacking in the EU with regard to human rights, it is difficult to *lead by example*.

Generally, bills of rights empower the judges to protect liberty and hinder that democracy by means of majority vote crushes individual rights (Brennan 1989: 432). A charter, even when it is no more than the codification of existing law, decreases the room for discretion of the ECJ and national courts when dealing with EC law of fundamental rights. The EU Charter is, however, found wanting. It is weakly developed with regard to citizenship rights, as a person must be a citizen of a member state to qualify as a citizen of the Union, and with regard to political rights. The onus is on human rights, which undoubtedly has been strengthened but it has not introduced 'any concrete policy changes nor altered anything significant within the existing legal, political and constitutional framework' (de Búrca 2001: 129).

There are other limitations to the Charter: it only applies to the actions of the EU institutions and the member states' authorities, and it is not designed to replace other forms of fundamental rights protection. Section 1 states that the

Charter will only be made to apply to the 'institutions and bodies of the Union' and only to the member states 'when they are implementing Union law'. Article 51 (section 2) states that the Charter does 'not establish any new power or task for the Community or the Union, or modify powers and tasks defined by the Treaties'. Moreover, certain human rights concerning the right to asylum, social rights and minority rights are contested at the EU level. Many of the rights clauses of the Charter have the status neither of fundamental nor of ordinary rights but are merely policy clauses (Menéndez 2003). This hampers the impression of a fully credible external rights policy. But most importantly, the Charter was not made binding. It was not included in the Nice Treaty – only solemnly proclaimed. The institutionalization of a human rights policy in the EU is weak.

> The real problem of the Community is the absence of a human rights policy, with everything this entails: a Commissioner, a Directorate General, a budget and a horizontal action plan for making effective those rights already granted by the Treaties and judicially protected by the various levels of European Courts.
> (Weiler 2004: 65)

Even though the Charter already has some legal bite[4] the question with regard to whether it subscribes to cosmopolitanism is whether it actually feeds into the reform process of the Union itself and becomes binding.

CONSTITUTIONALIZING EUROPE

The (Laeken) Convention on the Future of Europe started its work in February 2002 and concluded in June/July 2003. It is now widely depicted as a *Constitutional Convention*. It was modelled on the Charter Convention, with a majority of parliamentarians. Forty-six out of sixty-six voting members, and twenty-six out of thirty-nine from the candidate countries were parliamentarians. Its mandate was broader, its working method included working groups, and the applicant states had a number of representatives present, as active, participating, observers. The Convention succeeded in forging agreement on a single constitutional proposal in 2003, which incorporated the Charter of Fundamental Rights as Part II,[5] and which the Heads of States adopted on 29 October 2004,[6] and which is going to be subjected to hard-won ratification processes in the member states.

Efforts have thus been taken to make the emerging constitutional structure comply with democratic principles. Further, the weakening of the pillars, the strengthened role of the EP and the generalization of co-decision and qualified majority voting as decision-making procedures improve the coherence and the democratic quality of the Union. And so does the strengthening of national parliamentary involvement in EU activities as well as the citizens' right initiative (Article I-47.4). The legal order of Europe confers rights upon the citizens and subjects law-making to the will of the citizens. The EU has achieved an element of supranational normativity based on the principles of fundamental rights, rule of law and democracy, and the ECJ represents a firm dispute resolution mechanism whose foundation is now bolstered by the entrenchment of 'the primacy of Union law'. However, the member states remain key players. Among other things they retain control of the Union's sources of funds, unanimity is demanded as regards fiscal policy and Common Foreign and Security Policy (CFSP) and Common Security and Defence Policy (CSDP), and the Council still controls constitutional amendment. '[A]lso in future, Treaty amendments will require unanimity and ratification by all the member states' (Kokott and Rüth 2003: 1343).

The Constitutional Treaty establishes a Union Minister for Foreign Affairs who will be both the Vice-President of the Commission and be part of the Council (Article I-28). Wolfgang Wagner (2006) argues that the Europeanization of security and defence policy leads to a democratic deficit as it increases executive dominance – and further that 'the EP can . . . hardly compensate for the weakening of parliamentary control at the national level' (Wagner 2006: 209). But in this regard the Constitution represents an improvement from a democratic perspective as it provides for more clarity and transparency. This is so, first, because the EP's supervision is increased. Its consultant role is formally entrenched according to Article I-40.8: 'The European Parliament shall be regularly consulted on the main aspects and basic choices of the common foreign and security policy. It shall be kept informed of how it evolves.' Secondly, the CFSP, whose institutional structure is formally intergovernmental (Pillar II), has been in the making for a long time, making it increasingly difficult for the national foreign ministries to control the policy-making process. Many important decisions are made at the European level. The Constitutional Convention mandated by the Laeken IGC (2000) included the foreign and security policy on its agenda. This meant that this policy was debated in a *transnational forum* and not in an intergovernmental body, and thus reduced the executives' leverage on foreign and security policy. This is welcomed from a cosmopolitan point of view as it embodies a constraint on the 'unilateralism' of the member states. A clause to preclude independent action of member states is firmly stated in Article I-40.5 of the Constitutional Treaty: 'member states shall consult one another within the European Council and the Council on any foreign and security policy issue which is of general interest in order to determine a common approach.' Thirdly, when it comes to specific provisions concerning a CSDP it is firmly stated that the Union's peace-keeping and conflict-preventing missions shall be 'in accordance with the principles of the United Nations Charter' (Article I-41.1). The United Nations Charter is mentioned in several places in the Constitution as it has been in previous treaties, hence underscoring the respect for higher ranking principles. Now the question is whether cosmopolitanism actually informs the external relations of the Union.

COSMOPOLITAN POLICIES?

For a long time the Community has subscribed to democracy and human rights as the basic criterion for membership. Portugal, Spain and Greece were not admitted before they had abolished totalitarianism and changed their form of government. In a report to the June 1992 Lisbon European Council, the Commission restated that there were certain fundamental conditions for membership: only European states could become members of the EU; candidate states must have a democratic constitution and they must respect the principles of the rule of law and human rights. This is reiterated in the criteria for membership set by the Copenhagen European Council (1993). These conditions may be 'slippery' (Grabbe 2002: 251f.), and the mechanisms for achieving them inconsistent (Schwellnus 2005: 255ff.), but they nevertheless point to the principled basis of the Union.

Also, when it comes to trade and international co-operation in general, there is a commitment to democracy and human rights. The EU insists on the respect of minority rights in third countries – non-European countries – and there is political conditionality on aid and trade agreements.[7] Since 1995 the 'human rights clause' is supposed to be incorporated in all co-operation and association agreements. In 1998 the Union launched an initiative on the death penalty and torture and raised the issue on a bilateral and multilateral basis worldwide, and through the UN. The list of countries which have abolished capital punishment as a result of EU pressure is impressive. The EU has affected the human rights situation, in particular with regard to the abolishment or reduction of capital punishment in Cyprus and Poland, Albania and Ukraine, Azerbaijan and Turkmenistan, Turkey and Russia through different kinds of means and measures (Manners 2002: 249–50). In Turkey there has been a political avalanche with respect to democratization and human rights, especially since 2002 (Avci 2005: 137). Further, the Union has cut direct budgetary support to Zimbabwe, the Ivory Coast, Haiti and Liberia. The EU has stalled on deepening relations with Russia, Croatia, Pakistan and Algeria because of breaches of basic human rights.

The Commission has adopted several co-operation instruments for regional and bilateral relations and the EU holds regular summit meetings with its main partners. It has developed so-called partnership and co-operation agreements, 'aiming to establish an area of prosperity and good neighborliness',[8] with many countries. It has, so to say, prompted a *new regionalism.*

> New regionalism appears to constitute a relatively safe space within which Europe can display identity and norm difference from the US: The EU can lay down an identity marker of what it perceives to be a more humane governance model in its relations with the developing world, without having to confront or contradict US power head-on.
>
> (Grugel 2004: 621)

As mentioned, it is as a regional entity that the EU can be justified cosmopolitically.

The EU, whose biggest members have been colonial powers, now exports the rule of law, democracy and human rights (Rosecrance 1998: 22). These policies are reflective of the value basis of the Union. However, one may ask whether this is mainly cheap talk. Is the EU consistent, do the member states apply the principles consistently on third countries – or merely in places where it is not very costly? The EU is certainly not consistent as non-European countries are being treated differently. For example, Russia is merely marginally sanctioned for its wars in Chechnya (although the EU threatens to impose stronger sanctions). Israel is being threatened with sanctions because of its policies towards the Palestinians, but sanctions have not been carried out. Uzbekistan is another example of a country where *the essential elements clause* is not upheld rigorously despite widespread torture and lack of reform.[9] These examples indicate a lack of consistency in EU external policies; hence the criticism of hypocrisy and window-dressing. There is also the complaint that there is more emphasis on the protection of civil and political rights compared to social and economic ones and that commercial interests take precedence, which the present plea by some member states to lift the weapon embargo on China seems to substantiate.

JUST CHEAP TALK?

Adrian Hyde-Price (2006) takes, in his contribution to this issue, the latter examples as evidence of the EU as a normal interest-maximizing power; one that only uses 'soft power' and 'second-order' concerns when they are not costly or detrimental to 'national interests'. After the Cold War, 'the EU was used by its most influential member states as an instrument for collectively exercising hegemonic power, shaping its "near abroad" in ways amenable to the long-term strategic and economic interests of its member states' (Hyde-Price 2006: 226–7).

Such a realist approach faces difficulties. First, in empirical terms the data presented can be countered by examples suggesting that rights protection costs. It is beyond doubt that the human rights politics of the Union have a cost and are not without sacrifices, as both the enlargement and the support of the former Yugoslavia illustrate (cf. Sjursen 2002). In numerous documents, declarations and policy statements the EU has distanced itself from the power politics of traditional states in international relations. The primary goal of the CFSP is 'to safeguard the common values, fundamental interests, independence and integrity of the Union in conformity with the principles of the Union Nations Charter'.[10] The EU Commission represents 12 per cent of all international financial aid world-wide and, combined with the aid of the member states, the figure is more than 55 per cent (Petiteville 2003). Europe is the largest contributor to the promotion of democracy in the world (Börzel and Risse 2005). With regard to the abolition of the death penalty 'the EU often finds itself at odds with other developed OECD states, such as the US and Japan' (Manners 2002: 253). In addition, the EU has been very supportive of the UN and has also been a driving force in its reform process.

Second, on methodological terms, to reduce all behaviour to interest maximization and security motives makes it hard to make robust predictions. On such a basis, how do we comprehend the ideological warfare of the US after

11 September, as well as the decision to enlarge as a normative commitment? Regarding the fact that the EU and the member states are the world's biggest contributors to democracy, does this really pay off? How can one make cost–benefit calculations at all in such fuzzy questions? Security threats as well as security maximization are highly dependent on psychological factors that cannot be rationally calculated on a means–ends basis. In general it is hard to establish what constitutes equilibrium when it comes to non-quantifiable entities such as soft security. It is difficult to assess whether the used means are optimal or not as there is no objective metric available.

The upshot is that in theoretical terms one should avoid an approach that predetermines the result as does the 'civilian power' approach as well as that of the realists. The objection with regard to the former pertains to the problem of explaining change or variation. When behaviour is seen as driven by fixed identities or given norms, there is no conceptual outfit for explaining deviation or reflection over the putative rationality or legitimacy of the policies. With regard to the latter the well-known criticism of rational choice assumption of preference or interest-maximization applies. States conceived of as actors should not merely be seen as *rational* in the sense that they form preferences and pursue them consistently, but also as entities having the capacity of being *reasonable* in the sense that they possess a notion of what is just and fair (Rawls 1993: 49) and what is communicatively rational (Habermas 1996: 5). Only on the basis of the latter can one understand the international order as one made up of normative rules and mutually supportive behaviour of the actors. Whichever way we understand such a system, in whatever form it is seen to come – be it in the sense of a strict non-intervention principle, contractual law or the protection of human rights – it is only understandable on the basis of some norms that command respect in and of themselves. The international order is thus not 'an anarchical self-help system' but *a delimited normative order*: 'the legal order of each state, each national legal order, is organically connected with the international legal order and through this order with every national legal order, so that all legal orders merge into an integrated legal system' (Kelsen 1944: 354). This is what makes for the putative stability of the international order and hence makes transactions, contractual agreements, strategic bargaining possible. Co-operation as well as competition require a stable and predictable order that makes promises credible. Such an order sets the 'fair' terms of co-operation but then also limits the actors' sovereignty: 'For the rule *pacta sunt servanta*, the legal basis of all international treaties, as a rule of positive international law, corresponds only in a limited way to the principle of autonomy' (Kelsen 1944: 354).

It is such preconditions, that preference maximization is parasitic on, which are overlooked by many realists and which make the analysis of the present world order 'not realistic enough'. This is clearly seen in the tendency to analyse normative utterances as merely *window-dressing* or information-reducing mechanisms – neglecting the force of normative commitments in international interaction. The fact that public deliberation does not necessarily eliminate egoistic motives, but rather forces the actors to hide them, testifies to the force and autonomy of norms. That parties at least are hypocrites – they pay homage to norms in order to reach agreement – underlines the autonomy, validity and importance of norms. 'The force of norms – the feature that makes manipulation and interpretation worth while – is that they do have a grip on the mind; otherwise, there would be nothing to manipulate' (Elster 1989: 100).

From this follows that one cannot from the very outset deem the well-known rhetoric of the Union about democracy and human rights as mere window-dressing (even though some actors obviously are behaving strategically), as do realists who generally conceive of ideas as information-reducing means, and political talk as strategic communication: cheap talk intended to seduce the audience. Regardless of whether normative commitments are 'really' intended as window-dressing or not, they can have behavioural consequences according to *the civilizing force of hypocrisy* (cf. Elster 1998: 111f.). Irrespective of the actors' intentions, in so far as they appeal to norms that are widely accepted, they in fact also confirm their validity. *Cheap talk* often strikes back as it becomes impossible to withdraw promises or refute pledges in an open debate, once they are made public. The mechanisms of soft power related to peer pressure and reputation – blaming and shaming according to standards espoused by transnational civil society – work effectively to expose norm-breakers to public attention (Nye 2004). Non-compliers are not left unsanctioned in the international area owing to the formation of *communicative power*. Increasingly, power-wielders are held accountable to standards espoused by transnational public discourse and protest and also the 'creeping' legalization of human rights.

One may certainly question whether the EU actually is a regional power with a cosmopolitan imprint, but the assessment should be based on sound criteria and not be foreclosed by choosing a conceptual strategy that rules out this very possibility. As we have seen, the EU has committed itself to a law-based view of international relations. Yet the question remains whether it can avoid the dangers of an unchecked delegation of power to a supranational organization, which is the well-known danger of unconstrained cosmopolitanism.

COSMOPOLITANISM RESTRAINED

A real republic depends on bodies above the nation state that citizens can appeal to when their rights are threatened. In order to ensure justice at the world level, or at least to be able to sanction norm breaches such as human rights violations and crimes against humanity, there is a need for a system that lays down the law, equally binding on all. It is a rather thin normative basis for such an order as it must be based only on what human beings have in common, namely, their right to freedom, equality, dignity, democracy and the like, listed in human rights declarations and basic rights stipulations of modern constitutions. The question is, then, how much power the custodian of such an order – the EU, the UN – should have and what kind of organization it should be. It follows from the preceding analysis that the threat of sanctions is an intrinsic part of the law.

The legitimacy of the laws stems, as mentioned, from the very fact that they are obligatory and coercive. The law is a means to compel compliance, but it can only do so without unleashing the potential threat of force when it applies equally to all and when it is in compliance with moral principles, which, under modern conditions, means that it must be just and made by the people. An association is only democratic to the extent that it relies upon the alleged legitimate use of force to ensure compliance with its norms and only democratically made law can claim to be legitimate. Also, an organization above the nation-state level equipped with enforcement mechanisms – namely, capacity to make threats credible – can rightly do so only in so far as its actions are democratically regulated. The codification and positivization of human rights represent *juridification* as they are made and adjudicated by legal bodies. Such bodies are in need of democratization as rights should be given by the rights-holders themselves or their representatives. In a democracy it is the citizens who give themselves the rights. Hence, no humanitarization without representation.

Moreover, when it comes to implementation there also is the requirement of democratic procedures, as norms need procedurally regulated bodies for their interpretation, specification and adjudication. Norms, also legal norms, are rooted in practice, are contested and require argumentation and interpretation with regard to concrete interests and values in order to be properly applied. In concrete situations of norm violations, often more than one justified norm may be called upon. To choose the correct norm requires interpretation of situations and sometimes also the balancing and weighting of rights (Günther 1993; Alexy 1996). Individuals' rights are limited by others' rights and concerns, and the abstract law enforcement by a *world state* runs the danger of glossing over relevant distinctions and differences. A world state with far-reaching competencies – with an executive government – thus faces severe difficulties as it necessarily must leave much discretionary power to the world executive. It would imply the risk of unchecked delegated politics and a stern democratic deficit. A world state would lack any peer to relate to and hence be an unconstrained sovereign.[11] Consequently, there is a problem with cosmopolitan law in contrast to the existing 'international law' with regard to the *legal protection* (Scheuerman 2002: 448). It faces significant difficulties with regard to the legal protection of freedom rights. It is the principle of the rule of law – *das Rechtsstaat* – that safeguards against states' infringement of individual liberties as it requires the government to act on legal norms that are general, clear, public, prospective and stable. How can the rights of the citizens be protected at the supranational level?

The democratic constitutional state is not limited to rights protection. Its task is also to make sure that the regulation of interests as well as the realization of collective goals can be rendered acceptable by taking stock of a whole range of norms, interests and values. I have conceived of the EU as cosmopolitan in the sense that it subjects its actions to the constraints of a higher ranking law and not as an emerging world organization. This is underscored by the fact that the EU does not possess a system for norm implementation of its own.

It depends on national political systems – national administrations – in order to put its measures into effect. This diminishes the tremendous leeway for legislators and courts at the supranational level. Moreover, the democratic features of the system of law-making and norm interpretation at the European level, constrained by the power of the member states, warrants that the EU does not become an unchecked entity – one that does not run the risk of being a world despotic Leviathan. It does not grant the citizens unmediated and unchecked membership in a world organization but rather respects the allegiance to particular communities – the nation states. The EU represents a constraint upon brute state power and excessive nationalism but is itself balanced by the states that have the upper hand in legislative matters.

CONCLUSION

The criterion of a legitimate foreign policy can be derived from a cosmopolitan approach stating that only under the review of a higher ranking order can one know whether or not actions are normatively defensible. In addition, to establish this criterion I have argued that the opposition between democracy and human rights can only be solved by establishing supranational institutions. Furthermore, the threat of force is needed to ensure equal rights for all but can only find justification when used to protect human rights. Hence the defining feature of a legitimate polity cannot be the absence of military force, but rather the specific way in which it is used – never autonomously or at will.

On the theoretical underpinnings of this perspective I have argued that actors in the international order should not be seen merely as interest maximizers but also as able to act out of a sense of justice or duty. Increasingly, this obligation is structurally entrenched; hence infringement of human rights is not left unsanctioned in the international order. On assessing whether the EU actually abides by this criterion the findings are mixed. On the one hand, inconsistency and double talk are not infrequent. On the other hand, the EU is the most promising example of a post-national powerful regional organization and one which increasingly becomes a role model for other regions. The effort to include the EU Charter of Fundamental Rights in the new Constitutional Treaty is a strong indication of heightened consistency between externally projected and internally applied standards. The parameters of power politics have already changed in Europe, a fact that actually seems to have influenced the external relations of the Euro-polity.

Biographical note: Erik Oddvar Eriksen is Professor of Political Science at ARENA – Centre for European Studies, University of Oslo, Norway.

Address for correspondence: Erik O. Eriksen, ARENA – Centre for European Studies, University of Oslo, PO Box 1143 Blindern, 0317 Oslo, Norway. Tel: +47 22 85 59 57. Fax: +47 22 85 78 32. email: e.o.eriksen@arena.uio.no

NOTES

1 An earlier version of this paper was read at the EUSA Ninth Biennial International Conference 31 March–2 April 2005 in Austin, Texas. I am grateful for comments from A.J. Menéndez, M. Lerch, H. Sjursen, A.E. Stie, K.E. Jørgensen and an anonymous reviewer.

2 See Beck and Grande for a different take on what a cosmopolitan Europe means. Their 'kosmopolitische Europa' is one which does not distinguish between empire and civilian power, and one that is not confined to the EU but stretches from Los Angeles and Vancouver to Vladivostok (Beck and Grande 2004: 23).

3 Council Regulation (EC) No. 381/2001 of 26 February 2001 creating a rapid-reaction mechanism [Official Journal L 57 of 27.02.2001].

4 See http://www.arena.uio.no/cidel/cwatch/bibliography.html

5 The content was included basically unaltered as Part II of the Constitutional Treaty.

6 *Treaty establishing a Constitution for Europe*, CIG 87/2/04 REV 2, Brussels, 29 October 2004.

7 'The offer of trade and association agreements, technical and development assistance, political dialogue, diplomatic recognition, and other instruments is now usually made conditional on respect for human rights' (Smith 2003: 111).

8 Article I-57.1 of the Constitutional Treaty; see also Communication from the Commission, European Neighbourhood Policy, Strategy Paper, Brussels, 12 May 2004, COM(2004) 373 final.

9 *European Voice*, 18–24 March 2004: 15.

10 The Treaty on European Union (TEU, Title V, Article 11).

11 There is no uncontested blueprint for the design of a cosmopolitan order to which the argument over the proposal of David Held *et al.* testifies; see e.g. Habermas 1998, 1999, 2001. See further Bohman and Lutz-Bachmann 1997; Brunkhorst 1999; Brunkhorst *et al.* 1999; Höffe 1999; Apel 2001; Archibugi 2003b; Grant and Keohane 2005.

REFERENCES

Alexy, R. (1996) 'Discourse theory and human rights', *Ratio Juris* 9(3): 209–35.

Alston, P. and Weiler, J.H.H. (1999) 'An "ever closer union" in need of a human rights policy: the European Union and human rights', in P. Alston (ed.), *The EU and Human Rights*, Oxford: Oxford University Press, pp. 3–68.

Apel, K.O. (1998) *Auseinandersetzungen in Erprobung des transzendental-pragmatischen Ansatzes*, Frankfurt: Suhrkamp.

Apel, K.O. (2001) 'On the relationship between ethics, international law and the politico-military strategy in our time', *European Journal of Social Theory* 4(1): 29–39.

Archibugi, D. (2003a) 'Cosmopolitical democracy', in D. Archibugi (ed.), *Debating Cosmopolitics*, London: Verso, pp. 1–15.

Archibugi, D. (ed.) (2003b) *Debating Cosmopolitics*, London: Verso.

Avci, G. (2005) 'Turkey's EU politics: what justifies reform?', in H. Sjursen (ed.), *Enlargement in Perspective*, ARENA Report 2/05, Oslo: ARENA, pp. 129–49.

Axelrod, R. (1990) *The Evolution of Co-operation* [reprint 1984], New York: Penguin Books.

Beck, U. and Grande, E. (2004) *Das kosmopolitische Europa*, Frankfurt: Suhrkamp.

Beitz, C.R. (1979) *Political Theory and International Relations*, Princeton, NJ: Princeton University Press.

Bohman, J. and Lutz-Bachmann, M. (eds) (1997) *Perpetual Peace. Essays on Kant's Cosmopolitan Ideal*, Cambridge, MA: MIT Press.

Börzel, T. and Risse, T. (2005) 'One size fits all! EU policies for the promotion of human rights, democracy and the rule of law'. Paper presented at the EUSA conference, Austin, Texas, 31 March–2 April.

Brennan, W.J. (1989) 'Why have a Bill of Rights?', *Oxford Journal of Legal Studies* 9(4): 425–40.

Brunkhorst, H. (1999) 'Menschenrechte und Souveränität – ein Dilemma?', in H. Brunkhorst, W.R. Köhler and M. Lutz-Bachman (eds), *Recht auf Menschenrechte*, Frankfurt: Suhrkamp, pp. 157–75.

Brunkhorst, H., Köhler, W.R. and Lutz-Bachmann, M. (eds) (1999) *Recht auf Menschenrechte*, Frankfurt: Suhrkamp.

Dannreuther, R. (ed.) (2004) *European Union Foreign and Security Policy: Towards a Neighbourhood Strategy*, London: Routledge.

de Búrca, G. (2001) 'The drafting of the European Union Charter of Fundamental Rights', *European Law Review* 26: 126–38.

Duchêne, F. (1972) 'Europe's role in world peace', in R. Mayne (ed.), *Europe Tomorrow: Sixteen Europeans Look Ahead*, London: Fontana, pp. 32–47.

Elster, J. (1989) *The Cement of Society*, Cambridge: Cambridge University Press.

Elster, J. (1998) 'Deliberation and constitution making', in J. Elster (ed.), *Deliberative Democracy*, Cambridge: Cambridge University Press, pp. 97–122.

Eriksen, E.O. (2004) 'The EU and the right to self-government', in E.O. Eriksen, J.E. Fossum and A.J. Menéndez (eds), *Developing a Constitution for Europe*, London: Routledge, pp. 33–58.

Falk, R. and Strauss, A. (2003) 'The deeper challenges of global terrorism: a democratizing response', in D. Archibugi (ed.), *Debating Cosmopolitics*, London: Verso, pp. 203–31.

Fassbender, B. (1998) 'The United Nations Charter as constitution of the international community', *Columbia Journal of Transnational Law* 36: 529–619.

Grabbe, H. (2002) 'European Union conditionality and the *acquis communautaire*', *International Political Science Review* 23(3): 249–68.

Grant, R.W. and Keohane, R.O. (2005) 'Accountability and abuses of power in world politics', *American Political Science Review* 99(1): 29–43.

Grugel, J.B. (2004) 'New regionalism and modes of governance – comparing US and EU strategies in Latin America', *European Journal of International Relations* 10(4): 603–26.

Günther, K. (1993) *The Sense of Appropriateness: Application Discourses in Morality and Law*, New York: State University of New York Press.

Habermas, J. (1996) *Between Facts and Norms. Contributions to a Discourse Theory of Law*, Cambridge, MA: MIT Press.

Habermas, J. (1998) *The Inclusion of the Other*, Cambridge, MA: MIT Press.

Habermas, J. (1999) 'Bestiality and humanity: a war on the border between legality and morality', *Constellations* 6(3): 263–72.

Habermas, J. (2001) *The Postnational Constellation*, Cambridge, MA: MIT Press.

Habermas, J. (2004) *Der gespaltene Westen*, Frankfurt: Suhrkamp.

Held, D. (1995) *Democracy and the Global Order. From the Modern State to Cosmopolitan Governance*, Stanford: Stanford University Press.

Held, D. (2002) 'Law of states, law of peoples: three models of sovereignty', *Legal Theory* 8(2): 1–44.

Hill, C. (1998) 'Closing the capabilities–expectations gap?', in H. Sjursen and J. Peterson (eds), *A Common Foreign Policy for Europe? Competing Visions of the CFSP*, London: Routledge, pp. 18–38.

Höffe, O. (1999) *Demokratie im Zeitalter der Globalisierung*, München: C.H. Beck.

Honoré, T. (1993) 'The dependence of morality of law', *Oxford Journal of Legal Studies* 13: 1–17.

Hyde-Price, A. (2006) '"Normative" power Europe: a realist critique', *Journal of European Public Policy* 13(2): 217–34.
Kant, I. (1784/1991) 'Idea for a universal history with a cosmopolitan purpose', in I. Kant [ed. H. Reiss], *Political Writings*, Cambridge: Cambridge University Press, pp. 41–53.
Kant, I. (1797/1991) 'The metaphysics of morals', in I. Kant [ed. H. Reiss], *Political Writings*, Cambridge: Cambridge University Press, pp. 131–75.
Kelsen, H. (1944) *Peace through Law*, Chapel Hill: University of North Carolina.
Kokott, J. and Rüth, A. (2003) 'The European Convention and its Draft Treaty Establishing a Constitution for Europe: appropriate answers to the Laeken questions?', *Common Market Law Review* 40(6): 1315–45.
Luhmann, N. (1995) *Das Recht der Gesellschaft*, Frankfurt: Suhrkamp.
Manners, I. (2002) 'Normative power Europe: a contradiction in terms?', *Journal of Common Market Studies* 40(2): 235–58.
Manners, I. (2006) 'Normative power Europe reconsidered: beyond the crossroads', *Journal of European Public Policy* 13(2): 182–99.
Menéndez, A.J. (2003) '"Rights to solidarity": balancing solidarity and economic freedoms', in E.O. Eriksen, J.E. Fossum and A.J. Menéndez (eds), *The Chartering of Europe*, Baden-Baden: Nomos, pp. 179–98.
Morgenthau, J.H. (1993) *Politics among Nations*, New York: McGraw-Hill.
Nye, J. (2004) *Soft Power: The Means to Success in World Politics*, New York: Public Affairs Press.
Petiteville, F. (2003) 'Exporting "values"? EU external Co-operation as "soft diplomacy"', in M. Knodt and S. Princen (eds), *Understanding the European Union's External Relations*, London: Routledge, pp. 127–41.
Rawls, J. (1993) *Political Liberalism*, New York: Columbia University Press.
Rosecrance, R. (1998) 'The European Union: a new type of international actor', in J. Zielonka (ed.), *Paradoxes of European Foreign Policy*, The Hague: Kluwer Law International, pp. 15–23.
Scheuerman, W.E. (2002) 'Cosmopolitan democracy and the rule of law', *Ratio Juris* 15(4): 439–57.
Schmitt, C. (1996) *The Concept of the Political* [reprint 1932], Chicago: University of Chicago Press.
Schwellnus, G. (2005) 'The role of argumentative coherence in the EU's justification of minority protection as a condition for membership', in H. Sjursen (ed.), *Enlargement in Perspective*, ARENA Report 2/05, Oslo: ARENA, pp. 247–74.
Sjursen, H. (2002) 'Why expand? The question of justification in the EU's enlargement policy', *Journal of Common Market Studies* 40(3): 491–513.
Smith, K.E. (2003) *European Union Foreign Policy in a Changing World*, Cambridge: Polity Press.
Wagner, W. (2006) 'The democratic control of military power Europe', *Journal of European Public Policy* 13(2): 200–16.
Weiler, J.H.H. (2004) 'Human rights, constitutionalism and integration: iconography and fetishism', in E.O. Eriksen, J.E. Fossum and A.J. Menéndez (eds), *Developing a Constitution for Europe*, London: Routledge, pp. 59–68.

Anchoring Europe's civilizing identity: habits, capabilities and ontological security[1]

Jennifer Mitzen

INTRODUCTION

Will the deepening of the Common Foreign and Security Policy (CFSP) and greater military capabilities compromise the European Union's (EU's) identity as a 'civilian' and a 'civilizing' power? Interestingly, the United States (US) has long seen itself as a civilizing power, whose military power is subordinate to its moral identity and mission. As the 2002 National Security Strategy (NSS) puts it, 'our Nation's cause has always been larger than our Nation's defense'. This suggests that another way to pose the question might be, would military capabilities make the EU (eventually) like the US, whose subjective sense of self is perhaps increasingly at odds with the way it is perceived by other states? There certainly are enough similarities between the US and the EU to make the question salient: both share the universalistic values of democracy and capitalism, and both have given themselves civilizing missions toward the rest of the world. If the primary difference is one of capabilities, i.e. if civilian means are the core of civilian power, then once the EU gets those capabilities, it risks a similar disjuncture between subjective sense of self and how others see it. It is in light of the potential

EU–US comparison that I consider the implications of a deepening CFSP for the EU's identity. I suggest that fears that it would threaten the EU's civilizing identity, raising the specter of 'great power Europe', may be unwarranted.

The collective identity of a 'civilizing power' is related to the notion of 'civilian power', which is rooted in the initial goal of European integration: making war among member states unthinkable. François Duchêne in 1972 first called Europe a 'civilian power', a 'special international actor whose strength lies in its ability to promote and encourage stability through economic and political means' (Sjursen 2004: 122). Duchêne's starting point was Europe's relative military weakness, but the shared understanding of what makes Europe distinctive on the world stage has always pointed beyond particular foreign policy instruments to that larger founding goal. For example, the 1973 Copenhagen Declaration on European Identity taps into that 'civilizing' goal when it speaks of Europe's responsibility to serve as 'an element of equilibrium and a basis for cooperation' in world affairs. Europe's civilizing identity is associated with multilateralism, or 'diplomacy first', and with commitments to pursuing representative democracy, the rule of law, social justice, and human rights in its foreign policy (e.g. Maull 2000; Manners 2002a).

In the debate over the impact of growing military capabilities on this identity, two views particularly stand out. On the one hand, Karen Smith (2005: 12) argues that military capabilities threaten civilian identity, suggesting that the EU will 'fold to the supposedly superior hand of military force', perhaps eventually to become 'a larger version of a sovereign state', an 'armed superpower of sorts'. On the other hand, Stelios Stavridis (2001: 49–50) suggests that military means might be essential to realizing effective civilian power, that goals of human rights and democracy, not tools, determine whether the EU is civilian. Military capabilities compromise the EU as a civilian power, or they are necessary for it. There seems an important, if implicit, shared premise in this debate: identity stability depends on military power, i.e. material forces drive identity.

In contrast, I argue that habits not capabilities determine identity. Identities are anchored in routines with significant others, and actors – even corporate actors such as states – become attached to or invested in these routines. This is because routines give individuals an important form of security, which, following Anthony Giddens (1991), I call 'ontological security'. The idea is this: actors value their sense of agency, the ability to make choices and pursue favorable outcomes. That ability rests on knowing one's own preferences and interests. In other words it rests on an identity, which means that actors need stable identities to be 'actors' or 'agents' at all. In any given social environment, actors solidify identity and learn to be 'agentic' through routinized relations with significant others. From a platform of stable routines, aspiring agents come to know who they are and therefore can act. Then, because routines anchor identity, actors become attached to, or invested in, their routines. Building on research in a number of experimental and theoretical fields, elsewhere I have proposed that alongside physical security-seeking, states seek ontological security through routinizing relations with their primary strategic partners

(Mitzen forthcoming). States not only seek to secure their territory and govern-ance structure; they also seek to secure their identity as a particular kind of actor. The assumption that states seek ontological security suggests a cognitive-affective source of resistance to identity change in world politics.[2]

Applied to the EU case, the proposition that states need ontological security and achieve it through interstate routines suggests that a militarily powerful Europe will not undermine 'civilizing power Europe'. This is because the collec-tive aspirational identities of civilian and civilizing are constituted not so much by their relationship to military power, but by intra-European routines of multi-lateral security cooperation, which began with European Political Cooperation (EPC) and deepened in the 1990s with the CFSP. Through these routines, EU member states enact their collective identity and recognize it in one another, keeping it salient even for external action. Insofar as 'civilizing power Europe' rests on these routines and states aspire to that identity, EU states will be attached to them.

In this article I first summarize the proposition that states seek ontological security. From here, I develop the hypothesis that the EU's identity as a civiliz-ing power is anchored by internal routines of foreign policy cooperation that are deliberative and reflexively held. If true, the hypothesis suggests that Europe's civilizing power will not be compromised by increased military capabilities. Rather than 'test' the hypothesis, my aims are twofold: to establish its plausi-bility and to spur further research on the centrality of the EU's foreign affairs routines for its identity as a civilizing power.

ONTOLOGICAL SECURITY IN WORLD POLITICS

We are accustomed to thinking about security monolithically, as physical security, of the body. But there is another fundamental form of security, ontological security, or security of one's identity, which, as others have argued (e.g. Huysmans 1998; McSweeney 1999; Manners 2002b), has implications for world politics. All actors need a stable sense of who they are, an 'identity', in order to act; for example, to have goals, assess environments, make choices. Agency is an accomplishment that requires ontological security. This means that ontological security is just like physical security: a primary drive, in every social actor.

Understanding ontological security as a primary drive requires first acknow-ledging a relationship between uncertainty and identity. Namely, uncertainty can make it hard to act, and since the ability to act is crucial for our identity, uncertainty can make it difficult to be one's self, to sustain an identity over time. The uncertainty is not like that foregrounded in rational choice theory. There, uncertainty is equated with 'risk', so that it is always possible to assign probabilities and to make an educated guess about what might happen (e.g. Kreps 1990: ch. 3). The uncertainty I am talking about begins instead with the proposition that there are some outcomes, or relations between strategies and outcomes, that decision-makers cannot know or even think they know. Where events are novel or infrequent actors cannot assign probabilities; there is not enough information even to form an educated guess about the likelihood of an outcome or the link between cause and effect (e.g. Knight 1971 [1921]; Dequech 1997). This type of uncertainty reduces – objectively – the confidence that actors can have in their probability assignments, which calls into question their ability to act rationally.

On an instinctive level, all individuals are aware of, and fear, the possibility of such radical or deep uncertainty because of its impact on agency. As Giddens (1991) puts it, all social actors know that behind the comfortable routines of our daily life, 'chaos lurks'. In fact, everyday life is full of possible dangers: both physical – your neighbor might attack, a car might run you down – and social – you might be fired, your spouse might leave you. Being consciously aware of all these possibilities all the time would generate tremendous anxiety. It would make an actor ontologically insecure, unable to act or 'be' herself. Ontological insecurity is the deep, incapacitating fear of not being able to organize the threat environment, and thus not being able to get by in the world.

A tragic example of such ontological insecurity is 11 September, in the immediate aftermath of which people in the US found it difficult to do anything: go to work, cross a bridge, ride the subway. It was hard to leave the house, but it was also hard to stay home, because the sense of uncertainty and threat was pervasive. No one knew where the threat was from or what might happen, whether you might be a target, your family, or your friends. People could not cognitively organize the threat environment, in that whatever you decided to do could cause harm. Or, at least, you could not prevent it.

In normal times, one strategy in particular holds this profound uncertainty at bay: routinization. By 'routines' I mean responses to stimuli that are relatively automatic or habitual. For a range of things that happen, the actor does not weigh alternatives or 'rationally update'. She does not 'choose' what to do; she simply responds. We hit the gas pedal when a light turns green, or intensify competition when rivals make overtures. When a set of stimuli evoke routinized responses a whole realm of possible questions and options is taken off the table, i.e. out of our primary, discursive consciousness and moved into our practical consciousness (Giddens 1991: 30). Since actors cannot consider and respond to all possible dangers at once, the cognitive capacity to choose how to respond to any subset depends on these routines. Thus, by systematically removing some questions from the table, routines help us to bring our threat environment under cognitive control. Routines therefore solve the chaos problem, allowing the actor to maintain a sense of self (Giddens 1991: 39–40). In short, they provide ontological security, which enables agency. That is why in the days after 11 September, government and media urged us to go back to our routines: go to work, fly, spend money. The message was that the first step to getting back to normal, much less getting over the tragedy, was to re-establish routines.

We all need ontological security, which means that we all need, and are attached to, our routines. Giddens (1991: 38) refers to individualized sets of routines that actors develop as a 'basic trust system'. A basic trust system is a 'cognitive cocoon' that 'brackets, at the level of practice, the knowledge of all possible events that could be threatening'. It enables the aspiring actor to see herself as a unitary, coherent, self with identities and interests to pursue. The routines of a basic trust system act as a sort of firewall against chaos and the dissolution of identity. As such, individuals become attached to the routines that constitute their basic trust system. Individuals like to feel that they have agency, and become attached to practices that make them feel agentic. Letting go of routines would amount to sacrificing our sense of agency, which would be hard to do.

This said, we gain ontological security in different ways, i.e. our attitudes toward routines vary in ways that are consequential for action. Broadly speaking, actors can develop one of two types of basic trust, rigid/maladaptive and healthy (Willmott 1986), and these particularly tell us how actors respond to novel situations and highly uncertain environments.

Actors with rigid basic trust treat their routines as ends in themselves, relying on them blindly or compulsively, without reflection. All 'agentic' energy is directed to maintaining routines, rather than toward experimentation, learning, and growth. When faced with profound uncertainty, actors with rigid basic trust respond by clinging to routines. Catarina Kinnvall (2004: 753 ff.) develops this idea as the 'securitization of subjectivity', the bounding or defining of one's self through 'one stable identity' rather than accepting a multiplicity or fluidity (Kinnvall 2004: 749). Uncertainty threatens self-boundaries, and an actor with rigid basic trust feels the urgent need to secure her self-conception. This is done especially by projecting negative aspects of the Self onto an Other or otherwise essentializing Self and Other, such as through stereotyping, relying on enemy images, resurrecting national myths, etc. When subjectivity is securitized, learning about the Other – or the Self – through interaction becomes impossible.

The alternative is healthy basic trust, which implies the ability to maintain a critical distance from routines. Routines are there and enable agency, but are reflexively held, so that the actor does not focus on them so much as on particular choices. With healthy basic trust, rather than avoiding disintegration, the actor can create or enact her identity(ies) and pursue her interests. Actors then can tolerate a certain measure of uncertainty; they do not respond to it by hardening self-boundaries, or 'securitizing subjectivity', but by, for example, reflecting on their practices and experimenting with new ones. As such, healthy basic trust is the precondition for creativity and complex learning (Giddens 1991).

Healthy basic trust manifests a sense of feeling at home in a threatening world. For this, Kinnvall and others (Dupuis and Thorns 1998) stress the role of the material environment in which routines are enacted, and in particular having a home or stable private space. A home provides refuge from the threats and surveillance of the outside world. Homes provide constancy, stable spaces to perform the routines of daily life and thus to reproduce self-conceptions. Knowing there is a space in which it is possible to be one's self provides the confidence necessary to assert one's self and to experiment with new identities.

Positing ontological security as a primary need suggests that all agency rests on routines; but the fact that there are two types of basic trust indicates that agentic capacities vary systematically. In a sense, this is intuitive: some of us are capable of complex learning and social trust, others are not; some are paralyzed by uncertainty, others are never more alive and creative. What these two types of basic trust tell us is that the character and location of routines condition an actor's ability to learn and realize her aspirations. It suggests that where agency is anchored by routines that permit reflection and critical distance from participation, and where these routines can be performed in a stable environment or 'home', actors have healthy basic trust. They can adapt to situations of novelty and high uncertainty, and they can learn.

EU FOREIGN POLICY COOPERATION: SECURING A CIVILIZING IDENTITY

Applying this theoretical framework to the EU case suggests that acquiring greater military capabilities and even using them selectively would not necessarily undermine Europe's identity as a civilizing power. The EU need not become a 'neocolonial' or 'great power Europe', because its collective identity as a civilizing power is anchored in intra-European foreign policy routines that permit deliberation and reflection, and this sphere of cooperation has a home. In other words, the EU's civilizing identity is supported by healthy basic trust, which guards against the securitization of subjectivity that 'great power Europe' implies. Healthy basic trust implies that European foreign affairs cooperation might just continue to grope toward something new in world politics – perhaps what others have called the post-modern state.

In this section I substantiate that intuition with evidence from the existing literature on the evolution of the EU's foreign policy cooperation (e.g. Nuttall 1992; Jørgensen 1997; Glarbo 1999; Tonra 2003; Smith 2004). The proposition that military capabilities will not erode the identity of 'civilizing power Europe' is strengthened if we see indicators of healthy basic trust: interstate habits that permit deliberation and reflection on foreign policy and that are not easily disrupted; and material locales for participants to retreat from public glare, or a 'home'. Ultimately, however, civilizing power is about external more than internal relations, and Europe is certainly not alone in having a civilizing mission toward the world. Often one state's civilizing mission is another state's colonial, hegemonic project: but I propose that the healthy basic trust anchoring intra-European relations makes Europe perhaps uniquely capable of 'externalizing' its civilizing mission. Of course, this does not mean that Europe will be an effective foreign policy actor, or will even choose to act at all; the claim is simply that when it does act externally, the identity of 'civilizing power' will discipline its instruments and outputs in ways we would not necessarily see for a traditional Westphalian state.

Europe's basic trust

Many analysts and practitioners have noted that cooperation among EU member states is so ingrained that in many issues national interests can be difficult to disentangle from European ones. Moreover, this cooperation is not just at the level of behavioral outputs, but also at the level of process, i.e. of how cooperation is achieved. Namely, it is now unthinkable not to meet to discuss foreign affairs prior to decisions – indeed it would be more difficult not to do so.

Of course this has not always been the case. Prior to EPC, European Community member states treated meetings with one another, which were 'irregular' and 'intermittent', as they did meetings with other states. Indeed, regularized multi-lateral action among European states differed little from that in the North Atlantic Treaty Organization (NATO) (Glarbo 1999: 39). National interests came first and states maintained a certain level of mutual suspicion, as we would expect in anarchy. The failures of the European Defense Community (EDC) in the early 1950s and Fouchet proposals in 1962, not to mention the deep disagreements over responses to the Six Day War, show that member states did not view the European context as primary, much less act with an eye toward any collective European identity (Smith 2004). By 1970, however, a consensus had emerged that member states should at least search for a common interest on matters of global concern, if only to 'prevent international problems from disrupting the Community' (Smith 2004: 4). Thus EPC was born with the minimal goals of pooling and exchanging information, to find consensus and build mutual trust. It was at first no more than a forum, which institutionalized opportunities to learn one another's reasons and positions. What it became, however, was the basis of member states' basic trust. Two aspects of this intra-European foreign policy cooperation stand out as indicating healthy basic trust: states are attached to the routines, and it has a home in Brussels.

Routines and attachment
The main accomplishment of EPC was to establish the habit of talking to one another about foreign affairs, or the 'coordination reflex'. From the start, foreign ministers met more often than was formally required and introduced additional twice-yearly (since 1974) Gymnich meetings, the small, face-to-face meetings guided by no fixed agenda. In addition to that uppermost level, Political Directors of the ministries, official liaisons ('European Correspondents'), and EPC working groups also began regular discussions; and connecting them all was the COREU, a dedicated encrypted telex network through which member states could keep one another constantly informed (Smith 2004: 197).

Together these created, by the early 1980s, a 'decentralized but authoritative network of deliberative forums' for discussing foreign policy, at ministerial and ambassadorial levels (Smith 2004: 105). As Tonra notes, increasingly

> national foreign policy actors sought out the views and opinions of partners before arriving at defined national positions. Thus, the first point of cognitive reference became, "what will the European partners think?" rather than "what is our position on this?"
>
> (Toura 2003: 740)

'The national position is not clear until the partner's anticipated views have been considered.' Tonra argues that the 'habit of thinking in terms of consensus', which began with EPC and deepened with the CFSP, suggests that decision-makers began to see themselves as no longer representing purely national views, but 'seeking to internalize the views of colleagues in order to see that their own positions are at least complementary in the common and shared endeavor of the CFSP' (Tonra 2003: 740). Glarbo (1999: 644) similarly discusses this 'reciprocal, yet in-built, disposition of national diplomacies' to consult with European member states. '[W]ithin EPC, coordination is not a deliberatively chosen means of pursuing preferences; it is ... a naturally "done thing".'

Three aspects of EPC in particular seem to have fostered the coordination reflex. First, EPC had no decision-making mechanism beyond the consensus principle and was kept wholly separate from Community institutions. Member states agreed to take no final position without prior consultation, but the final position need not be a unified one, and no foreign policy actions were specified. Taking away the pressure to decide made the institution non-threatening to national interests, and removed an important incentive to bargain and dig in, leaving more room for brainstorming and compromise. Second, the institution had an informal 'club atmosphere'. In other words, these were not formal diplomatic consultations. This facilitated viewing one another as colleagues or peers rather than as national representatives promoting national goals. Additionally, the commitments to privacy and discretion made it possible to speak freely.

Third, EPC provided an ongoing forum and forums have effects on problem-solving (Mitzen 2005). Speaking in public causes speakers to moderate their interest claims toward the common good (Elster 1995), and empirical research confirms that face-to-face talk has beneficial effects on joint problem-solving (e.g. Ostrom 2000). It is true that EPC outputs were generally no more than consensus and did not result in collective action. But participants placed much importance on the meetings and agreements. In a sense these meetings instantiated the collective identity, so that, as Tonra (2003: 747) puts it, the goal of maintaining the collective both drove members' action and was realized through it.

The consultation reflex exhibits healthy basic trust. It is a habit in which participants can reflect on their practices in light of the identity they share, and therefore provides the type of ontological security that can ground complex learning. One can certainly imagine foreign policy cooperation without deliberative routines: member states might agree to routinely accept a particular state's positions as authoritative, or to routinely circulate their prepared policy statements, and so on. What EPC set in motion, instead, was a habit of vetting foreign policy positions to one another, and even exchanging rationales as they were forming these positions.

A habit of deliberation might seem paradoxical. After all, deliberation is about scrutinizing taken-for-granted norms and practices, or undoing habits. Indeed, the promise of deliberative processes is to re-anchor social life on the basis of reasoned consensus on the common good, rather than on the preferences of the powerful, or social custom. The ontological security generating power of habits, on the other hand, rests on their automaticity: habits substitute for reflection and choice. But what is important here is the specific type of habit that was internalized: European states became habituated to meeting and talking through foreign policy positions with one another. The automaticity is at a procedural, not a substantive level. Policy-makers do not 'choose' each time whether to meet or give reasons; it does not cross policy-makers' minds *not* to meet. Indeed, if communicative action is the 'micro-mechanism' of this security community, as Sjursen (2004) argues (see also Risse 2000; Tonra 2003), it would seem that this mechanism, and the substantive promise of deliberative processes overall, rest on the procedural habituation to them. Participants must take for granted that their deliberative processes are in some sense temporally open-ended, that they will be exchanging reasons again and again, in order to allow themselves to be persuaded or to learn.

If the consultation reflex is an indication of healthy basic trust, states should be attached to it and it should be difficult to disrupt. One way to gauge attachment is to consider how deeply member states have internalized the reflex. The fact that EPC's informal norms have been increasingly institutionalized and codified, and that the reflex is not simply among ministers but extends to the embassy level as well, indicate a deepening 'taken-for-grantedness', or internalization. Another indication of internalization is the re-orientation of national level bureaucracies and foreign ministries toward Europe. Tonra (2003: 740) argues that national foreign policy bureaucracies are increasingly linked structurally to the 'collective foreign policy machine' (see also Jørgensen 1997: 178–9). Of course, there is variation in adaptations made by particular member states. But even in larger, more powerful states there is a downgrading of unilateral foreign policy initiatives relative to collective ones. Jan Irlenkauser (2004: 8) points out, for example, that German strategic planning has nothing like the European Security Strategy (ESS). There is no 'political will to clearly define national interests', and the most recent defense white paper was back in 1994. Lisbeth Aggestam (2004: 10) argues that regular interaction between foreign policy decision-makers has resulted in a 'nationalization of European identity'. In the 1990s, British, French, and German policy-makers did not simply adapt to EU membership, as one might adapt to an external force impinging on national interests. Rather, they conceived and constructed foreign policy differently than they did while acting strictly as independent nation states (Aggestam 2004: 238). Aggestam finds that, in the 1990s, there was:

> lack of reference made to independent foreign policies, and (greater) emphasis on the fact that unilateral action was neither an attractive nor feasible option ... European cooperation in foreign policy was considered the norm and national action the exception.
>
> (Aggestam 2004: 242)

But ontological security suggests that attachment is not just internalization. That is, it suggests a cognitive–affective dimension – a motivational glue – to routines that internalization alone does not quite capture. Actors want to hold onto identities, and will hold onto routines that reproduce those identities, even if holding onto the identity becomes more difficult. With this in mind, one way to get at this glue empirically would be to look beyond the institution of EPC/CFSP itself and ask, how has the EU responded to threats, or to changes in the threat environment? As we have seen above, extreme change or uncertainty can threaten routinized cooperative relationships by causing some actors to securitize their identities: actors with rigid basic trust will tend to create a monolithic Self and cast out the Other. In the EU context this securitization could take one of two forms. Member states might re-nationalize, withdrawing from intra-European routines; or they might band together to cast out the non-European, threatening Other.

Importantly, this did not happen in the 1990s with the end of the Cold War. Instead, Europe's response supports the hypothesis of healthy basic trust. For example, faced with the breakup of the former Yugoslavia, in late 1991, Germany unilaterally recognized Croatia. The move was widely criticized, and certainly did not exhibit deliberative routines, but member states did not respond by 'going national' themselves, distancing themselves, or viewing the German action as threatening. State identities were not securitized. Instead member states asserted the authority of the group. As Aggestam (2004: 244–5) argues, the breakup of Yugoslavia 'opened the discursive space for the reasoning of new rules of action', and while arguably Europe did not find a satisfactory joint response, struggling with it did not destroy the Union but led states to become more 'deeply committed to the idea of Europe as a civilizing process that eventually should comprise the whole European continent'. The result was a deeper norm of cooperation and consultation among European states, not a securitization.

Home

Another factor that I have argued is important for healthy basic trust is a stable, secure private space, a 'home', in which one can safely practice self-maintenance. 'Brusselization' (Allen 1998: 56–8), the 'shift in the physical and psychological locus of national decision-making to Brussels-based intergovernmental institutions' (Tonra 2000: 147), stands out in this regard. Initially, the 1981 London Report established a proto-secretariat, an administrative aid that moved with the presidency and working groups every six months. But by the 1986 Single European Act (SEA), the EPC secretariat was given a permanent home in Brussels. Transgovernmental foreign policy cooperation in the 1990s became less club-like and more like other EU cooperation as working group practices 'harmonized' in Brussels; for example, through the merging of CFSP groups with those of the Committee of Permanent Representatives (COREPER) (Tonra 2000).

It is tempting to view Brusselization in negative terms, as greater bureaucratization, with all the attendant unreflexive routinization, task duplication, and turf battles that we associate with bureaucracies. But while the Brussels-based institutional forums still need to work out the distribution of responsibilities for foreign affairs and security policy (Howorth 2001), as Tonra (2000: 159) points out, it is significant that diplomats and not national civil servants are the participants in the 'Brussels machine'. In general, diplomats are recruited and trained differently than national civil servants, namely with an eye toward developing empathy toward others. '[D]iplomats ... share a culture and mode of thought which is at least distinct from that of national civil servants and is perhaps more open to the possibilities of shared and mutually beneficial interests.' In other words, diplomats might be more oriented to consensus and joint solutions than national civil servants. What Brusselization does is to give European diplomats a 'European' home to supplement their national home, and this can be seen to provide a secure space for being 'Europe' together. That is, having a place devoted to maintaining their conversations gives ontological security.

Of course, a sphere of privacy in foreign policy decision-making might not be desirable for other reasons – shielding decision-makers from the public eye can call into question the democratic legitimacy of a foreign policy output. But that important issue can be bracketed for now, especially because in general, governments tend to be more secretive in foreign policy than in domestic policy. So even if we might question the normative implications of this privacy, it is not the case that the European home by itself is causing a loss of input from national mass publics. Rather, it provides a space in which states can be 'public in private', i.e. visible to one another as part of the collective identity of Europe, while relatively insulated from the surveillance of their own publics, or of other states.

Europe's civilizing power

Thus far I have proposed that the intra-European routines of foreign policy cooperation manifest healthy basic trust, which suggests that a changing or uncertain threat environment will not lead to internal fragmentation or to Othering. But the latter is worth examining more closely. The EU's civilizing identity is a self-conception about its relationship to and treatment of a non-European Other, but historically, civilizing missions have been colonialist projects, rooted in military power. So the question is, can Europe sustain a civilizing identity if it acquires military capabilities, or do military capabilities necessarily bias such missions?

Indeed, one might be skeptical that the EU (or any polity) could be a civilizing power. Internal habits are not necessarily exported. Realists would argue that any civilizing mission runs up against the imperatives of anarchy; relativists might argue that one state's civilizing mission is another state's hegemonic imposition of values. For example, US domestic politics are premised on public deliberation among member states and the identity as a civilizing power is often invoked; but the US does not necessarily produce the identity as a civilizing power deliberatively in its relations with others. Indeed, its ambivalent relationship toward multilateralism suggests that the self-conception as a civilizing power can remain in a bubble, insulated from interstate practices, and thus be nothing more than a fantasy identity (Adler 2005). This suggests that even if the EU's civilizing identity is anchored in healthy basic trust among member states, there is no reason to expect that this identity could be exported.

However, the analogy from US to EU is not direct. The EU is not a Westphalian state, a hierarchical structure with the ability to coerce its members. Some 1990s developments certainly looked like a trend toward hierarchy or federalization, such as the Commission's joint right of initiative or the High Representative of the CFSP. But neither the Commission, the European Parliament nor the European Court of Justice participate in CFSP decision-making, which is still nearly completely governed by unanimity rules and permits states to opt out of EU foreign policy positions.

Thus, EU foreign policy is not determined in a hierarchical state-like environment and then projected, fully formed, into an anarchic one. Rather, within the EU there is always a little bit of anarchy going on. A crucial function of EU deliberative routines is to manage or tame the anarchic space that remains between the European states themselves. Thus, while for EU member states war might be unthinkable, there is a fundamental difference in the way war is unthinkable between Illinois and Wisconsin versus between France and Germany. For the latter, the security dilemma is never completely overcome. War is unthinkable only by being continually produced as such, through the habits and routines of European cooperation.

I propose that because the habit of deliberation tames anarchy 'inside', it also produces the potential to civilize EU relations with the 'outside': EU foreign policy is not only 'inter-action' with outsiders but also always 'intra-action', and this makes all the difference. So as long as EU member states premise external relations on their habits of deliberation, it would be difficult to keep that identity divorced from interstate practice. There is a greater chance that external practices will be disciplined by that identity. This does not mean that the EU will be an effective actor, or even successfully implement a given policy. But it does mean that it will be difficult to take security actions that are inconsistent with an internationally accepted notion of what it means to be civilized (cf. Manners 2002a).

Some support for my hypothesis that Europe's internal mode of securing basic trust conditions its relations with the world can be found by comparing the recent US NSS to the ESS. These documents respond essentially to the same post-11 September threat environment, where terrorism and the proliferation of weapons of mass destruction (WMD) loom large. But both the process by which the doctrines were made and the substance of the doctrines themselves differ considerably, and arguably the different processes help to account for the substance.

The NSS is mandated by law and emerges from the National Security Council essentially fully formed. It is not made in consultation with other states. Some of the principles of the current NSS – such as the US responsibility to shape the world and its goal of preventing the rise of another superpower – have been percolating since around 1990, but they only became dominant after 11 September. Substantively, as Felix Berenskoetter (2005: 76) shows, in the NSS, US primacy is portrayed as the result of its victory in the Cold War, and as rooted in its domestic constitution: American freedom, democracy and capitalism. The key threats that the US faces to its primacy – and to global order altogether – are terrorism, rogue states and WMD. While the document does not explore the causes of these threats, the causes, like the threats themselves, are outside the US and the Western world. Terrorists and rogue states are deviants; they have nothing to do with the US and are expelled from its self-identity (Berenskoetter 2005: 78–9). Instead, these threats are depicted as thriving in the not-US, where freedom is lacking. Faced with this radical, evil Other, the US must respond forcefully, and unilaterally if necessary. The document is by no means insular: the US ought to help spread its successful model throughout the world. But the NSS portrays this as a distinctly 'American internationalism', i.e. where universal responsibility can be carried out alone. There is little mention of multilateralism, the UN or international law (Berenskoetter 2005: 84). In other words, US identity is securitized – the Other is cast out – and the response is unilateral and military.

The ESS differs both procedurally and substantively. First, consider the sheer novelty of the ESS. Security strategies are tools of states for guiding foreign policy; there is no precedent for a group of states to produce a doctrine. Moreover, the various EU member states have different strategic cultures and may view their threat environments quite differently. As Hill and Wallace (1996: 8) point out, foreign policy requires a shared identity and sense of 'place in the world', which comes from 'national history and myths'. In this respect, Europe's collective identity is weak relative to those of its member states, and so there is no reason to expect a 'Europe-first' response to a threat. This is the context in which Javier Solana, as High Representative of the CFSP, initiated the ESS. He circulated a draft to member states in June 2003, after which Europe's deliberative habits took over. The ESS's content and terms – such as the controversial use of the word 'pre-emption' – were debated, the document was altered, and EU member states voted and accepted it six months later in December (Bailes 2005).

Four substantive differences – nicely highlighted by Berenskoetter (2005) – between the ESS and the NSS stand out. First, rather than frame the document in terms of a democratic victory, the ESS situates Europe's role as arising from its own past, using that history of rivalry and conflict as 'a source of critical self-reflection' (Berenskoetter 2005: 89–90). Second, the threats of terrorism, rogue states and WMD do not 'dominate' the document the way they do the NSS; indeed, rather than highlight uncertainty and fear in the post-11 September world, the ESS notes that Europe has 'never been so secure'. Terrorism and WMD proliferation have complex causes, and the real threat is more general: globalization, instability and failed states threaten everyone. Third, where specific threats are considered, they are not 'expelled' from Europe itself. The ESS notes that modernization, crises and alienation can cause terrorism and these are part of all European societies. Threats to stability are caused by us as much as them: the ESS does not equate threats with the 'not-us' as the NSS so pointedly does (Berenskoetter 2005: 81). Finally, for dealing with these threats, cooperation and multilateralism are crucial; indeed, the ESS 'does not leave room for an alternative' to multilateral action. The document replaces any reference to pre-emption with the notion of fostering a 'culture of prevention', to address the causes of instability and failed states, and build post-conflict peace. Military capabilities are mentioned solely in the context of post-conflict situations, not as instruments for taking offensive action (Berenskoetter 2005: 85). In sum, the ESS links security practices, including the use of force, to Europe's civilizing identity without Othering the non-European. Rather, the threatening Other is made a part of itself.

Arguably, the fact that the ESS was produced deliberatively, by participants who themselves have one foot in anarchy, helps to account for this substantive difference. European states can only be themselves by performing their deliberative routines; there would be no ESS without European deliberation. But because Europe's routines are among separate states, they cannot help but keep salient Europe's own conflictual history. This, in turn, disciplines its strategies against expelling the non-European Other. What is expelled instead are the impulses to renationalize, and the impulse to action that might be received as aggression.

In sum, Europe's routines of foreign policy cooperation are deliberative and internalized, and member states are attached to them. Moreover, even in a highly uncertain threat environment, member states continue to turn to deliberation and cooperation and the results are anything but a securitization of European identity. All of this suggests that Europe's civilizing identity is supported by healthy basic trust. If that is true, then changes in EU instruments, such as greater military capabilities, will not themselves undermine that identity.

CONCLUSION

Positing that states need ontological security suggests that habits more than capabilities anchor identity. With this in mind, examining the character of the routines through which European member states achieve ontological security, I have argued that EU foreign policy cooperation can maintain a non-colonialist civilizing identity even as the EU gains greater military capabilities. Unlike the US, which can define its civilizing mission wholly internally, EU member states cannot even define Europe as 'civilizing' without confronting some degree of anarchy.

Of course, incorporating military capabilities into a civilian identity is difficult on many levels, and finding a way to reconcile the use of force in particular instances with the identity as a civilizing power will be an ongoing challenge. It is not yet clear precisely how the EU will assimilate military tools into its civilizing mission, and I certainly do not mean to understate the challenge. But the point is that, on their own, military capabilities need not threaten the EU's civilizing power. Because the particular habits supporting the EU's civilizing identity are healthy and increasingly robust, the EU may be uniquely able to project its civilizing identity outward. Great power Europe, it seems, is not on the horizon.

Biographical note: Jennifer Mitzen is Assistant Professor in the Department of Political Science, Ohio State University, USA.

Address for correspondence: Jennifer Mitzen, Department of Political Science, Ohio State University, 2140 Derby Hall, 154 North Oval Mall, Columbus, OH 43210–1373, USA. Tel: 614-292-7400. email: mitzen.1@osu.edu

NOTES

1 For helpful comments, many thanks to Knud Erik Jørgensen, Morten Kelstrup, Ian Manners, Srdjan Vucetic, Alex Wendt, Børge Romsloe, and participants in the CIDEL Workshop, Oslo, Norway, October 2004. I am especially grateful to Helene Sjursen both for inviting me to join this project and for detailed comments and guidance on successive drafts. An earlier version was presented at EUSA, Austin, Texas, March 2005.
2 Even if individuals need ontological security, it is a leap to suggest that states need ontological security in an analogous way. But the argument developed here does not necessarily rest on that broad claim, since many of the points are made about individuals rather than states.

REFERENCES

Adler, E. (2005) *Communitarian International Relations*, London and New York: Routledge.
Aggestam, L. (2004) 'A European foreign policy? Role conceptions and the politics of identity in Britain, France and Germany', doctoral dissertation, Stockholm University.
Allen, D. (1998) 'Who speaks for Europe? The search for an effective and coherent external policy', in J. Peterson and H. Sjursen (eds), *A Common Foreign Policy for Europe?*, London and New York: Routledge, pp. 41–59.
Bailes, A. (2005) 'The European Security Strategy: an evolutionary history', SIPRI Policy Paper 10.
Berenskoetter, F.S. (2005) 'Mapping the mind gap: a comparison of US and European security strategies', *Security Dialogue* 36(1): 71–92.
Dequech, D. (1997) 'Uncertainty in a strong sense: meaning and sources', *Economic Issues* 2(2): 21–43.
Dupuis, A. and Thorns, D.C. (1998) 'Home, home ownership and the search for ontological security', *Sociological Review* 46(1): 24–47.
Elster, J. (1995) 'Strategic uses of argument', in K. Arrow *et al.* (eds), *Barriers to Conflict Resolution*, New York: W.W. Norton, pp. 236–57.
Giddens, A. (1991) *Modernity and Self-Identity*, Cambridge: Polity Press.
Glarbo, K. (1999) 'Wide-awake diplomacy: reconstructing the common foreign and security policy of the European Union', *Journal of European Public Policy* 6(4): 634–51.

Hill, C. and Wallace, W. (1996) 'Introduction: Actors and actions', in C. Hill (ed.), *The Actors in Europe's Foreign Policy*, London and New York: Routledge, pp. 1–16.

Howorth, J. (2001) 'European defence and the changing politics of the European Union: hanging together or hanging separately?', *Journal of Common Market Studies* 39(4): 765–89.

Huysmans, J. (1998) 'Security! What do you mean? From concept to thick signifier', *European Journal of International Relations* 4(2): 226–55.

Irlenkauser, J. (2004) 'A secure Europe in a better world – the European Union's Security Strategy. A German perspective', in M. Overhaus, H. Maull and S. Harnisch (eds), 'The European Security Strategy: paper tiger or catalyst for joint action?', *German Foreign Policy in Dialogue* 5(13): 7–14.

Jørgensen, K.E. (1997) 'PoCo: the diplomatic republic of Europe', in K.E. Jørgensen (ed.), *Reflective Approaches to European Governance*, New York: St Martin's Press, pp. 167–80.

Kinnvall, C. (2004) 'Self, identity, and the search for ontological security', *Political Psychology* 25(5): 741–67.

Knight, F. (1971) [1921] *Risk, Uncertainty, and Profit*, Chicago: University of Chicago Press.

Kreps, D. (1990) *A Course in Microeconomic Theory*, Princeton, NJ: Princeton University Press.

Manners, I. (2002a) 'Normative power Europe: a contradiction in terms?', *Journal of Common Market Studies* 40(2): 235–58.

Manners, I. (2002b) 'European [security] Union: from existential threat to ontological security', IIS Working Paper.

Maull, H. (2000) 'Germany and the European security and defence policy: a time for reflection?', *German Foreign Policy in Dialogue* 2 (July): 1–3.

McSweeney, B. (1999) *Security, Identity and Interests: A Sociology of International Relations*, Cambridge: Cambridge University Press.

Mitzen, J. (2005) 'Reading Habermas in anarchy: multilateral diplomacy and global public spheres', *American Political Science Review* 99(3): 401–17.

Mitzen, J. (forthcoming) 'Ontological security in world politics: state identity and the security dilemma', *European Journal of International Relations*.

Nuttall, S. (1992) *European Political Cooperation*, Oxford: Clarendon Press.

Ostrom, E. (2000) 'Collective action and the evolution of social norms', *Journal of Economic Perspectives* 14(3): 137–58.

Risse, T. (2000) '"Let's argue!" Communicative action in world politics', *International Organization* 54(1): 1–39.

Sjursen, H. (2004) 'Changes to European security in a communicative perspective', *Cooperation and Conflict* 39(2): 107–28.

Smith, K.E. (2005) 'Still "civilian power EU"?', European Foreign Policy Unit Working Paper, 2005/1.

Smith, M.E. (2004) *Europe's Foreign and Security Policy: The Institutionalization of Cooperation*, Cambridge: Cambridge University Press.

Stavridis, S. (2001) '"Militarising" the EU: the concept of civilian power revisited', *International Spectator* 36(4): 43–50.

Tonra, B. (2000) 'Committees in common: comitology and the common foreign and security policy', in T. Christiansen and E. Kirchner (eds), *Committee Governance in the European Union*, New York: St Martin's Press, pp. 145–60.

Tonra, B. (2003) 'Constructing the common foreign and security policy: the utility of a cognitive approach', *Journal of Common Market Studies* 41(4): 731–56.

Willmott, H. (1986) 'Unconscious sources of motivation in the theory of the subject: an exploration and critique of Giddens' dualistic models of action and personality', *Journal for the Theory of Social Behaviour* 16: 105–21.

'Our size fits all': normative power Europe and the Mediterranean

Federica Bicchi

INTRODUCTION[1]

These are interesting times for analysts of the European Union's foreign policy. As the days of 'is there such a thing as a European foreign policy?' finally recede into the past, much attention is being focused on the issue of what exactly such a thing is and what it does. The debate has acquired substantial momentum thanks to the argument put forward by Manners, according to which the EU can be conceptualized as a 'normative power'. In his view, the EU is normatively different and promotes 'universal norms and principles' in its relations with non-members (Manners 2002: 241). This argument has also taken to a new level the already thriving debate about the variety of principles and norms exported by the EU (e.g. Youngs 2001; Knodt and Princen 2003).

Less noticed but equally interesting, another argument has recently been voiced. It refers to the tendency of the EU to 'reproduce itself' (Bretherton and Vogler 1999: 249) in its relations with non-members. The argument goes that the EU addresses patterns of interdependence 'through the external projection of internal solutions' (Lavenex 2004: 695). The projection might reflect an embellished or selective model of governance, but it is 'an operational one' (Nicolaïdis and Howse 2002: 768), which does contribute to promoting a European understanding of principles of substantive justice.

Where do we stand, then? Is the EU a 'normative power', promoting universal norms, or is it a 'civilizing power', projecting its own understanding of norms on to the rest of the world? Where do the principles enshrined in European foreign policy (EFP) come from? Are they the product of 'normative globalization' or are they linked to 'the internal dynamics of the Union itself' (Smith 2003: 17)? What is the role of third parties towards which the EU's action is directed? Why do member states, together with the Commission and at times the European Parliament, 'select' certain norms to be exported? To put it more specifically: How can we explain the normative connotation of EFP?

In addressing these questions, this article will make two points. First, it will suggest limiting the category 'normative power Europe' to cases in which the EU's stance has been shown to be intentionally inclusive.[2] The two broad criteria of inclusiveness and reflexivity, which will be explored below, will be used to classify theoretical approaches and arguments about the EU and the promotion of norms. As I am going to argue, cases where EFP lacks one or both of these conditions comprise a distinct category, better captured by the label 'civilizing power Europe'.[3] The second point I will put forward in this article is a sociological institutionalist interpretation of the EU as a 'civilizing power'. I will suggest that EFP-making is often unreflexively eurocentric. My understanding is that much of the EU's action can be characterized as an unreflexive attempt to promote its own model *because institutions tend to export institutional isomorphism as a default option* (DiMaggio and Powell 1991; Finnemore 1996; Jepperson 2002). While EFP can be seen as an intentional action aimed at changing the external environment in the EU's favour, or as an intentional attempt to promote universal norms, it can also be seen as unreflexive behaviour mirroring the deeply engrained belief that Europe's history is a lesson for everybody. Put shortly, EFP is informed, at least partially, by the idea that 'our size fits all'.

I will illustrate the utility of a sociological institutionalist approach by analysing the promotion of regionalism in the Euro-Mediterranean Partnership (EMP). The EU aims at promoting regionalism as the 'normal way' for neighbouring countries to address issues of common interests. Regionalism thus is a policy, given that the EU promotes a sense of regional awareness and community, as well as interstate arrangements and organizations (cf. Fawcett 2004: 433). It is also a norm in the sense that the EU aims at establishing a standard of proper behaviour around which actors' expectations would converge (cf. Jepperson et al. 1996: 54). The EU 'does it regional' towards the four corners of the globe to an unparalleled extent (Smith 2003: 69), as is particularly evident in relations with developing countries (Grilli 1993: 65 ff.). Successive waves of multilateral agreements with the African, Caribbean and Pacific (ACP) countries have enshrined the regionalist norm, which the current Cotonou agreement watered down only in part (Forwood 2001). The contrast between EU and US attitudes towards Latin America is revealing. While the US re-engaged with its southern neighbours in the 1990s by developing a regionalist approach to economic governance, the EU has built on its longer history of involvement to develop a thicker notion of partnership within regionalism (Grugel 2004). Similarly, the EU approach towards Eastern European countries after the end of the Cold War quickly developed a strong regional dimension, shown, for instance, in programmes like PHARE. The main exception to the regionalist rule is the EU's bilateral relations with the US, which remain outside any multilateral framework despite their 'transatlantic' format.

The Mediterranean is a particularly hard case for regionbuilding. The EU has pursued the regionalist project by formalizing a series of institutional links between the EU and its southern partners. But it is difficult to justify the idea of a 'Mediterranean region' on 'objective' grounds. Leaving aside the thorny issue of the northern border of such a region, the southern Mediterranean has been polarized between Arab countries and Israel. Moreover, Israel's unsettled identity has made it an unlikely partner in regionbuilding even if the peace process was placed on a better footing (Del Sarto 2003). Arab regimes have consolidated national sovereignty at the expense of regional co-operation (Barnett 1995). Paradoxically, the Middle East, stretching from Morocco to Iran, is unified by its 'perennially conflictual character' (Buzan and Wæver 2003: 217). As a consequence, there has never been a request to the EU on the part of Mediterranean non-members to participate in or orchestrate a regional environment. On the contrary, Mediterranean countries have tried to play against their neighbours in order to develop tighter relations with the EU, as in the case, for instance, of Morocco and Turkey. Shortly before the EMP was launched, the Mediterranean was defined as 'un mythe, un paradoxe' (Henry 1991). Why then did the EU embark upon regionbuilding?

The article proceeds as follows. I will first address the main arguments that aim at explaining the EU's promotion of norms. I will distinguish them according to how inclusive and how reflexive they describe the EU to be. I will then present a few indicators supporting a sociological institutionalist analysis of regionbuilding in the Mediterranean. I will conclude by returning to the discussion of 'normative power' and 'civilizing power'.

EU, HOW REFLEXIVE AND INCLUSIVE ARE YOU?

Two criteria are particularly useful in distinguishing among the various arguments about the nature of EFP and the normative connotations read into EFP. The first is the inclusiveness of the foreign policy-making process. By this is meant the extent to which EU foreign policy-makers permit a role (in theory or in practice) in EFP-making for external actors affected by EFP. The second is institutional reflexivity, meaning the capacity of EU foreign policy-makers to critically analyse the EU's policy and adapt it according to the effects the policy is expected to have on the targeted area. While inclusiveness is about involving non-members, institutional reflexivity is about anticipating effects on non-members and pre-emptively adapting to them. I will analyse the two criteria, before focusing on the arguments made on their basis.

The issue of inclusiveness is crucial in order to evaluate the normative connotation of EFP. According to Manners (2002) and, from a different perspective, Sjursen (2006), the normative value of Europe's power rests on the universal character of the principles it promotes. More specifically, the EU behaves normatively when it promotes values that *empower* actors affected by EFP. Normative power is, as any form of power, relational, and in order to be normatively justifiable, it must give a voice to people outside of the EU. There is, however, a thin line between 'giving voice to' and 'speaking for'. Given the EU's tendency to be eurocentric, the normative meaning of Europe's action is therefore to be assessed against its capacity to give non-members a role in EFP. This has two aspects. Normatively, it entails scrutinizing the norms promoted by the EU, to assess whether they are hypothetically inclusive and potentially shared by everybody. Empirically, it calls for the analysis of how inclusive the process of EFP-making is, in order to determine its outcome. While it goes beyond the scope of this article to analyse the impact of EFP, the issue of the normative value of EU's action thus entails asking questions such as: To whom do exported norms apply or are intended to apply? Does discussion within the EU take into account the views expressed by actors whose 'normality' is going to be affected (Manners 2002)?

The issue of reflexivity helps to distinguish between teleological and intentional behaviour, on the one hand, and routine-based behaviour, on the other. In the definition by Giddens, institutional reflexivity refers to the 'regularised use of knowledge about circumstances of social life as a constitutive element in its organisation and transformation' (Giddens 1991: 20). Reflexive behaviour thus springs from an ongoing reflection about the action, its context, its effects on such a context and the feedback of those expected effects on the action.[4] Therefore, reflexivity is based on a broad definition of rationality, which not only includes bounded rationality, but also encompasses a logic of justification. In the latter perspective, rationality 'means the ability to adopt a reflective attitude, the ability to redeem presuppositions of knowledge, the possibility to learn, to alter behaviour and to change preferences when faced with better arguments' (Eriksen 1999: 233). Reflexivity is thus expressed by the possibility of redemption through context-specific knowledge and action based thereon. Routine-based behaviour is, on the contrary, founded on practices that have lost their original meaning (if they ever had one) to become ritualized and symbolic. While behaviour can still be seen as intentional, it is 'not willful' (March and Olsen 1989: 160). The fundamental logic of political action is appropriateness, within a concept of identity, and order is created thanks to the capacity of institutions to give meaning and to attribute appropriateness to behaviour, rather than agents setting tasks for institutions (March and Olsen 1989: 38; cf. Müller 2004). For analysing EFP, reflexivity entails asking questions such as: To what extent is the action of the EU based on a 'conscious' effort on the part of the EU foreign policy-makers to critically analyse the expected consequences of norm promotion for all parties involved and adapt EFP accordingly?

The issue of reflexivity is also linked to the concept of power. Here too, the different relationship posited in the case of reflexive or unreflexive behaviour between the agent and individuals on the 'receiving end' establishes a different type of power between the two. If we use the typology suggested by Barnett and Duvall (2005), we see that reflexivity (or lack of it) cuts across several types of power. Reflexive behaviour can thus stem from and support the 'power over' somebody, as well as a more constitutive understanding of power, based on the 'power to' call agents and their interests into being. Unreflexive behaviour belongs more squarely to the constitutive type, by which the agential leeway is significantly constrained by the structure in which it takes place (and which explains the unreflexive behaviour on the part of the agent). Still, such a structure can establish a clear and direct hierarchy between social roles, as in Marxist interpretations of capital and labour, or a more diffuse understanding based on discourse and knowledge. Therefore, the issue of power remains at the centre of the picture in the various theoretical arguments that we are going to examine, something hardly surprising when examining normative *power* and civilizing *power*.

Inclusiveness and reflexivity can be used to classify the arguments that have been put forward to explain the nature of EFP and 'normative power Europe' in particular. If we cast them in a 2 × 2 table, we come up with the following (Table 1). On the left-hand side of the table, rationalist and sociological institutionalist accounts portray the EU's action as eurocentric, leaving little room to outsiders. On the right-hand side, constructivism has tended to depict instead an inclusive picture.[5] Reflexivity, however, divides sharply between rationalist accounts and sociological institutionalism, according to their different emphasis on reflexive and unreflexive processes, respectively. Constructivist arguments have straddled the demarcation line between reflexive and unreflexive behaviour. It should be noted that this table is not a proper typology, as types are not mutually exclusive and positions reflect more the state of the debate than

Table 1 Arguments explaining the nature of European foreign policy

	Eurocentric	Inclusive
Reflexive	Rationalist accounts	
		Constructivism (cosmopolitan; historical institutionalism)
Unreflexive	Sociological institutionalism	

ontological or epistemological actuality. It is useful, though, to summarize the relative emphasis of the various arguments.

According to a rationalist interpretation of norms promotion, the answer is relatively straightforward: the EU intentionally exports norms from which it benefits, with only enough attention to the receiving end for the beneficial effect to occur. This explanation rests on a logic of consequentialism and the expected outcome of rational choices. This is the direction indicated, for instance, by Youngs (2004), in his account of the EU's promotion of democracy and human rights, as well as Hyde-Price (2006) and Haddadi (forthcoming). According to Youngs, the EU knows what it does when it promotes human rights as part of a more general strategy, where the goals are to consolidate regimes and encourage third-party support for the EU. Similarly, Haddadi has suggested that the EU has been promoting democracy in the Maghreb countries as a security strategy for the stabilization of the area. Hyde-Price depicts the EU as a regional hegemon, seeking to shape its external milieu through a mix of hard and soft power. From an economic perspective, the EU's normative action would stress the value of economic gains. Regionbuilding would become the means to deliver benefits such as improvements in terms of trade, access to new markets and the creation of a stronger regional economic bloc. This in turn would have positive, general effects in terms of development and, in the end, security for Europe. Several authors, though criticizing the limits of the EMP, have expressed interpretations of current Euro–Mediterranean relations along these lines (e.g. Hoekman 1999) and a large part of the EU's official rhetoric also mirrors this argument.

In the variegated world of constructivism, issues of inclusiveness and reflexivity receive a more nuanced answer. Constructivism sits on the fence separating reflexive and unreflexive behaviour, as one of its main tenets is that the border between reflexivity and unreflexivity is subordinate to time. What starts off as intentional behaviour tends to be routinized over time, as the early rationale for action is subsumed by the repetitive pattern of routine-based behaviour. This habit-forming pattern follows quite closely the path dependency argument elaborated by historical institutionalism.[6] This hypothesis has been used to explain how and why human rights spread (Risse et al. 1999), as well as the potential of the EMP in Euro–Mediterranean relations (Adler and Crawford, forthcoming). By 'talking the talk' and 'practising the practices', the repetition of social communication leads to change in actors' reciprocal disposition. Authoritarian regimes, under the pressure of transnational networks, put up a semblance of care for human rights, but over time their conformative discourse increasingly constrains their actions and then moulds their way of thinking so that despite their original intentions they fall into a pattern defined by human rights principles. Therefore, standardization of practices, regardless of their inclusiveness, is justified by the attempt to change 'nasty' regimes, such as those existing in the majority of Mediterranean non-members.

Moreover, from this perspective, 'normative power Europe' is much more based on inclusiveness than is evident in rationalist or sociological explanations, as inclusiveness is defined as a condition of normative power. This perspective puts the emphasis on the universal character of the norms promoted by the EU. According to Manners (2002), the key principles that constitute the normative core of 'normative power Europe' are democracy, rule of law, social justice and human rights. They are specific norms because they have a historical context. At the same time, they are universal because 'the EU, in its external action, refer[s] to reasons that can be expected to gain approval in a free and open debate in which all those affected are heard' (Sjursen 2006: 243). The normative part of this argument thus suggests that inclusiveness is guaranteed if the norms at stake have universal character, i.e. by the fact that if individuals were to have the possibility to speak out, they would agree. Normative power is, therefore, defined on the basis of the universality of values, which in turn guarantees the (indirect) protagonism of third parties.

'Indirect protagonism', however, does not travel well beyond an uncontested, narrow set of universal principles, and then we are stuck with the practical, rather than normative, question of how to involve third parties. The issue is complicated by the absence of democracy at the international level (Eriksen 2006) as well as at the domestic level. How then can EFP be inclusive in addressing non-democratic states in a still anarchical international environment? The empirical way out of this apparent stalemate, according to the cosmopolitan perspective, can be found in the attitude of the EU. As long as the EU aims for a strengthening of the international legal system, its behaviour can be labelled as normative. Such an attitude seems to mark the distinction between the action of 'normative power Europe', on the one hand, and historical empires and other international actors, on the other. As internationally binding cosmopolitan citizenship would give international subject status to external actors, formalization of international law is a guarantee of the inclusiveness of EFP.

Sociological institutionalism starts from the premise that institutional isomorphism tends to be the rule, rather than the exception (DiMaggio and Powell 1991).[7] Unreflexive transfer of knowledge and of patterned practices is 'normal', as exemplified by the number of similarities among institutions across the world. Culture, and its thick layer of institutionalized norms, routines and practices, tends to define 'what has meaning and what actions are possible' (Zucker 1983: 2). Organizations are thus embedded in a broader context of institutionalized meaning, and that context infuses them with a form and a mission, largely irrespective of the specific function they are meant to perform.

In this perspective, norms are exported not because they are efficient or have universal value, but because they are legitimated by the spread of Western culture and as such they are (unreflexively) embraced by third parties. Norms, in a sociological perspective, are equal to scripts, entailing constitutive and regulative effects (cf. Jepperson et al. 1996: 54). Their diffusion is linked to inter-organizational influence, the persuasiveness of cultural frames and to a logic of appropriateness. Sets of norms can be transferred from one organizational practice to another because 'institutionalized elements can "infect" other elements in a contagion of legitimacy' (Zucker 1987: 446). The process can flow from the state level to the international level, but also from the international level to the state (Klotz 1995; Finnemore and Sikkink 1998). In the case of EFP, the EU can be said to apply to non-member states the same norms it applies to members on the basis of an unspecified general legitimacy that it commands as the EU, rather than because of any defined rationale attached to these norms, or the specific context in which they are applied. According to sociological institutionalism, the direction of norms diffusion tends to show the spread and the increasing dominance of a Western cultural model (Jepperson 2002: 239–45). The claim of Western culture to universalism and rationality contributes to its expansive potential (Finnemore 1996: 331). Differently from the rationalist perspective, the hegemonic reach of Western institutions is a manifestation not of strategic or compulsory power, but rather of power on the border between structural power, as in direct hegemonic power, and productive power, aiming to produce subjects through knowledge, social discourse and social relations (Barnett and Duvall 2005).

The sociological argument thus suggests that 'normative power Europe' exports its own norms unreflexively, with a single model promoted to all its partners regardless of their context. The account by Börzel and Risse (2004) of EU policies for the promotion of human rights, democracy and rule of law goes in this direction. The EU is described as projecting 'its own identity of a democratic polity into its relations with third countries'. Börzel and Risse (2004: 26, 28) remark on the similarity of the various policies, to the point that the EU seems to follow 'one single cultural script' and exhibits a 'one size fits all' attitude. Following the tenets of sociological institutionalism, I suggest refining this interpretation, by making the link between domestic and international norms more explicit and labelling the attitude of European foreign policymakers as '*our* size fits all'. In the Mediterranean case, an 'our size fits all' argument explains norm promotion not by the expected benefits in terms of economics and/or security for the EU, nor by the intrinsic value of regionalism as a universal norm but by the EU's specific and internal experience as a regional organization, parlayed as a required form of behaviour for external actors.

To summarize, therefore, there are three different arguments about the normative connotation of EFP. First, the rationalist approach suggests that the EU promotes its norms because it expects to benefit from their adoption, and as such EU behaviour is both reflexive and eurocentric. Second, according to the constructivist perspective, the EU promotes norms of universal value, thus by definition inclusive, and the process by which it does so starts reflexively but drifts into unreflexivity through path dependency. Third, a hypothesis based on sociological institutionalism argues that the EU promotes its own norms because institutions promote institutional isomorphism, and this is particularly the case from the West towards the rest of the world. Therefore, there is only a small recognized possibility that Europe behaves both inclusively and reflexively – and only in that case, which falls in the upper right-hand corner of Table 1, is it appropriate in my view to characterize the EU as 'normative power Europe'.

As this brief review of the literature has shown, however, there is a vast variety of cases in which EFP, while normatively connotated, is neither reflexive nor inclusive and is better captured as an instance of 'civilizing power'. Sociological institutionalism in fact argues that this is often the case. What I am going to focus on next is how this argument can be linked to empirical evidence.

DOWNLOADING A MEDITERRANEAN REGIONAL MODEL

What I will present here is a series of indicators that go in the direction of supporting a sociological institutionalist interpretation of the region-building policy of the EU towards the Mediterranean, as enshrined in the EMP. A quick glance at indicators for rationalist and constructivist hypotheses reveals that these two approaches do leave a number of issues pending. The case for a rationalist argument, from an economic perspective, looks *prima facie* very strong. Since the launching of the EMP, there has been a flurry of free trade agreements signed not only between Mediterranean non-members and the EU, but also among Mediterranean countries (Handoussa and Reiffers 2001). The trend, however, has been more symbolic than substantial. While bilateral agreements between the EU and single Mediterranean countries have a substantial transformative potential, South–South agreements, which would cement the regional Mediterranean dimension, are riddled with exceptions and rarely implemented (Radwan and Reiffers 2005). In the end, the replication of free trade agreements among Mediterranean non-members seems to symbolically mimic the institutionalized pattern of relations with the EU, a point going in the direction of sociological institutionalism more than of a rationalist explanation.

Constructivist explanations also leave the door open to sociological institutionalism, as they tend to be more convincing on the unreflexive side, rather than on inclusive aspects. Path dependency is certainly a strong factor in contemporary Euro–Mediterranean relations. The process by which the EU has conceptualized its southern neighbours as a region unfolded at the beginning of the 1970s (Bicchi, forthcoming) and despite the southern enlargement, the end of the Cold War and lack of visible progress, the regional dimension has remained a characteristic of EFP towards the Mediterranean up to now. The case for the universal value of regionalism is still to be made, though. In spite of noble intentions of bringing peace and prosperity to the area, the EU has tended to justify its region-building efforts mainly by referring to its own history.[8] Moreover, it rates badly in terms of inclusion of third parties in the definition of regionalism for the Mediterranean. The EU is in fact remarkable for its incapacity to empower citizens of Mediterranean countries and to engage with the very civil society that it allegedly wishes to encourage.[9] Therefore, constructivist explanations are so far stronger on the issue of unreflexivity, which they share with sociological institutionalism, than on inclusiveness.

There is thus reason to look at a sociological institutionalist interpretation of the EU's action as a promoter of regionalism in the Mediterranean. Given the emphasis placed on isomorphism between institutions, this perspective high-lights how practices, norms and organizational arrangements travel from a Western centre to the periphery with little adaptation. To check the utility of this approach, I will analyse two main indicators of institutional isomorphism between the EU and the EMP, namely the similarities between their insti-tutional frameworks and between their agendas. I will complement them by tracing how a specific issue, Justice and Home Affairs, has migrated from the EU agenda to the EMP.

The multilateral institutional framework is at the heart of the EMP.[10] It dis-plays a remarkable predictability for people familiar with the EU institutional format. Ministers of Foreign Affairs of all the twenty-seven participant countries meet in the so-called Euro-Mediterranean conferences, including the Palestinian Authority in representation of the future state of Palestine, and the European Commission. Originally expected to take place once every two years, alternately in a European and in a non-European venue, Euro-Mediterranean conferences are now organized in the EU territory every semester. Among the reasons for this accelerated tempo is the agency behind these conferences, which lies predomi-nantly with EU presidencies. At the beginning of a presidency semester, the habit has developed for that country to state its programme for the EMP and to organize a 'mid-term' meeting. Other ministerial meetings have also been organized, with a remarkable similarity between the topics they address and the topics around which sectorial EU Councils are organized (see below). Despite attempts, there is no equivalent of the European Council in the EMP, because of the conditions of Arab–Israeli relations.[11] This, however, is the only type of meeting that tensions in the Middle East have made impossible. In fact, bringing all Mediterranean countries around the same table and having them talk business despite unresolved grievances is probably one of the main successes of the EU in its attempt to create a region in the Mediterranean.[12]

Below the ministerial level, similarities develop further. The Euro-Mediterranean Committee, made up of one ambassador from each country, has the task of arranging and deciding EMP activities between Euro-Mediterranean conferences. It meets once a month. Originally, this committee was, according to the Work Programme annexed to the Barcelona Conference, to consist only of the EU troika, flanked by the Commission and the Council Secretariat, and one representative from each Mediterranean partner country. What has prevailed instead is the practice of admitting 'as observers' all EU member states, de facto recreating a Euro-Mediterranean conference at a lower hierarchical level, as well as mirroring the composition of the EU's Committee of Permanent Representatives (COREPER). A new (i.e. not originally conceived in Barcelona) layer in the multilateral structure extends the parallel with the EU Council structure further. A 'gap' was perceived to exist between the Euro-Mediterranean conferences and the Euro-Mediterranean Committee, in the sense of limited opportunities for high-level dialogue not involving the Minis-ters of Foreign Affairs. Accordingly, in 2002 it was decided to hold ad hoc meet-ings among General Directors of Ministries of Foreign Affairs with the participation of the Commission. The pattern resembles the composition of the Political Committee, under European Political Cooperation and the pre-military times of the Common Foreign and Security Policy. The institutional practice of the EMP has also seen the creation of a broad set of working groups and meetings of senior officials, which contribute to the work of the EMP. Again, these gatherings mirror the ones within the EU Council structure at lower levels.[13]

This could be a case of 'rational' institutional design, if it was not for two reasons that point instead in the direction of institutional isomorphism. The first is the shift in the institutional setting from the original conception agreed in Barcelona to the current framework: all the changes point to a closer resemblance to the EU model. The pace, the venue and the participants in the meetings mirror now more than in 1995 the EU institutional structure. Second, while it could be argued that meetings among representatives of participant countries are hardly specific to the EU, as only the EU displays such a rich variety of venues at all levels of the hierarchy. There is thus room to argue that the EU has exported its own institutional model to the EMP.

What is the agenda fostered by this array of multilateral institutions? If we look at the frequency of meetings at the ministerial level (meetings devoted to general affairs as well as sectorial meetings), in comparison to EU Council meetings, the parallel develops further. Since the launching of the EMP in late 1995, ministers within the EU have met much more frequently than ministers within the EMP, the total being over 700 and thirty-six meetings respectively.[14] This raises several methodological questions about comparing the two sets. Moreover, the small number of Euro-Mediterranean sectorial conferences represents another limitation to any generalization. However, if we use the comparison for heuristic reasons only and we express these numbers as a percentage of the total, as in Figure 1, an intriguing pattern emerges. There is a strong similarity in the attention devoted to trade and economic affairs, infrastructure, culture, and social and environmental issues. In other words, the agenda of the EMP is largely similar to the agenda of the EU, which is based on economic matters but with a social flavour.

The issues that stand out because of their different importance in the EU and in the EMP are foreign affairs, agriculture and fisheries, and justice and home affairs.[15] The first two could also be explained by a rationalist account. The predominance of meetings devoted to foreign affairs in the EMP framework is an indicator that the core of the EMP remains grounded in international co-operation, more so than in the EU. Agriculture is a topic that the Mediterranean partners would be more than happy to discuss with European countries, but there is a staunch resistance on the part of the latter. Discussions are taking place, but the pace is determined by the reform of the Common Agricultural Policy. As reforms speed up, it is likely that more ministerial meetings will be organized.

The story of justice and home affairs is a micro case that shows how the agenda can travel from the EU to the EMP, along the lines of sociological

| Euro-Med Conferences | Council of the European Union |

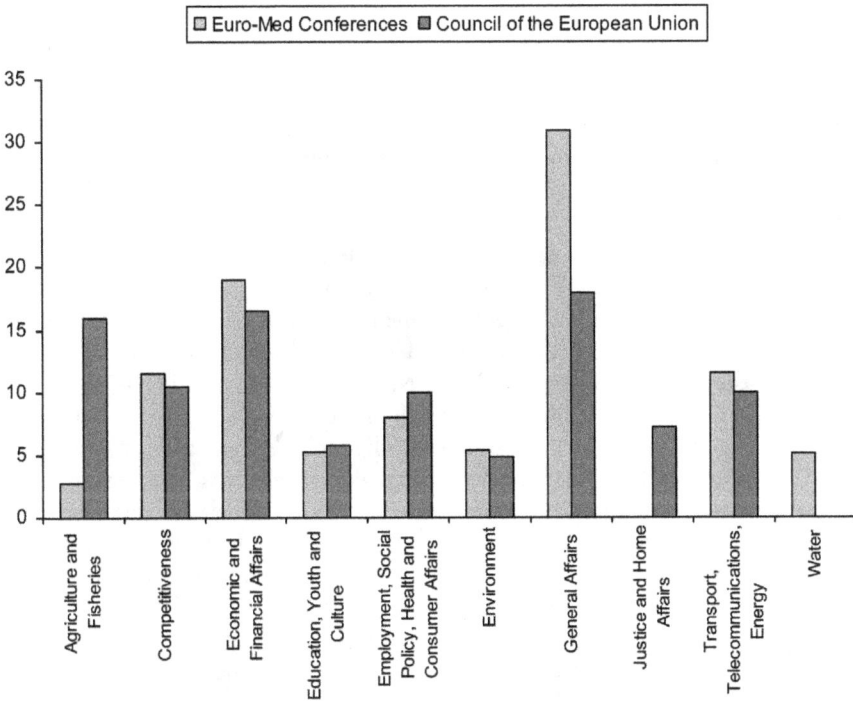

Figure 1 Ministerial meetings, percentage of the total, EMP and EU, 1996–2005
Source: For Euro-Med Conferences: Euro-Med Monthly Calendar, European Commission. For Council of the EU meetings: Press Reports, Council of the EU.

institutionalism. At the time of the Barcelona Conference, in 1995, the reluctance to address this type of topic at a multilateral level was mutual. Resistance, however, has shrunk in proportion to the momentum acquired by the Justice and Home Affairs chapter within the EU. Rather than by its formalization within the Maastricht Treaty, the issue of co-operation in justice and home affairs within the EU was put at the top of the EU agenda in October 1999, at the Tampere European Council. Since then, not only has the EU agenda increasingly allowed room for it, but there has been a clear, if still partial, transfer to the EMP agenda, as is evident from the below.

The first relevant mention of a development in this direction came in the Common Strategy for the Mediterranean, in June 2000. While largely reflecting the Barcelona Declaration, the Strategy also 'caught up' with areas in which the EU had developed common competences not enshrined in the Barcelona document. It thus mentioned Justice and Home Affairs, listing as specific initiatives the promotion of transparency and correspondence of legal systems, the fight against organized crime and drug trafficking, migration and the fight against terrorism. Shortly afterwards, in November 2000, at the Marseilles Conference, the twenty-seven EMP participants officially recommended the concerted preparation of a regional programme in the field of justice and home affairs. This input led to the creation of a group of Senior Officials on Justice and Home Affairs, which began its meetings in 2001. The programme they elaborated was then approved at the Euro-Med Conference in Valencia in April 2002, under the complicated name of 'regional cooperation programme in the field of Justice, in combating drugs, organised crime and terrorism as well as co-operation in the treatment of issues relating to the social integration of migrants, migration and movements of persons'.[16] While reference to 'home affairs' has been skipped to accommodate the sensitivities of Mediterranean partners, the content of the rapidly evolving programme closely mirrors the EU agenda.

Whereas this case could be interpreted as an example of strategic behaviour, in which the EU progressively involves Mediterranean countries in managing migration and terrorism, its significance is more complex. The EU's interest in recruiting its southern neighbours as allies in the fight against migration and terrorism predates the EMP and actually was among the reasons that prompted its formulation.[17] After 1995, the subject was dealt with primarily in bilateral relations, both at the national level and between the EU and single Mediterranean countries (Lavenex 2004: 690). The interesting shift is thus represented by the upgrading of the issue to the multilateral level, which has occurred in parallel with the development of the EU agenda and of its institutional capacities, as marked by the Tampere Council and expected by sociological institutionalism.

The similarities in the institutional settings of the EU and of the EMP, as well as in the content of their agendas, support the sociological institutionalist perspective that highlights a close, unreflexive link from the EU to the EMP and a eurocentric transfer of norms from the EU to the Mediterranean. This brief sketch of regionalism is obviously not sufficient to close the debate. But my aim here is to show how empirical research could be done, as well as to point up the utility of such an endeavour.

CONCLUSIONS

In this article, I have made three points. First, I have followed the advice of, among others, Diez (2005) and Sjursen (2006) to specify the argument about 'normative power Europe'. I have suggested that the normative connotation of EFP varies according to the degree of inclusiveness and reflexivity that is granted to it. Whenever we encounter a case of EFP which is both inclusive (in theory or in practice) and reflexive, the category 'normative power Europe' is well justified, along the lines of that demonstrated by Sjursen (2006). The category thus depicts the upper right-hand corner of Table 1. There are several cases, however, which fall outside this scope, and they should be distinguished in order to clarify the different types of EU action. I have suggested bringing these cases under the category of 'civilizing power Europe', which expresses the fact that the EU's action is either eurocentric, or unreflexively inclusive, or both. While the label 'normative power Europe' is probably too enticing for the future debate on EFP to resist a widespread usage of the term, it should be carefully defined, especially with regard to what it is not, in order to capture the connotation of EFP and the type of power relationship it establishes by doing so.

The second point I have made is that there are several ways to analyse the EU's capacity to spread norms, and a sociological institutionalist approach offers an original contribution in this direction. While rationalist accounts suggest that the EU knows what it does, and is inclusive only in as much as it suits its goals, constructivist analyses tend to vary in emphasis. Historical institutionalists focus on the way the frontier between reflexive and unreflexive is watered down by time, whereas cosmopolitan scholars argue that third parties are central protagonists in the *a priori* EU approach to legalization of norms. The originality of sociological institutionalism consists of its emphasis on unreflexive behaviour and institutional isomorphism, by which the EU promotes its own highly successful model of Western integration. It highlights cases of 'our size fits all' attitudes. The third point of this article has shown the utility of this approach by analysing how regionalism is promoted in Euro–Mediterranean relations. It has highlighted evidence of unreflexive behaviour, not only in the form of path dependency, but also and especially in similarities between the EU and the EMP institutional frameworks and working agendas.

Does evidence of unreflexive behaviour undermine the argument in favour of 'normative power Europe'? There is a flavour to 'normative power Europe' by which the EU is 'a force for good', standing on a higher moral ground than other international actors, not only because of its history and successes (as a 'laboratory', to use Nicolaïdis and Howse's (2002: 771) expression), but also because of the foreign policy it conducts.[18] Sociological institutionalism offers a different interpretation of the EU's stance in foreign policy, more rooted in power and in a dominant cultural paradigm. It underlines the 'dark side' of the EU's action in international politics (although the 'darkness' refers more to absence of analysis in scholarly literature than to the 'Darth Vader' nature of the EU). While starting from the same premises of 'normative power Europe', namely that the EU projects its internal characteristics into its foreign policy, sociological institutionalism interprets this projection not as an intrinsically progressive endeavour, but rather as a conservative attitude. Accordingly, the EU does not promote (neutral) norms, but promotes 'Europe' (in the form of European norms). How far to bring this argument and how to turn it into a political evaluation is a matter of empirical evidence and personal judgement. To me, it reads principally as a call for closer scrutiny of what 'normative power Europe' actually does.

The cosmopolitan approach has a good point, but its utility cannot be determined *a priori* given the limitations of democracy at the domestic and international level. The cosmopolitan interpretation of 'normative power Europe' does offer a way out of the cultural and power conundrum of distinguishing among norms, as it equates universally recognized norms with 'good' norms, a move which can be easily agreed upon. It also avoids scrutiny of who represents whom, a question which is particularly difficult in cases of authoritarian regimes. But by doing so, it also limits the analysis to a very small and specific set of universal norms. How are we to interpret the normative action of the EU beyond these limits? Regionalism, for one, represents a norm that is promoted by the EU but is, almost by definition, not universal.

The main argument of this article is thus that while the normative connotation of the EU's action embraces a set of universal values that distinguishes 'normative power Europe' from other international actors, EFP also encompasses a broader set of principles requiring closer examination in order to evaluate the nature of the EU in international affairs. Two questions need to be tackled. The first refers to the theoretical and normative underpinnings of EFP, which constitute the yardsticks against which to evaluate the EU's action. The second is related to the empirical dimension of EFP, in order to locate the scope of 'normative power Europe' and, at the same time, to identify the magnitude and scope of the EU's 'civilizing power'. The good moment for analysts of EFP has just begun.

Biographical note: Federica Bicchi is Lecturer in the Department of International Relations, London School of Economics and Political Science, UK.

Address for correspondence: Federica Bicchi, Department of International Relations, London School of Economics and Political Science, Houghton Street, London WC2A 2AE, UK. Tel: +44 20 7955 7987. email: f.c.bicchi@lse.ac.uk

NOTES

1 I would like to thank for their helpful comments Mathias Koenig-Archibugi, Mary Martin, Michelle Pace, Helene Sjursen, an anonymous referee and all the participants at the CIDEL workshop in Oslo in October 2004.
2 On this, see also Sjursen (2006) and Diez (2005).
3 The 'civilizing' attribute has an ambiguous meaning, partly negative (as in France's 'civilizing mission'), partly positive (as in 'civilizing influence'). The meaning depends on the interpretation of 'power', on which more below.
4 Giddens (2001) further distinguishes between different types of reflexivity. On this, see Mitzen (2006).
5 However, there is no necessity for constructivism to focus on inclusive behaviour, as it is by definition neutral about the content of norms.
6 Path dependency has also been analysed by rational institutionalism, which links it to the sunken costs of changing institutionalized agreements. This perspective falls into the rationalist type.
7 Key texts focusing on sociological institutionalism include March and Olsen (1989); DiMaggio and Powell (1991); Scott and Meyer (1994). For a review, see Zucker (1987); Jepperson (2002); Müller (2004).
8 See, for instance, European Commission, 'Communication on European Community support for regional economic integration efforts among developing countries', COM (95) 219 final, Brussels, 16 June 1995.
9 For an analysis of this point in relation to human rights, see Stetter (2003).

10 On the institutional framework and its multilateral dimension, see Edwards and Philippart (1997).
11 The difficulties connected with the organization of such an event were highlighted by the fiasco of the Barcelona summit in November 2005. Intended to mark the ten years of the EMP, the summit was deserted by most Arab heads of state.
12 It is worth mentioning that Syria and Lebanon sent a low-profile delegation to ministerial meetings at the height of the second Intifada.
13 Other institutions that should be mentioned (and that continue the parallel with the EU) include the co-operation between national parliaments and the European Parliament and the periodic meetings of the Civil Forum.
14 I have included Euro-Mediterranean Conferences held between January 1996 and June 2005, and EU Council meetings held between January 1996 and May 2005. The exact number of EU Council meetings for this period is 720. See Press Releases, EU Council sessions on General Affairs and External Relations. In the EU framework, General Affairs Council meetings and External Relations Council meetings have been put in the same category of 'General Affairs'. Moreover, meetings of the EU Council lasting two days have been counted as one.
15 There is also no equivalent for meetings devoted to water, although coal would represent a good, if early, term of comparison.
16 Presidency Conclusions, Valencia, 23 April 2002.
17 See, for instance, an early Commission Communication 'From the Single Act to Maastricht and Beyond', COM(1992)2000: 15.
18 On this issue, see the critique by Jørgensen and Laatikainen (2004).

REFERENCES

Adler, E. and Crawford, B. (forthcoming) 'Normative power: the European practice of region building and the case of the Euro–Mediterranean Partnership', in E. Adler, F. Bicchi, B. Crawford and R. Del Sarto (eds), *The Convergence of Civilizations. Constructing the Mediterranean Region*, Toronto: University of Toronto Press.
Barnett, M. (1995) 'Sovereignty, nationalism and regional order in the Arab states system', *International Organization* 49(3): 479–510.
Barnett, M. and Duvall, R. (2005) 'Power in global governance', in M. Barnett and R. Duvall (eds), *Power in Global Governance*, Cambridge: Cambridge University Press, pp. 1–32.
Bicchi, F. (forthcoming) *European Foreign Policy Making towards the Mediterranean*, New York: Palgrave.
Börzel, T.A. and Risse, T. (2004) 'One size fits all! EU policies for the promotion of human rights, democracy and the rule of law'. Paper presented at the Workshop on Democracy Promotion, 4–5 October, Stanford University.
Bretherton, C. and Vogler, J. (1999) *The European Union as a Global Actor*, London: Routledge.
Buzan, B. and Wæver, O. (2003) *Regions and Powers. The Structure of International Security*, Cambridge: Cambridge University Press.
Del Sarto, R. (2003) 'Israel's contested identity and the Mediterranean', *Mediterranean Politics* 8(1): 113–26.
Diez, T. (2005) 'Constructing the self and changing others: reconsidering "normative power Europe"', *Millennium* 33(3): 613–36.
DiMaggio, P.J. and Powell, W.W. (1991) 'The iron cage revisited: institutional isomorphism and collective rationality', in W.W. Powell and P.J. DiMaggio (eds), *The New Institutionalism in Organizational Analysis*, Chicago: University of Chicago Press, pp. 63–82.

Edwards, G. and Philippart, E. (1997) 'The Euro–Mediterranean Partnership: fragmentation and reconstruction', *European Foreign Affairs Review* 2(4): 465–89.

Eriksen, E.O. (1999) 'Towards a logic of justification?', in M. Egeberg and P. Lægreid (eds), *Organizing Political Institutions*, Oslo: Scandinavian University Press, pp. 215–44.

Eriksen, E.O. (2006) 'The EU – a cosmopolitan polity?', *Journal of European Public Policy* 13(2): 252–69.

Fawcett, L. (2004) 'Exploring regional domains: a comparative history of regionalism', *International Affairs* 80(3): 429–46.

Finnemore, M. (1996) 'Norms, culture, and world politics: insights from sociology's institutionalism', *International Organization* 50(2): 325–47.

Finnemore, M. and Sikkink, K. (1998) 'International norm dynamics and political change', *International Organization* 52(4): 887–917.

Forwood, G. (2001) 'The road to Cotonou: negotiating a successor to Lomé', *Journal of Common Market Studies* 39(3): 423–42.

Giddens, A. (1991) *Modernity and Self-Identity*, Cambridge: Polity Press.

Grilli, E. (1993) *The European Community and the Developing Countries*, Cambridge: Cambridge University Press.

Grugel, J.B. (2004) 'New regionalism and modes of governance – comparing US and EU strategies in Latin America', *European Journal of International Relations* 10(4): 603–26.

Haddadi, S. (forthcoming) 'Political securitization and democratization in the Maghreb: ambiguous discourses and fine-tuning practices for a security partnership', in E. Adler, F. Bicchi, B. Crawford and R. Del Sarto (eds), *The Convergence of Civilizations: Constructing a Mediterranean Region*, Toronto: University of Toronto Press.

Handoussa, H. and Reiffers, J.-L. (2001) 'The FEMISE Report on the Evolution of the Structure of Trade and Investments between the European Union and its Mediterranean Partners', FEMISE Network.

Henry, J.-R. (1991) 'La France et le mythe méditerranéen', in H. el Malki (ed.), *La Méditerranée en question. Conflits et interdépendances*, Casablanca/Paris: Fondation du Roi Abdul-Aziz/Editions du CNRS, pp. 191–9.

Hoekman, B. (1999) 'Free trade agreements in the Mediterranean: a regional path towards liberalisation?', in G. Joffé (ed.), *Perspectives on Development. The Euro–Mediterranean Partnership*, London: Frank Cass, pp. 89–104.

Hyde-Price, A. (2006) '"Normative" power Europe: a realist critique', *Journal of European Public Policy* 13(2): 217–34.

Jepperson, R.J. (2002) 'The development and application of sociological neoinstitutionalism', in J. Berger and M. Zelditch (eds), *New Directions in Contemporary Sociological Theory*, Lanham, MD: Rowman & Littlefield, pp. 229–66.

Jepperson, R.J., Wendt, A. and Katzenstein, P.J. (1996) 'Norms, identity, and culture in national security', in P.J. Katzenstein (ed.), *The Culture of National Security. Norms and Identity in World Politics*, New York: Columbia University Press, pp. 33–75.

Jørgensen, K.E. and Laatikainen, K.V. (2004) 'The EU and the UN: multilateralism in a new key?'. Paper presented at the Second Pan-European Conference on EU Politics, Bologna, 24–26 June.

Klotz, A. (1995) *Norms in International Relations. The Struggle against Apartheid*, Ithaca, NY: Cornell University Press.

Knodt, M. and Princen, S. (eds) (2003) *Understanding the European Union's External Relations*, London: Routledge.

Lavenex, S. (2004) 'EU external governance in "wider Europe"', *Journal of European Public Policy* 11(4): 680–700.

Manners, I. (2002) 'Normative power Europe: a contradiction in terms?', *Journal of Common Market Studies* 40(2): 235–58.

March, J.G. and Olsen, J.P. (1989) *Rediscovering Institutions. The Organizational Basis of Politics*, London/New York: Macmillan/Free Press.

Mitzen, J. (2006) 'Anchoring Europe's civilizing identity: habits, capabilities and ontological security', *Journal of European Public Policy* 13(2): 270–85.

Müller, H. (2004) 'Arguing, bargaining, and all that: communicative action', *European Journal of International Relations* 10(3): 395–435.

Nicolaïdis, K. and Howse, R. (2002) '"This is my EUtopia . . .": narrative as power', *Journal of Common Market Studies* 40(4): 767–92.

Radwan, S. and Reiffers, J.-L. (eds) (2005) 'The Euro–Mediterranean Partnership, 10 years after Barcelona: achievements and perspectives', FEMISE Network.

Risse, T., Ropp, S.C. and Sikkink, K. (eds) (1999) *The Power of Human Rights. International Norms and Domestic Change*, Cambridge: Cambridge University Press.

Scott, R.W. and Meyer, J.W. (1994) *Institutional Environments and Organizations: Structural Complexity and Individualism*, London: Sage.

Sjursen, H. (2006) 'The EU as a "normative" power: how can this be?', *Journal of European Public Policy* 13(2): 235–51.

Smith, K.E. (2003) *European Union Foreign Policy in a Changing World*, Cambridge: Polity Press.

Stetter, S. (2003) 'Democratization without democracy? The assistance of the European Union for democratization processes in Palestine', in A. Jünemann (ed.), *Europe–Mediterranean Relations After September 11*, London: Frank Cass, pp. 153–73.

Youngs, R. (2001) *The European Union and the Promotion of Democracy*, Oxford: Oxford University Press.

Youngs, R. (2004) 'Normative dynamics and strategic interests in the EU's external identity', *Journal of Common Market Studies* 42(2): 415–35.

Zucker, L.G. (1983) 'Organizations as institutions', *Research in the Sociology of Organizations* 2(1): 1–47.

Zucker, L.G. (1987) 'Institutional theories of organization', *Annual Review of Sociology* 13(1): 443–64.

Normative by nature? The role of coherence in justifying the EU's external human rights policy

Marika Lerch and Guido Schwellnus[1]

INTRODUCTION

> The European Union is well placed to promote democracy and human rights ... Uniquely amongst international actors, all fifteen member states of the Union are democracies espousing the same Treaty-based principles in their internal and external policies. This gives the EU substantial political and moral weight.
>
> (European Commission 2001a: 3)

The above quotation from a Commission communication regarding the European Union's (EU's) role in promoting human rights and democratization in third countries strongly invokes the self-image of the EU as a normative force on the international scene. Since the 1990s, the EU has undergone a dynamic development both in terms of its internal constitutionalization and in its external promotion of human rights. This has also led to a renewed academic interest in the idea that the EU represents a 'normative power' (Manners 2002) on the international arena. The normative power concept neatly captures a prominent identity discourse at the EU level, but as an analytic concept it nonetheless suffers from a lack of clarity.

In its boldest formulation normative power refers to the *nature* of the EU, which supposedly 'predisposes it to act in a normative way' (Manners 2002: 252), and depends not on 'what it does or it says, but what it is' (Manners 2002: 252). Yet when looking at the nature of the EU empirically, one may well question whether the EU is really better equipped to act in a normative way than other polities. Although the constitutionalization of the EU may be an unprecedented process lifting its normative basis well beyond that of other international organizations, the Union's democratic and human rights credentials are in no way supreme when compared to democratic nation states. Certain specific characteristics of the EU as a 'hybrid polity' (Manners 2002: 240) even undermine its normative power, especially the parallel existence of supranational external relations, intergovernmental Common Foreign and Security Policy (CFSP), and independent national foreign policies of member states. Hence, one of the most important problems the EU's external policy faces in normative terms is coherence, a fact that has been recognized both by academic commentators (Alston and Weiler 1999) and by EU institutions, calling for a 'coherent and consistent EU approach' towards promoting human rights in non-member states (European Commission 2001a: 5).

While studies in the field of EU external relations have examined consistency and coherence either conceptually with regard to its basis in the Treaties (e.g. Duke 1999; Nuttall 2001) or empirically at the level of policy action (e.g. Szymanski and Smith 2005), we use it as a theoretical concept and focus on the level of argumentative justification accompanying the EU's human rights policy. We analyse the arguments provided by EU actors and documents in support of externally promoted policies, instead of simply assuming the Union to be a 'force for good' by nature. The argument proceeds in three steps: in the theoretical framework, we propose combining insights from argumentation theory and the classification of different types of arguments, namely utility- , value- and rights-based arguments, with the concept of coherence in order to analyse complex justifications of the EU's external human rights policy and to assess the normative power of the EU. The empirical case studies apply this framework to two fields in which the EU has been particularly proactive: the abolition of the death penalty and minority protection, respectively. The conclusion assesses the implications of our results for the argument that the EU is a normative power in the international realm.

THEORETICAL FRAMEWORK: THE STUDY OF ARGUMENTATION PROCESSES IN INTERNATIONAL RELATIONS THEORY

Among the International Relations (IR) scholars studying argumentative processes, three different approaches can be distinguished. As a first strand, constructivists have sought to utilize Habermas's 'Theory of Communicative Action' (Habermas 1984). A major aim for scholars working from this angle is to identify the role and conditions of sincere arguing processes in IR, and to trace the consequences for processes of persuasion, socialization and normative change (Risse 2000). Arguing in this perspective is not only a distinct mode of interaction (as opposed to bargaining), but is also based on a specific logic of action, in which actors are oriented towards reaching a reasoned consensus and prepared to be persuaded by the better argument.

Against this view, rationalists have developed the concept of 'rhetorical action', which can be defined as the 'instrumental use of arguments to persuade others of one's selfish claims' (Schimmelfennig 2000: 129), as an alternative theoretical approach to study argumentation processes. While supporting the constructivist claim that norms and justifications are not merely post-hoc rationalizations or epiphenomena to material factors, the rhetorical action approach retains a consequentialist logic of action, which means that actors engaged in arguing are not necessarily genuine and also do not internalize norms, even when they have to admit argumentative defeat.

It follows that both approaches, despite their antagonistic positions, share a commitment to establish the action-theoretical foundations of argumentative behaviour. A third perspective concentrates more on the structure, content and types of arguments at the intersubjective level than on the underlying motives and action-theoretical foundations at the subjective level (Wæver 2003: 199).

The use of utility- , value- and rights-based arguments in complex argumentations

Following the third strand of theory outlined above, we take an argumentation-theoretical (instead of action-theoretical) approach to assessing the EU's justification of its external human rights policies. To do so, we apply the distinction into three different types of arguments: utility- , value- and rights-based arguments (Habermas 1993; Sjursen 2002). Firstly, arguments can refer to the expected utility of an action in relation to a given purpose. Within this type of argument, a policy decision is presented as legitimate on the basis of its efficiency in reaching a given goal, or by referring to interests such as economic gains or increased security and stability. Secondly, the EU may refer to the particular values defining the European community, or values shared between the EU and other international agents. A policy decision is considered legitimate because it is appropriate in the given cultural context and in relation to the identity of the members of a community. In this case, external EU policies would be presented as fundamentally 'European' and backed with reference either to the internal *acquis* of the Union or other 'European standards', e.g. Council of Europe norms. In some cases other identities – e.g. the 'Western community of values' – can be invoked to support the claim. The precondition for the success of value-based arguments is that the addressee identifies with the proposed values, i.e. either considers herself as belonging or aspires to belong to the invoked community. Thirdly, a policy can be justified with reference to universal rights, i.e. overarching principles of justice, which are deemed to be universally valid and could be accepted by all parties concerned. References to the universality of human rights and to global UN standards are indicative of this type of argument (Sjursen 2002: 494–5).

The aim of our analysis is not to establish a dominant type of justification, which then serves as an indicator for the agents' reasons or motives for taking certain decisions. Linking arguments directly to actor motivations is problematic, because the fact that an actor predominantly or even exclusively justifies her actions with one type of argument does not necessarily indicate that this is the motive behind her action: a rhetorically rational actor might use value- or rights-based arguments for purely instrumental reasons. Conversely, an actor with strong normative reasons for promoting a policy (e.g. an environmentalist) might resort to utility-based arguments to persuade someone who does not share her conviction (e.g. an industrial manager).

Moreover, policy choices often have to be backed by multiple arguments to be persuasive, so that all three types of arguments might be deployed simultaneously within a complex argumentation (Crawford 2002: 23). There often is not one single convincing argument. Additionally, multiple arguments can be the result of the need to gain the support of a 'winning coalition' in a diverse audience, or be directed towards different audiences (Perelman and Olbrechts-Tyteca 1969: 23). The existence or even predominance of complex arguments highlights the importance of coherence between different types of arguments as one – often overlooked – aspect of the legitimacy and persuasiveness of policies promoted by a supposed normative power.

An argumentation-theoretical approach to coherence

In argumentation theory, mutually supporting arguments are termed convergent. If several arguments independently lead to the same conclusion, this can enhance the persuasiveness of the overall argument (Perelman and Olbrechts-Tyteca 1969: 471). This does not mean, however, that the persuasiveness of a convergent argumentation increases automatically with the number of arguments put forward. It can be assumed that the higher the number of arguments introduced, the greater the importance as well as the difficulty of achieving coherence of the overall argumentation. The concept of coherence has found its way into IR scholarship with Thomas Franck's claim that '[t]he degree of a rule's legitimacy depends in part on its coherence, which is to say its connectedness, both internally (among the several parts and purposes of the rule) and externally (between one rule and other rules, through shared principles)' (Franck 1990: 180). With regard to application of rules (Franck 1990: 143), coherence has to be distinguished from mere consistency. Coherence demands not simply that a rule is applied equally to everyone, but that any distinction or exception can be justified in principled terms, so that 'a rule's inconsistent application does not necessarily undermine its legitimacy as long as the inconsistencies can be explained to the satisfaction of the community by a justifiable (i.e. principled) distinction' (Franck 1990: 163). Still, if 'double standards' remain unjustified, they constitute a major incoherence and therefore severe challenge to the policy's legitimacy.

Although Franck takes a predominantly structural view, in which legitimacy (and therefore also coherence) figures as 'a property of a rule or rule-making institution which itself exerts a pull to compliance' (Franck 1990: 16; emphasis omitted), this is not how the concept was originally conceived of in Ronald Dworkin's writings on the 'integrity' of legal norms and decisions, from which Franck's notion of coherence is derived (Franck 1990: 143). Coherence in this perspective is not so much a structural feature of the rules themselves, but a political ideal or guiding principle at work both in the construction of norms and in their interpretation and application (Dworkin 1986: 176).

The most obvious form of argumentative incoherence is, of course, if arguments are not in fact convergent but controversial, i.e. support divergent or even mutually exclusive policies. If different EU bodies or member states advocate incompatible policies, the legitimacy of the Union's efforts to persuade external states to adopt any of the policies will be severely impaired. But even if all arguments seemingly push in the same direction of supporting the promoted policy, '[t]he convergence between arguments may cease to carry weight if the result arrived at by the reasoning shows up elsewhere some incompatibility which makes it unacceptable' (Perelman and Olbrechts-Tyteca 1969: 472). This is especially unfortunate in complex argumentations, because different types of arguments have different coherence conditions.

The following two case studies analyse the justification of the EU's foreign policy regarding the death penalty and minority protection, respectively – two fields in which the EU has proactively promoted normative policies externally. The analysis is guided by three leading questions: first, *how* does the EU justify its external human rights policies, i.e. *which types of arguments* are used in the complex overall argumentation? Second, *how coherent* are the arguments? And third, what are the *effects of incoherence* with regard to the EU's role as a normative power? The discourse analysis conducted for this purpose is based on a systematic evaluation of official EU documents such as human rights reports, presidency conclusions or Commission communications, as well as foreign policy documents searched through the European Foreign Policy Bulletin Database (EFPB) and speeches by prominent EU representatives, e.g. the Commission president or the commissioners for external relations and enlargement.

THE EU'S POLICY AGAINST THE DEATH PENALTY: EXPORTING AN INTERNAL POLICY

'The European Union ... has agreed to campaign for the universal abolition of the death penalty' (Patten 2000). Yet this normative and clearly change-oriented engagement of the EU is a rather recent phenomenon. The major policy statements from the early and mid-1990s did not refer explicitly to the abolition of capital punishment as an objective to be pursued in the framework of European Political Cooperation (EPC)/CFSP or Community action. Until 1997, neither the treaties nor the Copenhagen criteria made a specific reference to capital punishment. And the EPC/EU did not clearly and publicly appeal to third countries to generally abolish the death penalty.

In 1998 this rather reluctant position shifted towards a forceful, clear and public European commitment to strive for abolition worldwide. Several factors have led the EU to become an active promoter of abolition after 1997, including the Council of Europe's successful work in establishing abolition as a pan-European norm, the abolitionist trend in Europe and worldwide, and the efforts of European non-state actors and members of the European Parliament (see Manners 2002). In 1998 the EU adopted Guidelines on the Death Penalty, which clearly state the objective of the Union to 'work towards universal abolition of the death penalty as a strongly held policy view agreed by all EU member states' and describe methods for reaching this objective, including démarches, initiatives in multilateral fora, encouragement of relevant international organizations and collaboration with civil society (Council of the European Union 1999a: annex 7). Since the adoption of these guidelines, EU activities have expanded, an impressive number of démarches have been issued, and abolition has been made a priority objective supported by Community funds in the framework of the European Initiative on Democracy and Human Rights (EIDHR). From 1999 on, the EU has successfully sponsored a resolution on the death penalty in the United Nations Commission on Human Rights (UNCHR) at every session since. Yet, debates in the United Nations also illustrate the deep conflict marking the death penalty issue. In the UNCHR, an increasing number of countries have regularly dissociated themselves formally from the resolution, arguing that the imposition of capital punishment is a value question, protected by the rules of sovereignty and to be determined by each society. An EU initiative for a resolution on the death penalty in the General Assembly in 1999 foundered because of the staunch resistance by retentionist states (Bantekas and Hodgkinson 2000). The opposition against international rules on abolition highlights the need for the EU to present persuasive – i.e. coherent – arguments to legitimate its campaign against the death penalty.

Making the case for abolition

Using the analytical framework introduced above, one clear pattern in EU discourse stands out: it is dominated by arguments appealing to universal rights, i.e. references to the universal nature of human rights and to established international human rights law. The Union frequently stresses international agreements as the basis of its policy, and further institutionalization and legalization of human rights norms and procedures is deemed desirable (e.g. Council of the European Union 2001: 10; 2002: 12f.). This type of multilateral-legal argument is likely to mobilize support in the global arena because international law expresses a consensus achieved by legitimate (just) procedures. Yet, in the case of the death penalty, international law is not sufficient as a reference point for EU policy. Although international lawyers have identified a 'partial' ban of the death penalty (Schabas 1997: 219), no international norm generally defines legally sanctioned executions as a violation of human rights. In order to establish coherence between the European value consensus and the internationally accepted definition of the right to life, the EU must aspire to change the valid rules of international law. The EU is confronted with the challenge to present coherent arguments, which go beyond the legal status quo without undermining the fragile consensus on universal human rights already achieved.

This helps to explain the caution and gradualism characterizing the Union's argumentation. Firstly, the EU constantly refers to and supports the international rules on the conditions for the imposition and application of the death penalty. A frequent reference for the EU campaign is the Statute of the International Criminal Court, which does not even foresee the death penalty for crimes against humanity. Secondly, the death penalty *per se* is rarely directly condemned as a human rights violation. The typical argument – following a wording used in United Nations documents – instead underlines that abolition contributes to the 'enhancement of human dignity and the progressive development of human rights' (Council of the European Union 1999a: 59), or to the 'gradual growth of human dignity and to the development of human rights' (Council of the European Union 1999b). Thus, the EU leaves room for different human rights conceptions while pushing a debate and a gradual process towards a new international consensus on the interpretation of the right to life. Assertions clearly expressing the view that the death penalty conflicts with the very concept of human rights and human dignity complement rather than replace the gradualist discourse, as the following 2002 statement illustrates: 'The European Union considers that the abolition of the death penalty contributes to the enhancement of human dignity and the progressive development of human rights. The European Union finds this form of punishment cruel and inhuman' (European Council 2002). The latter quotation also reveals an additional rights-based argument employed by the EU to back up its policy in a coherent manner: the question of the death penalty is linked to the ban of cruel and inhuman treatment and punishment, a *ius cogens* norm which is most likely to be accepted as being universally valid.

The prevalence of universal rights-based arguments in international fora makes perfect sense from the viewpoint adopted here. In a pluralistic, multicultural context, a reference to European values or even identity would not go a long way in justifying foreign policy action. Generally, the EU discourse only indirectly evokes the internal value consensus by confirming rather laconically that all EU member states have abolished the death penalty, thus underlining that – in this area – the EU practises what it preaches (i.e. coherence between rhetoric and action).

However, there are at least three constellations where value arguments do play a prominent role in the justification of the Union's abolitionist policy, without leading to incoherence in the overall set of arguments. First, European norms are referred to in bilateral relations with (aspiring) members of the Council of Europe, since the latter self-consciously presents a value community based on a European canon of human rights. A second constellation amenable to value and identity arguments is the relationship between the Union and its accession candidates where the demand for abolition can be justified by the ethical consensus underlying the European community, e.g. towards Turkey. Finally, despite some ethical differences, which seem to have become more obvious and conflict-prone in recent years, the relationship between Europe and the US is frequently referred to as a community of shared liberal values, which forms an additional argumentative basis for the EU to justify its trans-atlantic call for abolition. An EU Memorandum forwarded to the US authorities in February 2000 (cf. Council of the European Union 2000a: annex 5), outlining in detail the reasons for abolition in Europe, relies on a complex set of different arguments. The Memorandum recalls that:

> for the European Governments the death penalty as a means of State punishment rapidly revealed itself as a denial of human dignity, which is a fundamental basis of the common heritage of the EU as a union of shared values and principles.
>
> (Council of the European Union 2000a: 82)

This memorandum, however, also draws strongly on the argument that the death penalty is ineffective for fighting crime: '[I]t is scientifically undemonstrated that the death penalty and its application deter criminality any more effectively than other forms of punishment' (Council of the European Union 2000a: 82). This type of argument is also used in culturally more diverse constellations. By appealing to the undisputed common interests of (almost) all governments such as the effective fight against crime, violence and terrorism, the universal rights-based arguments can be strengthened while circumventing a sensitive value conflict.

Summing up, we find a rather strong internal coherence between the different arguments the EU uses to justify its strive for the abolition of the death penalty, and also in relation to the argument put forward in the context of its general human rights policy. The 'price' paid for this degree of coherence and credibility has been the late beginning of the common proactive abolitionist policy. Until 1998, *de iure* abolition had not yet been achieved EU-wide. In five member states, complete legal abolition for all crimes was only achieved during the 1990s (Belgium, Ireland, Italy, Spain, United Kingdom).[2] This was problematic for justifying an active external policy in two ways: firstly, the EU could not forcefully argue that the death penalty was a violation of universal human rights as long as legal rules in the member states stood against this interpretation. Secondly, at member state level, the British government in particular held a position regarding the death penalty, which stood in outright contradiction to a European abolitionist campaign based on human rights arguments. The Conservative government considered abolition as a matter of national – or to be more precise, parliamentary – sovereignty. When this position changed and the last legal provisions providing for capital punishment were abolished from the British statute books in 1998, this tension between universal claims and European values dissolved. Only after this value consensus or 'acquis éthique'[3] had been reached within the Union could the EU and its member states make coherent human rights arguments externally without being accused of hypocrisy.[4]

The impact of argumentative coherence in the death penalty case

When we look at the actual policy in this issue area after 1998, we also find indications that its development has been affected by the need for argumentative coherence. Two aspects of the EU's policy against the death penalty may illustrate this: the scope of diplomatic engagement and the specific approach towards the US.

Firstly, the need for coherence is reflected in the carefully defined conditions of EU diplomatic interventions in the field of the death penalty. Implementing the discursive compromise outlined above, the diplomatic approach is equally gradual. The Guidelines contain a set of criteria determining when the EU will intervene with démarches on behalf of individuals. These so-called 'minimum standards' to be observed by states retaining capital punishment broadly follow the rules accepted as the *acquis* in international law. Normally, the EU does not intervene when these minimum standards are met, i.e. when the state concerned respects the norms set by the international community. Yet, the goal to progressively change these rules – which would make the careful approach obsolete – has not been lost sight of. Firstly, the EU makes general démarches to support abolitionist tendencies and discourage regressive steps in third countries, such as lifting a moratorium or extending capital punishment to new crimes. Secondly, the EU uses multilateral channels to keep up the international dialogue and promote a new, abolitionist consensus. Thirdly, the EU has enhanced the financial support for non-state actors pursuing abolitionist objectives,[5] thus supporting transnational intervention, which can go beyond the boundaries of the international legal status quo.

Secondly, the need for coherence helps to better understand the specific approach towards the US. The EU is particularly active in trying to convince its transatlantic partner of the abolitionist philosophy. This involvement can partly be explained by the fact that the US belongs to the group of the five major 'executioners' in terms of numbers (Hood 2002: 91), but it also reflects the pull towards coherence: first, the proactive approach to the US signals that the EU, in line with the universality arguments, criticizes Western democracies as harshly as developing countries. Second, the appeals to the US can contribute – if successful in the long run – to enhancing the coherence between human rights arguments of different partners belonging to the

'Western' camp. An abolitionist America would reduce the contradictions between the EU universality discourse and the US interpretation of the death penalty issue as a 'value' question of criminal justice to be answered by democratic procedures in each society.

MINORITY PROTECTION: THE PROBLEM OF 'DOUBLE STANDARDS'

The issue of minority protection acquired an important role in the EU's external relations after the end of the Cold War. This development started in 1991, when the Declaration on Human Rights adopted at the Luxembourg European Council dedicated a whole paragraph to minority protection (European Council 1991), and the guidelines for the recognition of new states after the breakup of Yugoslavia required 'guarantees for the rights of ethnic and national groups and minorities' (Council of the European Communities 1991: 119). Subsequently, references to minority protection were included in the Europe Agreements with Central and Eastern European countries, the Stability Pacts for Eastern (1995) and South-Eastern Europe (1999), and most significantly the political accession criteria spelled out at the Copenhagen European Council in 1993, which require 'respect for and protection of minorities' (European Council 1993).

This increasingly important external promotion of minority protection did not, however, follow the establishment of an internal EU minority standard. The EU has neither developed minority rights within the *acquis communautaire*, nor do the member states subscribe to a single standard (De Witte 2000; Pentassuglia 2001). At Community level, the issue of minorities is exclusively addressed through the concept of non-discrimination. This norm has been a long-standing principle within Community law in the form of gender equality and the abolition of discrimination on the basis of nationality between member states. Since the Amsterdam Treaty, the non-discrimination framework has been expanded to include ethnic and racial discrimination (Article 13 EC-Treaty). On this basis a Framework Directive on equal treatment in employment and occupation (Directive 2000/78/EC, OJ 2000 L303: 16–22), and a Directive on equal treatment between persons irrespective of racial or ethnic origin (the so-called 'Race Equality Directive' 2000/43/EC, OJ 2000 L180: 22–6) were adopted. Finally, 'membership of a national minority' was included in the non-discrimination article (Article 21) of the Charter of Fundamental Rights and thus has become part of the Treaty establishing a Constitution for Europe (Article II-81).[6] Despite the fact that the final version of the Constitutional Treaty for the first time mentions 'respect for human rights, including the rights of persons belonging to minorities' (Article I-2) among the fundamental values of the Union, the substantial provisions nevertheless do not go beyond non-discrimination.

In the enlargement context, the EU has demanded both non-discrimination and group-specific measures to protect minorities. There remains therefore a conceptual discrepancy between the internal non-discrimination-based approach and the external promotion of special minority rights beyond (and in addition to) this standard. Moreover, the EU applied differentiated pressure across applicants, dependent on whether minority protection was regarded as problematic and security relevant in the particular case. This is an indication that the EU's focus on minorities 'reflects pragmatic concerns for internal and external stability' (Pentassuglia 2001: 22) rather than a principled concern for minority rights as such (Kymlicka 2001: 375).

In summary, while the major goals behind the EU's external minority policy are considerations of security and stability, not the externalization of norms and values, this policy is pursued by civilian means (Manners 2002: 238), which rely predominantly on economic incentives and conditionality. However, the EU has also resorted to normative means, i.e. arguments to justify the policy in normative terms and persuade addressees of its legitimacy.

Justifying a double standard: coherent arguments for an incoherent policy?

In terms of our analytical framework, utility-based arguments could be expected to be predominant in the EU's discourse not so much because it is assumed that security concerns were in fact the primary motivation behind the EU's external promotion of minority protection (which is a plausible assumption but cannot be tested by argument analysis), but because a security-focused approach 'provides a rationale for the differential treatment of East and West' (Kymlicka 2001: 374) and could therefore be utilized to give a principled justification for double standards. Minority protection could be presented as a problem-solving approach specifically suited for the area of Central and South-Eastern Europe, where after the end of the Cold War resurging nationalism and the dissolution of multinational states have been identified as a major source of intra- and interstate conflict.[7] Moreover, security-related arguments would also give reasons for a pragmatic case-by-case treatment leading to differential treatment of third countries. Arguments justifying minority protection with reference to universal rights or particular European values, on the other hand, run the risk of exposing the discrepancies between the internal and external application of the minority norm, while leaving little room for a principled and coherent justification of double standards: if minority protection is a universal or specifically European norm, there is not much reason to deflect its application in current EU member states.

Arguments stressing the security threats posed by ethnic conflict and based on the assumption that minority protection is an effective measure to prevent the outbreak of ethnic violence indeed play an important part within the EU's argumentation: 'A substantial share of present conflicts derive from ethnic tensions and infringements of rights of persons belonging to minorities. Tolerance and non-discrimination build stability and security' (Council of the European Union 1999a: 34; see also European Commission 2001c: 5). Additionally, it is argued that the enlargement process, which provides an important framework for the EU's external pro-minority policy:

> has contributed decisively to achieving political stability, economic progress and social justice. Stable institutions ... reinforced protection of human rights, including rights of minorities ... are now common features. The enlargement process makes Europe a safer place for its citizens and contributes to conflict prevention and control in the wider world.
>
> (Verheugen 2001)

It is concluded that enlargement is in the EU's interest, because 'we profit from peace, stability and growth in this part of Europe' (Verheugen 2002).

The EU, however, combined utility-based arguments with other argument types. Universal rights-based arguments are put forward in two different ways: first, it is commonly stressed that '[t]he EU is committed to respecting the rights of persons belonging to minorities as part of universally recognised human rights' (Council of the European Union 2002: 116) and that minority protection therefore forms an inherent part of the EU human rights policy. Second, universal human rights and utility-based arguments are linked by stressing the role of human rights, part of which is the protection of minorities, in general to achieve and sustain internal and external stability (European Council 1991).

The use of universal rights-based arguments brings the problem of coherence to the fore. Although all EU members subscribe to global human rights documents, this consensus does not include minority protection. The problem is even more virulent in the case of value-based arguments. It is all the more surprising that the EU has emphatically and increasingly made minority protection a matter of specific European values. References to minority instruments to be implemented by candidate countries are exclusively to 'European standards', specifically the Council of Europe's Framework Convention on the Protection of National Minorities (FCNM), while universal instruments, which feature in general documents such as the annual human rights reports, are omitted (Pentassuglia 2001: 23). It is an obvious case of incoherence that the FCNM is presented as constituting the 'European standard' without being signed, let alone ratified, by all 'old' EU member states.[8]

The EU also resorts to explicit value-based arguments. Commission President Romano Prodi repeatedly referred to the EU as a 'Union of diversity and minorities' (Prodi 2003) and established a link between minority protection and the integration project itself: 'The European Union is an "alliance of minorities"' (Prodi 2002a). Respect for minorities is presented as a fundamental part of European identity:

> [T]olerance and mutual respect ... are deeply rooted in Europe's humanistic heritage ... We need these attitudes more than ever in today's Europe where we're all members of minorities. Indeed, given our centuries of experience of living together, we should be leading the world by example.
>
> (Prodi 2002b)

Such assertive language is also reflected in European Council statements that Europe 'is founded on respect for diversity and on tolerance' and should be based on 'the diversity of its cultures and languages, a Europe where social justice is promoted and the rights of minorities are protected' (Council of the European Union 1997). Furthermore, the protection of minorities is explicitly named to be part of 'fundamental European values, i.e. respect for human rights and the rights of minorities, international law, democratic institutions and the inviolability of borders' (European Council 1999). The promotion of minority rights is therefore presented as an externalization of internally shared values: 'The European Union is committed to encouraging ... the promotion of the values and models on which it is founded: in particular, democracy, respect for human rights and minorities, the rule of law and the market economy' (Council of the European Union 2000b: 54).

Reactions to incoherence: in search of an argumentative 'realignment strategy'

In order to realign these value-based claims with the *de facto* development of the EU, justifications for the external minority criterion are linked with norms enshrined in the internal *acquis*, namely non-discrimination, cultural diversity and the fight against racism and xenophobia. For example:

> Compliance with the principle of non-discrimination is an important element in the EU enlargement process. The European Council in 1993 included in the Copenhagen criteria that membership requires that the candidate country has established respect for and protection of minorities.
>
> (Council of the European Union 1999a: 36)

And: 'The notion of the respect for and protection of minorities is a key element in the fight against racism, xenophobia and anti-Semitism in the applicant countries' (European Commission 2000: 11). Furthermore, the Commission named '[c]ombating racism and xenophobia and discrimination against minorities and indigenous peoples' as a thematic priority for the EU's external human rights policy, because '[t]his is an area where the EU has significant internal as well as external policy competence' (European Commission 2001a: 17). As the argumentative backing for this claim the communication cites Article 13 EC-Treaty and the Race Equality Directive as well as the Charter of Fundamental Rights' provisions on equality before the law, non-discrimination and cultural diversity (European Commission 2001a; cf. also Council of the European Union 2002: 116).

Has this 'realignment strategy' been successful? This would only be the case if the externally promoted minority protection standard could in fact be subsumed under the established EU norms of non-discrimination, cultural diversity, and combating racism and xenophobia. This, however, is not the case. It follows that the EU's reliance on value-based arguments, justifying the external promotion of minority protection as being part of the fundamental 'European' values that underpin the Union, exposes the incoherent application of this particular norm within the EU. The EU's argumentation therefore exacerbates rather than diminishes the problematic character of the EU's external minority policy. In fact, it is precisely the resort to rights- and value-based arguments and the failure to provide a principled justification of the differential treatment of applicant states that render this policy incoherent.

CONCLUSIONS

What does the analysis of coherence in complex argumentations contribute to the argument of the EU as a normative power? Firstly, the discourse analysis elucidates a dimension of the EU's normative impact often underestimated in empirical studies. The question of *how* the Union justifies its policies, its demands and criticisms *vis-à-vis* third countries is an important aspect of the Union's legitimacy and persuasiveness, and therefore its role as a normative power. Secondly, the analysis of argumentation is important as it may have repercussions on the development of concrete policies, since the actors responsible for European foreign policy are aware of the need to bring their justifications in line with policy practice. While a discursive analysis of arguments does not aim to explain why the EU undertakes its external policies, and may not predict its effectiveness, as material incentives can induce compliance with ill-justified demands, it does offer insights into how much the EU can rely on its normative power to promote policies externally. And even scholars who conclude that incentive mechanisms 'work' concede that this may well have negative long-term effects (Schimmelfennig and Sedelmeier 2004: 675).

The two case studies have produced quite different results with respect to argumentative coherence and its effects. In the death penalty case, the EU relied predominantly on universal rights-based arguments complemented in a careful and coherent way by value- and utility-based arguments when addressing different audiences. It is also compatible with the coherence principle that the EU's external promotion of the abolitionist norm only became proactive and outspoken when it was securely established internally. In the minority protection case, by contrast, arguments had to justify a policy adopted in spite of a lack of value consensus among EU member states, a fact that led to serious problems with providing coherent justifications for the policy. Moreover, the EU has increasingly become entangled in a highly problematic identity discourse, especially when addressing membership candidates. This was reflected in the EU's rhetorical 'realignment strategy', i.e. the effort to link external policy justification back to internally established norms.

Hence, our findings with regard to the question as to how far the EU represents a normative power are mixed. The death penalty case seems to support the concept on all levels. The abolitionist policy was adopted for normative reasons, pursued with argumentative means and justified coherently. The minority protection case shows a different picture. The policy was adopted not so much for principled reasons but out of concerns about stability and security.

Although the EU tried to combine economic means in the form of conditionality with normative argumentation, it proved unable to justify the policy coherently as a result of the Union's community values. This did not render it ineffective (Schimmelfennig *et al.* 2003), but diminished the role of persuasion in diffusing minority protection norms, and thereby the EU's normative power in this issue area. It follows that the EU is not necessarily 'normative by nature' – its normative power depends heavily on the interaction between its policy goals, means and justifications, and therefore varies between different issue areas.

Biographical notes: Marika Lerch currently works in the European Parliament Information Office, Berlin, Germany. Guido Schwellnus is Researcher at the Center for Comparative and International Studies, Swiss Federal Institute of Technology (ETH) Zurich, Switzerland.

Addresses for correspondence: Marika Lerch, Zionskirchstrasse 33, D-10119, Berlin, Germany. email: marikaterch@web.de/Guido Schwellnus, Swiss Federal Institute of Technology (ETH) Zurich, Seilergraben 49, CM-8092 Zurich, Switzerland. Tel: +41 (0) 44 632 6369. Fax: +41 (0) 44 632 1289. email: schwellnus@eup.gess.ethz.ch

NOTES

1 The views expressed by the authors in this article are strictly personal.
2 Greece was until recently (2004) the only EU member state which – although abolitionist for ordinary crimes – had not yet abolished the death penalty from the statute books completely. For an analysis of abolition in Europe, see also Manners (2002).
3 The term '*acquis éthique*' has been used by the European Parliament in its resolution on the implementation of 'human rights/democracy' budget lines relating to campaigns in favour of a moratorium on capital punishment (European Parliament 2001: 395).
4 Until today, no treaty provision explicitly refers to capital punishment, but at the occasion of the Amsterdam Treaty revision, the Intergovernmental Conference adopted a declaration on the death penalty and Article 2.2 of the EU Charter of Fundamental Rights confirms that abolition forms part of the European 'ethical *acquis*'.
5 For the period 2002–2004 the Commission has earmarked 12 million euro for supporting respective projects under the EIDHR (European Commission 2001b).
6 Additionally, minority issues are addressed via two other, far less institutionalized norms: first, the EU is officially committed 'to respect and to promote the diversity of its cultures' (Article 151 EC-Treaty; cf. Article 22 Charter of Fundamental Rights and Article II-82 Constitutional Treaty). Second, the Union has started several policy initiatives to combat racism and xenophobia.
7 This security-based argumentation is in itself not unproblematic, given ethnic tensions in Western Europe, e.g. in Northern Ireland or the Basque country. Western governments have sought to deflect this counter-argument by distinguishing minority issues from terrorist activities and excluding the latter from being a concern for international minority protection instruments (Brett 1993: 158).
8 Among the old member states, the Framework Convention has been signed, but not yet ratified by Belgium, Greece and Luxembourg; France has not even signed it. Cf. http://conventions.coe.int/Treaty/EN/CadreListeTraites.htm (1 July 2005).

REFERENCES

Alston, P. and Weiler, J.H.H. (1999) 'An "ever closer Union" in need of a human rights policy: the European Union and human rights', in P. Alston, M. Bustelo and J. Heenan (eds), *The EU and Human Rights*, Oxford: Oxford University Press, pp. 3–66.
Bantekas, I. and Hodgkinson, P. (2000) 'Capital punishment at the United Nations: recent developments', *Criminal Law Forum* 11: 23–34.
Brett, R. (1993) 'The human dimension mechanism of the CSCE and the CSCE response to minorities', in M.R. Lucas (ed.), *The CSCE in the 1990s: Constructing European Security and Cooperation*, Baden-Baden: Nomos, pp. 143–60.
Crawford, N. (2002) *Argument and Change in World Politics*, Cambridge: Cambridge University Press.
De Witte, B. (2000) 'Politics versus law in the EU's approach to ethnic minorities', EUI Working Paper RSC 2000/4, Florence: European University Institute.
Duke, S. (1999) 'Consistency as an issue in EU external activities', EIPA Working Paper 99/W/06, Maastricht: European Institute of Public Administration.
Dworkin, R. (1986) *Law's Empire*, Cambridge, MA: Harvard University Press.
Franck, T. (1990) *The Power of Legitimacy Among Nations*, Oxford: Oxford University Press.
Habermas, J. (1984) *The Theory of Communicate Action, Volume One: Reason and the Rationalization of Society*, Boston: Beacon Press.
Habermas, J. (1993) *Justification and Application. Remarks on Discourse Ethics*, Cambridge: Polity Press.
Hood, R. (2002) *The Death Penalty. A Worldwide Perspective*, 3rd edn, Oxford: Oxford University Press.
Kymlicka, W. (2001) 'Reply and conclusion', in W. Kymlicka and M. Opalski (eds), *Can Liberal Pluralism be Exported? Western Political Theory and Ethnic Relations in Eastern Europe*, Oxford: Oxford University Press, pp. 347–413.
Manners, I. (2002) 'Normative power Europe: a contradiction in terms?', *Journal of Common Market Studies* 40(2): 235–58.
Nuttall, S. (2001) 'Consistency and the CFSP: a categorization and its consequences', LSE Foreign Policy Unit Working Paper 2001/3, London: London School of Economics.
Patten, C. (2000) Contribution to the debate in the European Parliament, 25 October 2000, Speech/00/404, available at http://europa.eu.int/comm/external_relations/news/patten/speech_00_404.htm (accessed 21 February 2005).
Pentassuglia, G. (2001) 'The EU and the protection of minorities: the case of Eastern Europe', *European Journal of International Law* 12(1): 3–38.
Perelman, C. and Olbrechts-Tyteca, L. (1969) *The New Rhetoric. A Treatise on Argumentation*, Notre Dame: University of Notre Dame Press.
Prodi, R. (2002a) 'Europe beyond the borders, Europe from below'. Speech at the ceremony organized by the city of Sarajevo, 6 April 2002, available at http://europa.eu.int/futurum/documents/offtext/sp060402_en.htm (accessed 21 February 2005).
Prodi, R. (2002b) 'The past and future of European integration'. Speech to the Instituto de Espana, Madrid, 7 February 2002, available at http://europa.eu.int/futurum/documents/speech/sp070202_en.htm (accessed 21 February 2005).
Prodi, R. (2003) 'Croatia's journey towards EU membership'. Speech in the Croatian Parliament, Zagreb, 10 July 2003, SPEECH/03/360, available at http://europa.eu.int/comm/external_relations/news/prodi/sp03_360.htm (accessed 21 February 2005).
Risse, T. (2000) '"Let's argue!": communicative action in world politics', *International Organization* 54(1): 1–39.
Schabas, W. (1997) *The Abolition of the Death Penalty in International Law*, 2nd edn, Cambridge: Cambridge University Press.

Schimmelfennig, F. (2000) 'International socialization in the new Europe: rational action in an institutional environment', *European Journal of International Relations* 6(1): 109–39.

Schimmelfennig, F. and Sedelmeier, U. (2004) 'Governance by conditionality: EU rule transfer to the candidate countries of Central and Eastern Europe', *Journal of European Public Policy* 11(4): 661–79.

Schimmelfennig, F., Engert, S. and Knobel, H. (2003) 'Costs, commitment and compliance: the impact of EU democratic conditionality on Latvia, Slovakia and Turkey', *Journal of Common Market Studies* 41(3): 495–518.

Sjursen, H. (2002) 'Why expand? The question of legitimacy and justification in the EU's enlargement policy', *Journal of Common Market Studies* 40(3): 491–513.

Szymanski, M. and Smith, M.E. (2005) 'Coherence and conditionality in European foreign policy: negotiating the EU–Mexico global agreement', *Journal of Common Market Studies* 43(1): 171–92.

Verheugen, G. (2001) 'The state of play of negotiations – where are we today?'. Speech at the DUPI Conference 'Approaching Copenhagen 2002: EU Enlargement and the Future of Europe', Copenhagen, 22 November 2001, available at http://europa.eu.int/comm/archives/commission_1999_2004/verheugen/speeches/sp22112001en.htm (accessed 21 February 2005).

Verheugen, G. (2002) 'Entering the final stage'. Speech, Vienna, 2 December 2002, available at http://europa.eu.int/comm/archives/commission_1999_2004/verheugen/speeches/sp02122002en.htm (accessed 21 February 2005).

Wæver, O. (2003) 'Discursive approaches', in A. Wiener and T. Diez (eds), *European Integration Theory: Past, Present and Future*, Oxford: Oxford University Press, pp.197–215.

Official documents

Council of the European Communities (1991) 'Declaration on the Guidelines on the Recognition of New States in Eastern Europe and in the Soviet Union', 16 December 1991, EC Bulletin 1991/12.

Council of the European Union (1997) 'Declaration by the Council and the Representatives of the Governments of the Member States, meeting within the Council, of 16 December 1997, on respecting diversity and combating racism and xenophobia', OJ 1998 C1/01, 3 January 1998.

Council of the European Union (1999a) 'EU Annual Report on Human Rights 1999', adopted October 1999, Luxembourg: Office for Official Publications of the European Communities.

Council of the European Union (1999b) 'Declaration by the Presidency on behalf of the European Union on Nepal', 2 June 1999, EFPB-Doc. 99/97.

Council of the European Union (2000a) 'EU Annual Report on Human Rights 2000', adopted 9 October 2000, Luxembourg: Office for Official Publications of the European Communities.

Council of the European Union (2000b) 'Council Joint Action 2000/717/CFSP of 16 November 2000 on the holding of a meeting of Heads of State or of Government in Zagreb (Zagreb Summit)', OJ 2000 L290, 17 November 2000: 54.

Council of the European Union (2001) 'EU Annual Report on Human Rights 2001', adopted 8 October 2001, Luxembourg: Office for Official Publications of the European Communities.

Council of the European Union (2002) 'EU Annual Report on Human Rights 2002', adopted 21 October 2002, Luxembourg: Office for Official Publications of the European Communities.

European Commission (2000) 'Commission Report on the Implementation of the Action Plan against Racism: Mainstreaming the Fight against Racism', Brussels, January 2000.

European Commission (2001a) 'Communication from the Commission to the Council and the European Parliament: The European Union's Role in Promoting Human Rights and Democratization in Third Countries', COM(2001) 252 final, Brussels, 8 May 2001.

European Commission (2001b) 'Commission Staff Working Document, European Initiative for Democracy and Human Rights Programming Document', Rev1-final, 20 December 2001.

European Commission (2001c) 'Communication from the Commission on Conflict Prevention', COM(2001) 211 final, Brussels, 11 April 2001.

European Council (1991) 'Conclusions of the Luxembourg European Council: Declaration on Human Rights', Luxembourg, 28–29 June 1991, Annex V, SN 151/2/91.

European Council (1993) 'Presidency Conclusions of the Copenhagen European Council', Copenhagen, 21–22 June 1993.

European Council (1999) 'Presidency Conclusions of the Berlin European Council. Part III: Statements on Kosovo', Berlin, 24–25 March 1999, SN 100/1/99.

European Council (2002) 'Declaration by the Presidency on behalf of the European Union on the recent death sentences in Sudan', 30 August 2002, EFPB-Doc. 02/219.

European Parliament (2001) 'Resolution on the implementation of "human rights/democracy" budget lines relating to campaigns in favour of a moratorium on capital punishment', B5-0804/2000, 26 October 2000, OJ C 197, 12 July 2001.

Comment: Crossroads or cul-de-sac? Reassessing European foreign policy

Michael Smith

INTRODUCTION

If it is true that European foreign policy stands at a crossroads between 'normative power and Great Power', it is no less true that the study of European Foreign Policy (EFP) also stands at a crossroads. Whereas the substance of policy seems to stand between civilian and military institutions, cultures and practices, raising major questions about the ways in which those institutions, cultures and practices are to develop in the future, the study of policy lies somewhat uneasily between European integration and international relations, feeding rather guiltily off both but incapable of taking the key steps towards their synthesis or even their mutual engagement. As Helene Sjursen points out in the introduction to this issue, there is a need to take into account relevant conceptual insights from adjacent disciplines such as law and sociology. Because the empirical and the conceptual domains of EFP studies lie across or in between a number of established and themselves often contested areas, they also partake of some of the much broader tensions between materialist and normative approaches to the social sciences more generally, and between the demands of theoretical discourse and the concerns of policy-makers.

Is this 'in-betweenness' of EFP studies a source of new analytical opportunities, or does it provide a rationale for the reassertion of conventional approaches both to analysis and to policy? More specifically, what does this issue clarify about the questions that relate the study of EFP to adjoining empirical or conceptual domains? What questions does it raise explicitly or implicitly about the ways in which EFP relates to broader considerations of international relations?

CONCEPTUAL HIGHWAYS AND BYWAYS

The explicit assumption behind this issue is that with the prospective acquisition of military means for EFP, some key questions need to be asked about whether the European Union (EU) is, will remain or can remain a 'civilian' power with a 'normative/civilizing' influence both on the foreign policies of its member states and on practices of international relations more generally defined. Many of the contributions take up these themes and explore them in distinctive ways. Here, I subject them initially to an evaluation based on three questions. First, what kind of vehicle is EFP, for what purposes? Second, what drives and steers the EFP project? Third, what direction is the EFP project taking? These questions are both conceptual and empirical in nature. In the final part I move on to consider some questions about EFP that seem to arise from the contributions as a whole, and to propose some initial directions for considering them.

First, what about the nature of the vehicle that is EFP, and about its purposes? Whilst only one of the contributors (Hyde-Price) uses the term 'vehicle' in assessing EFP, each of them implicitly refers to such an understanding of the phenomenon. I can identify three sets of themes that relate to this concern, some of which occur simultaneously in individual contributions. The first set of themes might be described as materialist, focusing on the ways in which EFP reflects the presence of power and preferences, and the ways in which it fits into the broader structure of international politics. Here, the vehicle is loaded with the priorities and relative bargaining power of the EU member states. Thus, for Hyde-Price, EFP is a vehicle for co-operation, and a repository for member state interests that are essentially 'second order': things which they value but which do not engage their perceived vital interests and which do not directly require the deployment of major resources. In taking this position, Hyde-Price is effectively representing a materialist conception of foreign policy and international politics, which is only infrequently represented in the other contributions. He stresses the external pressures and opportunities that create the space for collective action, without any pre-judgement of the forms such collective action might take. Although she approaches the problem from a very different angle, Sjursen takes up some of these questions by arguing that the pursuit of 'normative power' can be an essentially rational strategy – that is from the point of view of discourse theory. Such a possibility has lain behind a lot of recent debate about the relationship between 'hard' and 'soft' power and about the differences between conceptions and practices of power on either side of the Atlantic.

In a second set of themes, it is not so clear that EFP rests on member state choices and preferences; indeed, a key assumption of many of the contributions is that such choices and preferences are themselves reshaped by the process of co-operation in EFP, and that this is indeed one of the key (often implicit) purposes, or at least one of the results, of the exercise. The vehicle here is one with a highly complex control system reflecting several layers of institutionalization and mutual dependencies. Thus the tensions between national practices and the demands of entanglement at the European level emerge very clearly from the contributions of Manners, Wagner and Eriksen, and in their different ways these pieces create a number of important questions about the ways in which the ontologies of EFP 'work' for those implicated in them. The issue is explored further by Mitzen, who sees the notion of ontological security as key to the ways in which EFP is 'exported' or has an impact on the outside world. A key question that is sharpened by these contributions is that of the extent to which the 'internal' development of EFP is related to the 'external' impact of EFP in the international arena: is the 'internal' by its nature primary and thus the 'external' the almost accidental by-product of the search for internal consistency and institutional coherence, or is the 'external' a vital element in the co-constitution of EFP and the broader international order?

In a third set of themes, the key is not in the processes of interaction that characterize EFP, but rather in the processes of generation: in other words, the ways in which the discourse(s) surrounding EFP produce characteristic and distinctive patterns of articulation and communication. This attention to the generative characteristics of EFP is a central theme in its development and in its study: here, the vehicle is a means of conveying signs and symbols, and focusing argumentation which in the first instance is part of the essence of EFP itself, but in the second instance can be related to much broader processes of deliberation and argumentation in world politics. Such themes lead to a central focus on the logics of EFP, and the authors in this issue provide a rich vein of studies in the different expressions of these logics. Thus Manners focuses on the ways in which different discourses – civilian and martial – characterize the current stage of EFP development, and notes the ways in which these intersect with the evolution of transgovernmental élite networks in a move away from the 'sustainable peace' that has been both a major feature and a major asset of the EFP phenomenon. In juxtaposition to this, Mitzen presents the notion of ontological security as a key foundation for the articulation of a European identity in the global arena. Another strong sub-theme that emerges from the contributions is that of legalization: both Eriksen and Sjursen, for example, focus on the ways in which legal discourse and practices can shape the possibilities of EFP.

Accompanying these sub-themes and constituting a major focus of a number of the contributions is the conception of EFP as essentially a process of deliberation; this relates quite strongly to the range of questions that arise around institutions and social learning (see above), but it also leads on to a key area of critique in the context of actually existing EFP. The contributions by Bicchi and by Lerch and Schwellnus raise this issue in a very direct way by focusing on the contradictions and tensions in EFP and the way it is practised, and they also provide useful empirical explorations of the ways in which the tensions are (or are not) resolved.

As pointed out in the introduction by Sjursen, there is a basic tension not only in the substance of EFP but also in its study. To put it crudely, it could be argued that the study of 'civilian' or 'normative' power is itself normative or prescriptive, and that it presupposes commitment by the analyst to a particular perspective. Hyde-Price challenges this by deploying the tools of structural realism and emphasizing the spaces opened up for agency on the part of member states acting collectively, whilst from a different perspective Wagner applies a corrective to those who might argue that there is a kind of natural homogenization or convergence process occurring across member states through the EFP channel. Other contributors (Manners, Sjursen, and Lerch and Schwellnus, for example) challenge it by pointing to the contradictory currents in both theory and practices of EFP from an ideational standpoint; still other contributors take more for granted the fact that EFP exists in a way independently of the preferences of member states, or that those preferences have been so thoroughly reshaped by EFP that they are in effect becoming identical to it (for example, Eriksen and Mitzen).

Even if one takes the position that the process in EFP is 'ever onwards and ever upwards', this in itself does not make the process unproblematic, since there are many areas in which the generation of 'civilian' or 'normative' power creates tensions: between EFP as an élite project and notions of democratic control (Wagner), between the aspiration to cosmopolitan democracy and its institutionalization (Eriksen), between the concept of normative power and the question of its legitimacy (Sjursen), between EFP as a comforting arena for deliberation about international issues and the need for action (Mitzen), between the rationales provided for EFP actions and the untidiness or contradictions of engagement in specific policy arenas (Bicchi, and Lerch and Schwellnus).

These contradictions are heightened by the actual or impending acquisition of military capacity for EFP. This is clearly a key element – but not necessarily the only or the dominant element – in the notion that the EU is at a policy crossroads. Ian Manners confronts it directly, with his argument that the acquisition not only of military capacity but also of an embryonic military-industrial complex creates a new and demanding set of tensions within EFP. Other contributors (Sjursen, Mitzen, Eriksen) address the issues more indirectly, by stressing the challenges posed by issues of 'hard power' or coercion to the established discourses and practices of EFP. By doing so, they bridge the gap between questions about what kind of vehicle this is, and who or what drives and steers it. For Manners, EFP is driven largely by ideas and discourses of international action, but he sees these as being affected (corrupted?) by the injection of new ideas and discourses associated with militarization. The dangers in creating a European military-industrial complex, or of intensifying transgovernmental military networks, are seen as immediate and significant. Wolfgang Wagner takes this theme up and develops it in the context of democratic control: implicitly, the creation of a military apparatus around EFP sharpens the risks of authority leakage to a transnational military élite, and thus the case for control by parliamentary bodies at the European rather than the national level. Hyde-Price would no doubt point out that these dangers can be linked to the permissive structure surrounding EFP in the 'new Europe', where new ventures become possible but their risks are not as salient as they would have been in a Cold War world.

The other contributions pay rather less direct attention to the 'military turn' in EFP, but this does not mean that they neglect it. Rather, it means that they are concerned with long-term developments in which militarization and its accompanying institutional or ideational apparatuses have a less central place. Thus Sjursen points to the continuing discussion in EFP about the relationships between 'hard' and 'soft' power and notes that it cannot always be taken for granted that the one is bad and the other good (either for the EU or for broader international society). Other contributors raise important questions about the ways in which the 'military turn' is articulated; for example, Mitzen with her attention to the generation of the European Security Strategy. More indirectly, the focus of some contributions (Bicchi, Lerch and Schwellnus, Manners) on the 'reflexiveness gap' in EFP could be seen as raising important questions about the extent to which incipient militarization is placed in the broader context of its 'internal' or 'external' legitimacy.

Such arguments raise important questions about where EFP is going. For Manners, it is clear that one direction is towards militarization, 'Great Power' status and practices, the creation of dependencies and away from the 'sustainable peace' that has been key to the EU's civilian power status. Hyde-Price, from a very different perspective, might find some common ground here: the EU for him is an exercise in collective milieu-shaping, structuring the actions of states both within and outside the Union and in some areas exercising a kind of collective hegemony. Such external orientations create inevitable contradictions, such as those pointed out by Bicchi and Lerch and Schwellnus: the imposition of institutional forms on 'partners' in international agreements, or the apparent double standards expressed by the gap between rationales and practices in the area of human rights. For others (Wagner, Sjursen, Eriksen, Mitzen) the direction is essentially towards a new type of institutional or cultural settlement within the EU itself – a settlement that might be strongly legalized and focused on processes of deliberation, thus raising major questions about the extent of control over EFP deliberations available either to member states or to populations within the Union. It is of course inevitable that these two sets of directions (external and internal) will interact, either mutually to reinforce each other or to offset each other, as they have done in the past development of EFP. For both directions, as pointed out by a number of contributors, the question of legitimacy remains pressing and unresolved.

We are left with a powerful sense of the contradictions to which EFP is subject. From whichever angle it is approached, the subject raises major questions about the interaction between internal developments and external structures and pressures, about the boundaries of 'civilian' and 'normative' power and about the legitimacy claims of EFP. In the remainder of the space available to me, I would like briefly to raise other questions that are uncovered but not always fully explored in the contributions.

THE ROADS LESS TRAVELLED: OPEN QUESTIONS ABOUT EUROPEAN FOREIGN POLICY

Three questions stand out for me among the many prompted by the rich vein of thinking in this issue. Each of them could in itself constitute a research programme, but here they are simply stated and some implications explored. The three questions relate to: internal process and external impact; the notion of turning points; and the EU as a 'power' in international politics.

First, let us consider the internal/external relationship: given the focus of the 'normative power' debate predominantly on the generation of norms and an EU identity among the member states and other groupings, does this mean that external impact is relegated to a residual status? Does it mean that the politics of normative power is a politics of self-absorption?

Second, what about the notion of turning points? My view would be not that the turning point in EFP arises simply from the opening up of a militarized perspective, but also from the accumulation of engagements with external forces, choices and commitments that has emerged from three decades of EFP. Does this mean that in focusing on the militarization thesis we are likely to miss the far wider implications of a maturing in EFP?

Finally, the notion of the EU as a 'power': it seems to me that many of the contributions rest on the essential recognition that the EU and its member states will increasingly have to confront the implications of international status and impact. What kind of 'power' might the EU be and what roles might it play? How will this power be articulated, deployed and felt in the wider international arena? In work undertaken with Ole Elgström and Chris Hill, I have put the case for further investigation of these issues (Elgström and Smith, forthcoming; Hill and Smith 2005: chs 1 and 18).

The consequences of these questions are not just theoretical. To use terms used by some of the contributors to this issue, we are no longer in a situation where extreme internal reflexiveness and awareness of the dynamics of the EFP system can coexist with an absence of reflexiveness in relations with the outside world. In other words, we need to be aware that the internal development of EFP and the broader development of international issues and structures are co-constitutive. Where does all of this leave us: at a crossroads or heading down a cul-de-sac? I think it leaves us – and this issue – somewhere different altogether: heading down the entry ramp on to a far wider conceptual and empirical highway, where the study of EFP becomes more and more connected with the study of international relations more generally, and where the practice of EFP is seen increasingly as a 'normal' part of the global arena rather than as something exceptional and *hors de concours*. This does not mean, of course, that EFP does not matter; it just means that it matters rather less than we have thought in and of itself, and rather more for the broader picture of international relations than others might have imagined.

Biographical note: Michael Smith is Professor of European Politics and Jean Monnet Chair in the Department of Politics, International Relations and European Studies at Loughborough University, UK.

Address for correspondence: Michael Smith, Department of Politics, International Relations and European Studies, Loughborough University, Loughborough LE11 3TU, UK. Tel: +44 (0)1509 22 2640. email: M.H.Smith@lboro.ac.uk

REFERENCES

Elgström, O. and Smith, M. (eds) (forthcoming) *The European Union's Roles in International Politics*, London: Routledge.

Hill, C. and Smith, M. (eds) (2005) *International Relations and the European Union*, Oxford: Oxford University Press.

Index

For Product Safety Concerns and Information please contact our EU
representative GPSR@taylorandfrancis.com
Taylor & Francis Verlag GmbH, Kaufingerstraße 24, 80331 München, Germany